AUSTR.   ___
NEW ZEALAND BY RAIL

3rd Edition

Colin Taylor

Bradt Publications, UK
The Globe Pequot Press Inc, USA

First published in 1988 by Bradt Publications.
Third edition published in 1996 by Bradt Publications,
41 Nortoft Road, Chalfont St Peter, Bucks SL9 0LA, England
Published in the USA by The Globe Pequot Press Inc,
6 Business Park Road, PO Box 833, Old Saybrook, Connecticut 06475-0833

British Library Cataloguing in Publication Data
A catalogue record for this book is available from the British Library
ISBN 1 898323 46 1

Library of Congress Cataloging-in-Publication Data
Taylor, Colin, 1928-
    Australia and New Zealand by rail / Colin Taylor. -- 3rd ed.
    p. cm. -- (Bradt Guides)
    Rev. ed. of: Australia by rail. 1988.
    Includes bibliographical references and index.
    ISBN 0-7627-0011-4
    1. Australia--Guidebooks. 2. Railroad travel--Australia-
    -Guidebooks. 3. New Zealand--Guidebooks. 4. Railroad travel--
    New Zealand--Guidebooks. I. Taylor. Colin, 1928- Australia by rail.
    II. Title. III. Series.
    DU95.T29 1996
    919.404'63--dc20   96-34456
                                                          CIP

Cover photographs
Front: "The spirit of the outback" (Queensland Rail).
Back: Koala (Peter Baker).

Photographs
Australian National (AN), Adrian Baker (AB), Peter Baker (PB),
Hilary Bradt (HB), Robert Hayne (RH), Queensland Rail (QR),
Roy Sinclair (RS), Gordon Smith (GS), Tranz Rail (TR).

Maps
Steve Munns.

Typeset from the author's disc by Donald Sommerville, London W5 3TR.
Printed and bound in Great Britain by The Guernsey Press Co Ltd.

CONTENTS

THE AUTHOR

Colin Taylor, recently retired as associate professor in the Department of Geographical Sciences and Planning at the University of Queensland, has held town planning positions in Victoria, Tasmania and Scotland, and has given conference papers and talks on planning and transportation in Tel Aviv, Canberra, Hobart, Melbourne, Sydney, Broken Hill, Brisbane, Ipswich and Mackay. Dr Taylor has also produced articles and broadcasts on the fascination of railways. In the last 20 years he has travelled more than 4,000 rail journeys in Australia and overseas, covering some 480,000 kilometres. He compiles the biennial *World Speed Review* for *Railway Gazette International* and is also the author of *Great Rail Non-journeys of Australia, Steel Roads of Australia* and, most recently, *Traincatcher*.

ACKNOWLEDGEMENTS

Marvin Saltzman of California, author of the famous *Eurail Guide Annual*, encouraged the first edition of this book. Since then, I have had valuable assistance from the management and staff of the various rail systems of Australia, of Tranz Rail (New Zealand), and from numerous individuals and travellers.

Special thanks are due to Geoff Churchman of IPL Books, Wellington, publisher of *Traincatcher*, and Roy Sinclair of Christchurch for their assistance in providing information, for their hospitality and for their company on some New Zealand journeys. The personal interest and encouragement of Hilary Bradt, who has experienced some of Australia's best train trips, is also greatly appreciated.

Finally, without the patient tolerance of my wife Barbara, the guide could never have been produced in the first place, let alone run to four (including one German language) editions.

Introduction

Important Notes
for Travellers

As with all guide books, it is necessary to begin by explaining some general principles and issuing a few words of caution to the intending traveller.

First of all, before commencing any journey, without exception, double check the departure and arrival times given in this book or in any timetable, as they are subject to change without prior notice. Changes will usually be minor and have little effect on most of the trips described in this book, but Australia and New Zealand are not as well served by rail networks as Europe, and you would not want to miss the only train of the day or be stranded in the outback when your plane home takes off from Sydney.

Train schedules are particularly liable to change at weekends and during holiday periods. Most interstate and long distance trains run regularly throughout the year, but many shorter distance trains may not operate at Christmas (including both Christmas Day and 26 December/Boxing Day), New Year's Day and Easter (Good Friday/Easter Monday) or on other public holidays. Schedules should be checked particularly carefully during Australian "long weekend" holidays, some of which vary from state to state. Australia Day (26 January) and Anzac Day (25 April) are observed uniformly in all states. Labour Day and the Queen's Birthday are kept in all states also, but on different dates. Holidays in New Zealand in addition to Christmas, Easter, etc., include Waitangi Day (6 February), Anzac Day (25 April), the Queen's birthday (first Monday in June), and Labour Day (fourth Monday in October). The New Year holiday in New Zealand includes both 1 and 2 January.

There is a 30 minute time zone change between the eastern states of Australia and South Australia, and one of 90 minutes out in the Nullarbor. Usually the train conductor will tell you when to alter your watch.

Eastern Summer Time applies between late October and early

March in Victoria, New South Wales and South Australia, but not in Queensland. This affects the times of through trains to or from the other states, either regularly or erratically, because starting and finishing times can be inconsistent. Schedules to and from Western Australia are less likely to be altered but arrivals and departures at Adelaide to and from the west should always be checked in the summer season. All timings given for trains are local standard times unless otherwise stated.

No publication which includes railway (or any other) timetables can hope to remain long up-to-date. Not even those published by the railways themselves! As an official in one major railway booking office said to me "We'd be the last to know!". There are regular travellers who will swear that railway timetables should properly be classed as works of fiction. Some people even suggest that their main use is to show how late the train is! The fact of life is that trains can be, and often need to be, re-scheduled for all sorts of reasons which might or might not be understood if explained in detail at the time to the unfortunate travellers. This is not peculiar to the railways of Australia or New Zealand. It is a worldwide phenomenon.

The would-be traveller in Australia is strongly recommended to obtain a copy of *Travel Times Australia* (*see* page 9). Unfortunately this ceased to be produced in 1996 while this book was being prepared, but its final (fourth) edition remains a comprehensive reference to rail, road and ferry services throughout Australia with many route maps, addresses, phone numbers and other information which will remain helpful, even though the timetables shown will become outdated. Major services (that is, nearly all) for New Zealand as well as Australia are also summarised in the *Thomas Cook Overseas Timetable*. This is reviewed bi-monthly.

The timetables given in this book are extracts only and do not show complete schedules on most lines. In particular, the times given for any round trip excursions may not reflect all the departure times from either the base city or the destination city. On a particular route there may be later departure times from the base city and earlier departure times from the destination city than are shown, none of which would be applicable to the best one-day round trip, but which might be useful if an overnight stay were contemplated.

Services run daily, unless otherwise noted. Where it is stated that services are "frequent", this means at least once each hour during normal daylight hours or between the time limits indicated.

All departure, arrival or other times in this book are given in four figure 24 hour time. A departure at 1.10p.m. is shown as 13.10. Midnight is 24.00. Time between midnight and 1.00a.m. is shown as 00.01 to 00.59. This corresponds to the practice used in most railway timetables in other countries, and in the timetables published by Thomas Cook, although railways in both Australia and New Zealand mostly tend to use a.m. and p.m. instead.

Cross-references to the *Thomas Cook Overseas Timetable* and to *Travel Times Australia* are given at various places in this book, including many of the timetable extracts. These cross-references appear in a distinctive typeface like this (C 9032, T 410), where "C" refers to the Cook's publication and "T" indicates *Travel Times*.

This should help the traveller to make a preliminary check update before finalising travel arrangements and making bookings. (It does not obviate the need for a final check before actually going to the station for the train.)

Where Cook's or *Travel Times* tables do not cover all the places or trains referred to in any of these tables, the word "local" is used instead of or additional to the table numbers. Where a train does not call at a station listed in the timetable, a dash ($-$) is given in place of a timing in most of the tables in this book. Various of the entries in the timetables and itineraries have explanatory footnotes which are shown by a raised letter in the style "Melbourne[c]".

Where arrival or departure times vary on some days by less than five minutes from the normal, the differences are not always shown in the tables so as to save space and simplify the presentation. In such cases the departure times given will always be the earliest, so that you do not miss your train.

GETTING STARTED

Residents of Australia or New Zealand should have very little difficulty starting out on a tour by rail, since they will know, or can easily find out, where the railway station is and can telephone for information and to make bookings, provided, that is, they can get through in the first place.

Railway enquiry numbers, like so many other telephone enquiry services, tend increasingly to be engaged and to put callers in a holding queue listening to music or an advertising blurb until, frustrated, they give up. Until people rise up and complain forcefully about this, it is something we all just have to put up with. If at first you cannot get through, just try again.

Arriving in Australia or New Zealand

For the visitor, however, plans will usually have been made to some extent in advance. But what you need to know is how to get from the airport to the railway station, or maybe first to your hotel to recover from jet lag. If you are catching a train on the day of arrival in Australia or New Zealand, then you want to be sure you have time to catch it. Airports are notorious places for long waits, whether on leaving the country (when they insist you are there hours before the plane's departure so that you spend a lot of money at the duty free shops) or on arrival, when you have to wait for your baggage, go through customs, and perhaps change money into local currency.

Most airports – certainly all the main international ones – have airport bus services which conveniently wait outside the baggage collection areas and convey passengers and their luggage to city hotels and railway stations, at fairly reasonable prices and usually with a fairly frequent service. There are always taxis as well, which offer door to door service a little quicker at twice the price (or sometimes considerably more).

None of Australia's or New Zealand's airports at present has an airport-to-city rail link, although one is planned for Sydney in time for the Olympics in year 2000 and a long mooted (and at one time ineffectually existing) Brisbane airport link is again under "active consideration".

The following is a summary of the airport links that are currently available:

Australia

Adelaide Transit Mini Bus every half hour to and from city (hourly at weekends and public holidays); 7km (4 mile) journey, calling at hotels and Keswick rail terminal. For further details phone (08) 8381 5311.

Brisbane Coachtrans buses every half hour, on the hour and half hour from city, and after arrival of flights from airport. Half hour journey to/from domestic terminal, 40 minutes for international. Buses operate to and from Brisbane Transit Centre (Roma Street station) and call at hotels. Fare $5.40. For further details phone (07) 3236 1000.

Cairns Airport Shuttle Bus to city (7km/4 miles) departs following arrival of flights. Calls at hotels. Railway station is in the city centre. For further details phone (070) 359 555.

Melbourne "Skybus Express" services most flights. Calls at Spencer Street station and also at hotels on weekdays; 23km (14 miles) journey, allow at least one hour. For further details phone (03) 9335 2811.

Perth "Feature Tours" bus, calling at hotels and East Perth railway station en route to the city centre; 13km (8 miles) journey, allow 45 minutes from boarding the bus which meets all arrivals, interstate and international. For further details phone (09) 479 4804.

Sydney Kingsford Smith Airport Bus every 30 minutes from 06.00 to 20.00; 11km (7 mile) journey, allow half an hour. Calls at Central railway station and city hotels. Phone (02) 9667 3221.

Darwin and **Hobart**, although served by some international flights, are excluded from this summary since neither is on or near any railway system. Details of local transport can be obtained from the relevant airlines.

New Zealand

Auckland Auckland Airporter Service to and from Downtown Airline Coach Terminal, calling at hotels and Auckland railway station, every 20 minutes from 06.45 to 20.45 daily. The 20km (12 mile) journey takes 40 minutes and costs $10. Phone (09) 307 5210.

Christchurch "Canride" operates to and from the city centre half hourly on weekdays, hourly at weekends; 12km (7.5 mile) journey. Addington railway station is about 2 miles (3km) from the centre. Taxi fare around $7. Phone (03) 365 5655.

Hamilton There is an Airport Shuttle from the City Shuttle Coach Terminal, as well as a door-to-door service. The railway station at Frankton Junction is 1.7km (1 mile) from Hamilton Travel Centre. For further details phone (07) 847 5618.

Wellington Johnstons Shuttle and the "Super Shuttle" coaches link the front entrance of Wellington railway station direct to and from the airport. Service half hourly; 7km (4 mile) journey. Phone (04) 387 8787 (Super Shuttle) or (04) 384 7654 (Johnstons).

Air and bus connections

Some of the Australian itineraries suggested later in the book include an air hop between Alice Springs and Mount Isa. If this is not operating, it is possible (for a masochist) to travel overnight between these places by coach.

Except where coach services connect otherwise-isolated railheads or provide the only service to major destinations, coach services are not included in this book. *Travel Times Australia* (as well as *Thomas Cook Overseas Timetable*) give details of bus and ferry services.

Prices and fares

All prices and fares are given in Australian or New Zealand dollars as appropriate. All prices were up to date in 1996 when this book was being compiled but, like train timings, they also may be subject to change without notice.

Telephone numbers

All Australian and New Zealand telephone numbers given in this book include the relevant area code, given in parentheses: for example (04) is the New Zealand code for Wellington. For all international calls to Australia and New Zealand the initial "0" in the area code should be omitted and the country codes 61 (Australia) or 64 (New Zealand) used instead.

Chapter One

Discovering Australia and New Zealand

By the scale of European countries, Australia is vast – a continent on its own. Distances are more on the North American scale but even that comparison fails when the Australian climate and population distribution are taken into account. North Africa would be more the archetype. At least if you think of a vast empty desert populated only on the fringes and mostly dry, then you have some idea of Australia. Take North Africa, turn it upside down and flip it over like a page in a book, then there is a faint echo of the more densely populated Nile Delta and Algerian coast in the Australian southeast whilst the rainforest and tropical savannahs of Nigeria and the African west coast are matched by north Queensland and the Northern Territory.

Indeed, travelling on land in much of Australia is not unlike a journey on the African continent. You can experience it on a train – the same timeless bush, the same enervating heat, and the apparently careless disregard for time. Time ceases to have meaning – you just lie there and let it all happen. That is one reason why it is better to see Australia by rail than in a hired car. On the road the vast distances and the glare of the sky will induce drowsiness. The unsealed "gravel" roads of the outback are like the laterite roads of the African savannah – slippery when wet, loose-surfaced when dry, ridged like corrugated iron and infested with thundering great trucks hauling multiple trailers at breakneck speed. These are called road trains. They are as frightening to meet as the "Mammy wagons" of West Africa and more truly lethal than the snakes and crocodiles you will hear about but rarely see in Australia. What you will see of Australia by car is mainly an assortment of road signs, traffic lights, fuel stations (sometimes more than 100 miles/160km apart) and other people's vehicles. Assuming you survive, you will arrive at your destination hot, tired and thirsty, hating both the bush (Australian for the countryside) and the concrete jungle of the city. The visitor will find Australia's road rules confusing and the unwary motorist can easily fall foul of the law.

You are definitely better off by train. You may not get there quicker but you will get there safer and have a chance to look out at the scenery. Some say Australian scenery is boring but they are wrong. It may seem so after a while if you don't look at it closely, but if you do, the variety will surprise you.

By train you can see examples of almost every type of Australian landscape – from the dense rainforests of tropical Queensland to the unbelievable emptiness of the Nullarbor Plain, the deep canyons of the Blue Mountains and the sprawling suburbs of the major cities. You cannot go to the Barrier Reef by train – but you can get very close. You can see some of the islands from the Queensland coastal route and can go by rail to the main centres from which the reefs are accessible by air or sea.

There is no funicular or mountain railway to help you reach the top of Ayers Rock, but you can take a train to within an hour's plane journey of it. You can penetrate the remote outback in air-conditioned luxury on trains like Queensland's *Spirit of the Outback* or Australian National's *The Ghan* and you can travel through "Crocodile Dundee" country on the *Gulflander*. By tram, on the oldest passenger rail line in Australia, you can go down to Port Melbourne where the ships used to bring the migrants to Australia under the Assisted Passage Scheme.

You can go across the Sydney Harbour Bridge by train and look out at the hot, congested streams of frustrated motorists on the adjoining road – who have to pay a toll that is more than your train fare and who will take longer to reach their city destinations than you will on the state-of-the-art double-deck *Tangara* trains of Sydney's Cityrail network. Tedious though many suburban rail journeys can be, the train is clearly superior to driving a car or riding a bus in the rush hour. You can go by train up into the Blue Mountains or down to the beach at Cronulla. You can go by train and tram right into the Royal National Park south of Botany Bay or take the Perisher SkiTube funicular up to Mount Blue Cow in the Snowy Mountains of southern New South Wales.

Australia is a land of great contrasts. Not only is there a world of difference between the wheat fields of Victoria and the sugar plantations of Queensland, or the dry red desert of the interior and the torrential downpours experienced in the coastal ranges; there is a vast difference between the fastest and newest trains and some you may find on the lesser known branch lines.

Australia's vastness and diversity cannot be covered in just a few days. Be prepared for long distances from one major city to another – in fact from almost anywhere to anywhere else. From Brisbane northwards up the Queensland coast to Cairns is as far as from Paris to Naples; from Melbourne to Perth is farther than from Paris to Moscow, while a rail journey from Brisbane to Perth is not much shorter, in either time or distance, than one from Moscow to Mongolia.

You will then be glad to know that almost all Australian trains are air-conditioned. In fact, Australia had the first air-conditioned trains in the Southern Hemisphere. It was also among the first with double-deck suburban electric trains and the first (if not the only) country to provide on-train shower cubicles as part of the ordinary facilities for passengers holding only economy class tickets.

Australia's railways offer a unique way of seeing the country in comfort, style, speed and safety. You will have time to relax, enjoy the scenery, and converse with Australians and tourists from all over the world, while sitting in comfort without the constraining bonds of a seat belt. This book is especially for those overseas visitors who can take advantage of the low-priced Austrailpass (which is not available to residents of Australia) – for details *see* Chapter Two, page 16. It may also open the eyes of many Australians to what this big, wide country has to offer when they travel by rail, using some of the passes and other fare concessions offered by the railway systems of Australia.

New Zealand is as different again from Australia as Australia is from anywhere else, and despite its smaller size contains an amazing diversity of scenery. Some say it is more like Britain and this is a matter of perception, but no-one can travel very far in New Zealand without observing the differences in the landscape; some obvious, some ever so subtle yet unmistakeable. Where in the British Isles would you find, for example, fields bounded by tall shelter belts, often only the width of one row of trees, like a ten-metre high hedgerow – and even in Northumberland or Wales you will not see any landscape so full of sheep as you will in parts of both the North and South Islands of New Zealand.

Near Rotorua in the north you are in a land of hot springs and mud pools; in the Southland you could easily think you were somewhere in the European Alps, in the Rockies or among the fiords of Norway – that is, if you are looking at the natural scenery. Once there is evidence of adaptation of the environment to human needs, the illusion vanishes and if you look closely, even the flora and fauna give the game away.

New Zealand has an area of 265,150km^2 (103,000 square miles) and a population of about 3½ million people. So it is not surprising to find in a country approximately the size of the United Kingdom with less than one tenth the population, that the railway system comprises little over 4,000km (2,500 miles) (compared to over 17,000km/10,600 miles in the United Kingdom and almost 40,000km/24,800 miles in Australia), and that passenger trains operate only over some 2,400km (1,500 miles). Nevertheless, Tranz Rail offers a daily service or better on every route, including the Tranz Scenic long distance trains and the Tranz Metro services of Wellington and Auckland, as well as providing better than daily ferry services linking the passenger rail networks of the North and South Islands.Whether your destination is in the fiords and snow-clad Alps of the South Island, the thermal wonders of the North Island, or the lush green pastures famed for succulent Canterbury Lamb, you can reach most of the key points by rail, in comfort and without fuss. A New Zealand Travelpass (*see* Chapter Nine, page 161) is available covering coach and ferry as well as rail services.

To help the tourist make the most of an Austrailpass or a New Zealand Travelpass and to show residents as well as visitors how to make the best use of the state passes and other special tickets available locally, this book offers ideas not found in any official publications or ordinary travel literature. As well as giving essential details about the principal and most popular train services this book suggests a number of itineraries which should be useful both to those who stick to the main lines and those who like to wander off the beaten track.

TRAINS IN AUSTRALIA AND NEW ZEALAND

No Australian or New Zealand trains travel as fast as British or European expresses, nor are the rail networks anything like the intricate pattern of routes found in Europe, where there can be many different ways of going between one place and another. But provided you make judicious reservations it is possible to get around both countries very well by train and see, or at least get within striking distance of, most of the main scenic attractions.

Australia still suffers from a proliferation of rail gauges – a problem which took years to solve in Britain and was averted only with difficulty in North America's early railroad days. Queensland, from Brisbane north and west including Toowoomba, Townsville, Cairns and Mount Isa, has the narrow, substandard gauge of 3ft 6in (1067mm). So does Western Australia except between Kalgoorlie,

Perth and the port area of Kwinana. New South Wales, from Sydney west to Broken Hill, south to Albury and Canberra, and north to the Tablelands and coast and through the border ranges into Brisbane, uses standard gauge (4ft 8½in or 1435mm) while the Victorian system, radiating north, east and west from Melbourne, is mostly of the broader "Irish" gauge of 5ft 3in (1600mm). Australian National, serving Adelaide west and north to Kalgoorlie and Alice Springs and including most of South Australia, uses both standard and Irish gauge.

It is easy to picture the havoc this can cause for "through" trains. However, since 1995 the problem has been overcome on all the main interstate routes. Brisbane in Queensland, Sydney in New South Wales, Melbourne in Victoria, Adelaide in South Australia, Perth in Western Australia and Alice Springs in the Northern Territory are all now linked by the standard gauge network.

In contrast to Australia, New Zealand's national rail network is a uniform 3ft 6in (1067mm) gauge.

The narrow gauge of Queensland is one reason that state has the slowest trains in Australia, although in recent years there has been substantial line upgrading and realignment, with a consequent increase in average speeds. A Swedish X-2000 tilting trainset was trialled in New South Wales in 1995 and Queensland has its own tilt trains under construction, likely to enter service by 1997 between Brisbane and Rockhampton.

Sharp curves and stiff gradients on many routes contribute to Australia's generally slow average speeds. The vintage tourist train from Cairns to Kuranda in far north Queensland takes 90 minutes to go 33km (20 miles) but when you see where and how it goes it is no surprise!

Queensland has more stations per person than any other state and many of its trains are required to stop at small stations on request, making tight schedules out of the question. In Queensland it is also possible still to find the occasional "mixed" train – a freight train with one passenger car – and freight wagons are often attached to the principal passenger trains serving Western Queensland. Such curiosities make Australia a paradise for rail buffs and those who enjoy the unusual, while for the ordinary tourist the main intercity and interstate expresses live up to the best railway traditions.

Rail travel in Australia and New Zealand has much the same advantages over air travel as has rail travel in Europe. It avoids time otherwise spent going to and from the airport and the nuisance of being there long before flight departure time. You are not encased in a capsule high above the clouds with little or no view of the sights and scenery en route, and the tedious delays waiting to claim luggage at the destination are mostly avoided, or at least reduced. As is true of rail travel everywhere, the slowness of the actual journey compared to air is not important when there is more real sightseeing time for the traveller to enjoy.

The visitor armed with an Austrailpass, which, like the famous Eurailpass is a wonderful bargain, can take the *Indian Pacific* rail cruise across the whole continent and back and pay less than an Australian has to pay for a single one-way trip.

Even the additional luxury of a sleeping berth (not covered by the pass) is not prohibitively expensive. A twin-berth sleeper on an interstate train costs perhaps 30% less than a double room in a 4-star hotel in a city such as Melbourne. For the single traveller the difference is much greater. Although the train cannot offer quite the luxury or spaciousness of a good hotel it is still, with its air-conditioning, private toilet and shower, an attractive proposition for the traveller wishing to use limited time to the best advantage.

You can spend nights sleeping comfortably on a train and wake up in a new place every day with new things to see and do. Depending on where you want to start and finish your tour, you can visit all the mainland state capitals of Australia – Perth, Adelaide, Melbourne, Sydney and Brisbane – in less than three weeks and you can include a side trip to Cairns or Alice Springs as well. By spending some of your nights on the train, you will not only save money and cover more of the country, but have opportunities to meet, talk and relax with people far more than in a lonely suite in a big city hotel.

New Zealand currently has no sleeping car services but the Auckland–Wellington main line can be traversed by day or night in comfortable accommodation and with on-board refreshment. All other rail centres in New Zealand can be reached by day trains in a day or less either from Auckland, Wellington or Christchurch. Wellington to Christchurch or vice versa is also a day trip including the ferry between Wellington and Picton.

Chapter Two

Organising Your Trip: Australia

This chapter is designed to be helpful both to those visitors who will, as far as practicable, make travel plans in advance and also those individual travellers who prefer or who are compelled to make their arrangements at shorter notice. Knowing about the alternative rail journeys that are available can be fruitful for the tourist who has made no prior reservations and arrives in Australia to find the popular "named" trains have been fully booked months in advance. Sleeping accommodation on trains is particularly hard to find at short notice during December and January, the Australian summer holiday months. Travel agents do not always warn tourists of these problems and some may not even be aware of them. Prior reservations are essential if you have a tight schedule and want to travel on the best known trains over the main routes.

You may have heard the standard Aussie assurance that "she'll be right, mate". The railways will try hard to help a visitor who is in difficulty, but it is not sensible to leave everything to chance. Key bookings should be made before you leave home, through your travel agent or direct through one of the offices listed here.

INFORMATION AND RESERVATIONS

The overseas marketing of the railways of Australia is co-ordinated by an organisation called Rail Australia, whose head office is located in the headquarters of Australian National at Adelaide.

The address is Rail Australia, 1 Richmond Road, Keswick, SA 5035; phone (08) 8217 4321 and fax (08) 8217 4609. For calls from outside Australia the country code "61" is used to replace the initial "0" of the "08" Adelaide area code.

There are sales agents in Canada, Denmark, France, Germany, Hong Kong, Japan, Korea, Netherlands, New Zealand, Singapore, South Africa, Sweden, United Kingdom and U.S.A. Your travel agent should be able to obtain detailed information from these agents or you can contact them direct. Full addresses are given in the Appendix on pages 204-5.

The Australian Tourist Commission has offices in some countries (*see* listing in Appendix, page 207) and will also be able to help. Bookings may also be made through Thomas Cook offices, where timetables and rail maps can be obtained.

The Austrailpass may be purchased from the offices of Qantas, the Australian airline, or from Jetabout Tours offices anywhere in the world.

Each Australian mainland state capital has an information and reservation office at its main railway terminal. There are also rail travel centres in central city locations and at some suburban and provincial stations. The following should cover most needs.

Information offices

Countrywide
The nearest rail information office can be reached at local call rates from most places in Australia by dialling 132 232. No area code is required. Where no phone number is given in the listing below the 132 232 number applies.

Australian Capital Territory
Countrylink Travel and Booking Centre, Railway station, Canberra. Phone (06) 249 8159.

New South Wales
Countrylink Rail Travel Centre, City Booking Office, Transport House, 11-31 York Street, Sydney, NSW 2000. Fax (02) 9224 4513. Also at Main Booking Office, Sydney Terminal station, Railway Square, and at the central city underground stations of Town Hall on George Street, and Wynyard on York Street near the Rail Travel Centre.

Victoria
City Booking Office, V/Line Travel, Transport House, 589 Collins Street, Melbourne, Vic. 3000. Fax (03) 3619-2728. Also at Main Booking Office, Spencer Street station, which is opposite Transport House at the west end of Collins Street. Phone (03) 9620-0771.

Queensland
Queensland Rail Travel Centre, Ground Floor, Central station, 305 Edward Street, Brisbane, Qld 4000. Fax (07) 3235 2940. Also at Brisbane Transit Centre, Roma Street station. In Cairns, at Booking Office, Railway Station, McLeod Street, and in Townsville at Booking Office, Railway Station, Flinders Street.

South Australia

Australian National, Keswick Rail Passenger Terminal, Keswick, SA 5035 (GPO Box 1743). Fax (08) 8217 4567 and at City Booking Office, Australian National Travel Centre, 136 North Terrace, near City station.

Western Australia

Interstate Booking Office, Westrail Centre, East Perth, WA 6000 (GPO Box S1422). Also at Westrail Travel Centre, City Rail Station, Wellington Street, Perth. Fax (09) 326 2063.

Northern Territory

Booking Office, Railway Station (off George Crescent), Alice Springs.

Tasmania

Tasmanian Travel Centre, 80 Elizabeth Street, Hobart, Tas. 7000. Phone: (03) 6230 8233. There are no main line passenger railways in Tasmania.

With the notable exception of Thomas Cook Travel, most travel agencies in Australia offer little information on rail travel and are unenthusiastic about finding it for you unless a rail trip is part of a package tour they are promoting. The various state tourist offices mostly have branches in the capital cities of the other states. These are additional places to obtain useful information, particularly about accommodation.

The State rail authorities and Australian National all publish their own timetables, usually in the form of individual leaflets or booklets covering particular regions. These are free of charge. Rail Australia publishes a useful summary sheet of major services. Suburban timetables are also published separately and leaflets for particular lines can be obtained free at most railway stations.

The Australian section of *Thomas Cook Overseas Timetable*, which is obtainable through Thomas Cook travel agencies in Australia and overseas, provides the closest thing to an up-to-date Australia-wide rail timetable.

More detail is given in *Travel Times Australia*, published by Traveltime Publishing, 3 Goodwin Street, Glen Iris, Victoria 3146. Unfortunately the May 1996 edition of this useful publication will be the last. Even though the timetables it contains will become out of date it also contains much other valuable information which will not date so readily. The last edition is still available from the publishers, price $7.95.

RAIL FARES AND PASSES

Most Australian trains, other than suburban services, have both first class and economy seating, although it is sometimes hard to tell the difference, particularly in New South Wales. For the budget-conscious traveller the economy seating in most XPT carriages (Sydney to NSW North Coast, Dubbo, Brisbane and Melbourne) is virtually no different in standard from first class. Western Australia's *Australind* (Perth–Bunbury) has one class only and there is no differentiation when you travel on any remaining "mixed" trains of outback Queensland.

Sleeping berths in New South Wales require a first class ticket as prerequisite. Economy sleeping berths as well as first class are available on most long distance trains within Queensland, while "holiday class" berths are available to economy class ticket holders on the *Ghan* (Adelaide–Alice Springs) and the *Indian Pacific* (Sydney–Adelaide–Perth). These trains, as well as the *Sunlander* and the *Spirit of the Tropics* (Brisbane–Proserpine/Cairns) also have very comfortable economy seating and also carry shower compartments for sitting passengers.

You can obtain information on ticket prices from most stations, the travel centres in the capital cities, or direct from Rail Australia.

Although there are various regional or state rail passes obtainable by anyone in Australia, none compare in value with the Austrailpass which is available only to visitors. However, this may not be the answer for a visitor intending to spend a holiday mostly or only in one state.

The following passes can be purchased at all Rail Australia agencies and at the main railway stations in the states concerned by visitors and Australians alike. A leaflet published by Rail Australia called *National and State Passes* is available with updates of this information. The details given below were correct at 1 April 1996 but may be subject to change.

Western Australia

Westrail Premier Discovery Pass One class: $189 for 21 days. Covers scheduled services in Western Australia by rail or by coaches owned or contracted by Westrail. (Perth to Bunbury, Albany, Esperance, Kalgoorlie, Geraldton and Meekatharra and Bunbury–Albany) and the fare component of some local package tours. Not valid for the special *Wildflower* coach tours, for Perth suburban rail system, or on the *Indian Pacific*. Meals on the *Prospector* are additional.

Westrail Southern Discovery Pass One class: $109 for 28 days. Restricted to Westrail Southern Circle Route in one direction; i.e. Perth–Bunbury–Margaret River–Augusta–Pemberton–Albany–Esperance–Kalgoorlie–Perth (includes travel on all coaches and trains except the *Indian Pacific*).

Victoria

V/Line Victoria Pass First class: $130 for 14 days. Half price for persons under 16 or holders of a Railways of Australia student identification card. A 7-day version at $75 is also available but only to holders of foreign passports. Obtainable in Melbourne from V/Line Travel, 589 Collins Street; Victour in Collins Street; YHA Travel, 205 King Street; and at Spencer Street and Flinders Street stations; also at Geelong, Ballarat and Bendigo railway stations.

Covers all rail and coach services operated by V/Line within Victoria: Melbourne to Albury/Wodonga, Bairnsdale, Geelong, Warrnambool, Hamilton, Horsham, Ballarat, Mildura, Swan Hill, Bendigo, Echuca, Cobram, and many smaller towns.

Not valid for Melbourne City trains, bus or tram systems, for which separate daily and other passes at very reasonable rates are available. Not valid for any part of an interstate journey or to Albury on interstate trains. (*See* paragraph overleaf, "Restrictions on Interstate Travel").

Victoria Pass holders are entitled to 25% discount on Budget Car Rentals and 10% discount off the room rate at any Flag or Homestead Inn in Victoria if reserved in advance at V/Line booking offices.

New South Wales

Countrylink offers a one calendar month **Discovery Pass** at $249 and a YHA one month Discovery Pass at $224. Available from the Rail Travel Centre or Central Reservation Office, Sydney, main stations in New South Wales and the NSW Government Travel Centre in Brisbane.

Covers all trains and State Rail-operated buses in New South Wales (except the Brisbane route north of Kyogle) including Sydney to Tweed Heads, Grafton, Taree, Newcastle, Wollongong, Nowra, Cooma, Albury, Griffith, Broken Hill, Bourke, Lightning Ridge, Bathurst, Tamworth, and many smaller centres shown on maps included in free State Rail timetables or other leaflets. Valid for XPT services and Sydney suburban trains. Sleeping berths and meals not included. Not valid for interstate travel except to Canberra.

There is another special kind of ticket, rather misleadingly called a "Pass" and this is the **East Coast Discovery Pass**. It is simply a one-way economy class ticket at a special fare which can be used at any time (subject to the usual reservation restrictions) once only within a period of six months. It is available for Sydney to Brisbane or Surfers Paradise or vice versa, or Sydney to Melbourne or vice versa, at $76, Melbourne to Brisbane or Surfers or vice versa, at $152, Sydney to Cairns via Surfers or via Brisbane or vice versa, at $199, or Melbourne to Cairns or vice versa, again by either of the two routes, at $275.

Queensland

Sunshine Rail Pass First class, 14 days $388, 21 days $477, one month $582; economy, 14 days $267, 21 days $309, one month $388, with half price for children. Available from QR Travel Centres at Roma Street and Central stations, Brisbane, at Surfers Paradise, Rockhampton, Townsville and Cairns and at other main railway stations in Queensland.

Covers all Traveltrain and Citytrain rail services in Queensland, including the Gold Coast, Brisbane to Toowoomba, Charleville, Longreach, Mount Isa, Rockhampton, Townsville, Cairns and many smaller places. Valid for the Brisbane suburban system, and for all the coach services operated by, or on behalf of, Queensland Rail (Ipswich–Toogoolawah, Charleville–Cunnamulla/Quilpie, Longreach–Winton, Cairns–Ravenshoe and others), and travel by freight trains where passenger accommodation is sometimes attached (it is vital to check this before travel), but not for the standard gauge trains to the NSW border operated by Countrylink.

Surcharges apply for sleeping berths and supplementary charges apply for travel on the *Queenslander* (currently $233 Brisbane–Cairns or $206 Brisbane–Townsville) to cover sleeping accommodation, meals and other extras.

Valid for the Kuranda Tourist Train, the *Gulflander* (Normanton–Croydon) and the Forsayth train. Does not cover the "Sunshine Daylight Rail Experience" operated by the Queensland Government Travel Centre (196 Adelaide Street, Brisbane; phone (07) 331 2211).

Restrictions on interstate travel

It is important to note that these State rail passes do not overlap or even meet. The NSW rail pass is valid only as far south as Albury and as far north as Kyogle or Murwillumbah. Although the Victoria Pass extends to Albury the two cannot be used together for a through Sydney–Melbourne journey, unless of course you break it at the border when no-one else need find out or has the business to know. Nor can you use a NSW Discovery Pass to travel between New South Wales and Brisbane, even by offering to pay the fare difference north from Kyogle. You have to pay the whole fare or break the journey at Kyogle (or Tweed Heads on the Countrylink coach), involving an overnight wait.

Another inter-railway curiosity (commonly experienced by rail travellers in Europe) may also be faced in Australia in that journeys across a State border are sometimes surcharged when you buy an ordinary through ticket. If you do not mind a break of journey you can sometimes save money by getting out, then re-booking, and continuing on a different train. Perhaps because of criticism of this anomaly, the normal commercial principle of price reducing with quantity has recently been applied; for example travelling from Sydney–Melbourne, booking to Albury, then from there to Melbourne now totals $144.60 whereas the through fare is only $130. It all becomes very complicated. But if you have an Austrailpass, all such difficulties disappear.

THE AUSTRAILPASS

This pass is available only to visitors from overseas (including Australian passport holders living abroad and having a valid round trip air ticket to the country of residence). It allows unlimited first or economy class travel on all government-owned railways and all railway-operated or railway-contracted coach services in Australia, including suburban trains in Sydney, Melbourne, Adelaide, Perth, Brisbane and Newcastle, but not buses operated by the State Transport Authority of South Australia.

It is sold in the United Kingdom by the many branches of Thomas Cook and in most parts of the world by travel agents and by Tour Pacific/Australian Travel Service. The phone number for all of the U.S.A. except California is (800) 432 2880; for California (800) 232 2121. It can also be purchased worldwide at any office of the Australian airline Qantas or of Jetabout Tours as well as all Rail Australia agents (*see* Appendix, pages 204-5).

In Australia it can be purchased from Rail Australia and the rail travel centres of the state capital cities, by residents of countries where it is not distributed or by other visitors who have been unable to obtain one before arrival in Australia. The applicant must produce a passport and outbound flight tickets. In case of difficulty, contact the Rail Australia office in Adelaide; phone (08) 8217 4321.

Use of the pass must begin within six months of date of issue (12 months when issued in New Zealand) and be completed by midnight on the last day of validity. The pass must be presented with the passport at the departure station of the initial journey for validation. No refund is payable after use commences.

There are two varieties, the normal Australpass for consecutive days of travel, and the Austrail Flexipass for those wishing to select a set number of days within a longer period (up to six months). This is ideal for people wishing to visit Australia and travel between places by train but not every day.

With the Austrail Flexipass, a day is counted as a period of up to 24 hours from the scheduled departure time of the train on which that day's journey commences. For example, an overnight trip between Melbourne and Adelaide starting one evening and finishing the following morning would count as only one day of use – provided there was no other rail travel using the pass on either of the two days. This also applies to the last day of use, when, for example, the pass would be valid for a journey commencing in Longreach at 07.00 and finishing in Brisbane at 06.30 the next morning.

Prices from July 1996 (in Australian dollars) are:

Australpass

	First class	Budget
14 days	$780	$460
21 days	$985	$595
30 days	$1210	$720
7 day extension	$410	$250

Austrail Flexipass

	First class	Budget
8 days	$650	$380
15 days	$915	$550
22 days	$1270	$770
29 days	$1620	$995

The 8-day Flexipass is **not valid** for travel between Adelaide and Perth or between Adelaide and Alice Springs.

Both classes of the Australpass and Austrail Flexipass cover seat reservations but not ancillary charges such as sleeping berths and meals. There is no fare reduction for children. The first class Australpass and Austrail Flexipass may also be used for economy class travel. The budget Australpass covers economy travel only, and cannot be upgraded to first class except where no economy sleeping or sitting accommodation is available on the desired service, when the difference between normal economy and first class fare, plus sleeping berth charges if appropriate, will be payable. However, the budget Austrailpass also covers "holiday class" accommodation on the *Ghan* and *Indian Pacific,* subject to the payment of the appropriate berth charges.

To help you work out whether an Austrailpass is worthwhile for your itinerary, some ticket prices for major journeys are given below. To facilitate comparison, the charges for sleeping berths and meals have been excluded from these figures, even where they are a compulsory addition to the normal fare (as, for example, first class Sydney–Perth on the *Indian Pacific*).

Sleeping berth charges must be added to fares quoted, and are also payable by holders of State or National rail passes. The first class prices range from $50 a night in Queensland, $66 on Australian National services, to $90 on Countrylink services. Holiday class berths on Australian National (Sydney–Adelaide–Perth and Adelaide–Alice Springs) are $33 per night, while Queensland has economy class berths at $30 per night.

Meal costs vary. Where meal payment is compulsory (by first class sleeping berth holders on the *Indian Pacific*, the *Ghan* and the *Queenslander*) charges range from $34 Adelaide–Alice Springs on the *Ghan* to $122 Sydney–Perth on the *Indian Pacific*. On the *Queenslander* the meal, berth and other charges additional to first class fare amount to $233 Brisbane–Cairns, or $206 Brisbane–Townsville.

The meal surcharge on the first-class-only *Prospector* (Perth–Kalgoorlie) is $8.90. Optional meal charges on the other services vary from perhaps $5 for a simple fork meal to around $16 for a three-course table-d'hôte dinner or perhaps more for an à-la-carte selection.

Sample fares

Fares quoted in this guide are correct at the time of going to press. However, Rail Australia warns that: "All fares as well as time-tables are subject to alteration without notice."

Ticket prices shown are in Australian dollars and are for one way journeys without berths or meals as explained in the paragraphs above.

Sample fares

Journey	First	Holiday	Economy
Sydney–Perth (normal)	$796.00*	$628.00*	$360.00
Sydney–Perth (low season)◊	$690.00*	$554.00*	$360.00
Adelaide–Perth (normal)	$518.00*	$402.00*	$220.00
Adelaide–Perth (low season)◊	$448.00*	$354.00*	$220.00
Adelaide–Alice Springs (normal)	$400.00*	$292.00*	$144.00
Adelaide–Alice Springs (low season)◊	$350.00*	$258.00*	$144.00
Sydney–Adelaide via Broken Hill (normal)	$278.00*	$226.00*	$140.00
Sydney–Adelaide via Broken Hill (low season)	$242.00*	$200.00*	$140.00
Sydney–Melbourne	$125.00	N/A	$90.00
Sydney–Brisbane	$125.00	N/A	$90.00
Sydney–Canberra	$54.00	N/A	$40.00
Sydney–Murwillumbah	$117.00	N/A	$85.00
Sydney–Broken Hill (*Indian Pacific*)	$186.00	$148.00	$92.00
Sydney–Broken Hill (Countrylink)	$117.00	N/A	$95.00
Sydney–Albury	$98.00	N/A	$70.00
Melbourne–Albury	$51.00	N/A	$36.40
Melbourne–Adelaide	$104.00	N/A	$50.00
Brisbane–Cairns	$193.00*	N/A	$129.00
Perth–Kalgoorlie	$58.80#	N/A	$60.00

* The fares so marked are for comparison only: tickets are not available for such journeys without extra berth and meal charges.

◊ Low season fares on the *Ghan* or *Indian Pacific* Sydney–Adelaide–Perth or Adelaide–Alice Springs are to be discontinued after April 1997.

The anomaly in Perth–Kalgoorlie fares is due to the fact that first class seats are available only on the *Prospector*, while economy seats are available only on the *Indian Pacific*, which is dearer, even though the *Prospector* fare quoted above includes a meal.

The complication of fare/berth/meal packages makes comparisons difficult and some tourists are confused and disgruntled when they find the Austrailpass involves many additions (as most other rail passes do everywhere). However, a single calculation is sufficient to show the benefit of an Austrailpass.

From Cairns in northern Queensland to Perth in Western Australia via Melbourne, one way, using ordinary tickets, travelling first class including sleeping berths only on necessarily overnight parts of the journey, (that is, assuming day travel Brisbane–Sydney–Melbourne but not Kalgoorlie–Perth) would cost over $1300 in fares. This is without counting the costs of optional à-la-carte meals between Cairns, Brisbane, Sydney and Melbourne (which are an extra in either case).

Using a 14-day first class Austrailpass, the total for the same trip would be $1028, provided of course that the journey was completed in that time. This would be no problem so long as accommodation was available at the time sought; the full journey on the above basis could be completed in seven days commencing on a Monday, or eight days commencing on a Thursday. So that, even on such a limited use of the pass, a significant saving is achieved.

This is without taking into account the fact that the same 14-day Austrailpass could be used for numerous side trips in the capital cities or elsewhere en route. It could even cover the travel element (fare only) of a return journey from Perth to Cairns, which could be accomplished within the 14-day validity of the Austrailpass if the Monday departure from Cairns were selected and only one night were spent in Perth.

Standard fare conditions

Discounts

Except for special tickets like the Austrailpass, children under 16 are entitled to discounted fares, generally half the normal adult fare. Children under 4 travel free unless occupying a separate seat on interstate trains or occupying a sleeping berth. Students of Australian tertiary educational establishments and Australian old age pensioners can also travel at reduced fares. Round trip tickets normally cost twice the one way fare.

Discounted fares, varying from 10% to 40% off the normal, are available on some routes and some trains in New South Wales; details on application. A special "coach class" fare is available between Adelaide and Kalgoorlie or Perth and vice versa.

Seat reservations

There are no seat reservation fees on Australian railways and seats and berths on the principal trains may usually be reserved six months in advance, but fees are charged for late cancellations of sleeping berths.

Luggage
The passenger luggage allowance is 50kg/110lb (not counting hand luggage). Luggage may be checked in at all the major railway stations, usually not less than half an hour before train departure. Such luggage will be placed in the baggage car and will not be accessible during the journey. It will also be difficult to retrieve should you decide to change your destination en route.

Sitting and sleeping cars on long distance trains all also have ample space for luggage at the end of the carriage or in the compartments. Luggage may be left at stations either in lockers or depositories. Charges for this vary from $2 or more to nil at smaller stations, where you arrange it with the station master (if you can find one!).

Cars
Motor vehicles may be carried at reasonable rates on the *Queenslander* (Brisbane–Townsville and Cairns), the *Spirit of the Outback* (Brisbane–Longreach), trains from Adelaide to Melbourne, Sydney, Alice Springs or Perth and vice versa, and on the Melbourne–Mildura goods (this motorail service being the only relic of the former *Vinelander* sleeping car service, now replaced by an overnight bus).

Credit cards and money
Most credit cards are acceptable for rail bookings at major stations, and for meals or other refreshments on most major train services, usually subject to a $10 minimum. There are banking and exchange facilities at Thomas Cook and American Express offices in major cities, as well as at banks themselves. Banks or Autobanks are located at the main railway stations in Brisbane and Melbourne, but not Perth, Adelaide or Sydney.

Tipping
Tipping in Australia is optional; occasionally practised in some restaurants (and in dining cars), less often, if ever, in bars, rarely in sleeping cars, and almost never in taxicabs – where it is customary to sit next to the driver and engage in friendly conversation. A genuine "thanks, mate" will be more appreciated than a tip, which is regarded as patronising or even insulting.

Remember, the Australian ethic is that everyone is as good as you, and you as good as they, provided you don't ever commit the unforgivable sin of comparing Australia unfavourably with your own country!

Railway food

Sometimes you will have to indulge; there is nowhere else to find sustenance without taking your own (which, though not exactly prohibited, is frowned upon). Generally Australian railway food is good, some of it excellent.

You can get tasty hot snacks reasonably cheaply on trains like the XPT or *Xplorer*, and on Queensland long distance trains. V/Line's InterCity services and QR's *Spirit of Capricorn* have rather more limited fare but there is no need to starve.

Main meals in dining cars cost no more, often less, than they would in a comparable restaurant (one with sit-down service, not a pub counter lunch). Trains like the *Ghan*, the *Indian Pacific* and the *Queenslander* more than border on gourmet style food. Less extravagant is the humble railway pie, which has recently made a comeback, and is very tasty, inexpensive sustenance for the hungry, even if a trifle messy to consume.

As for breakfasts, the railways of Australia do better than most. Not all Australians really consume chunks of steak or chops with egg for their daybreak meal, but on some overnight long distance sleeper trains you would certainly think they did. Try it.

Chapter Three

Introducing
Australian Trains

Before considering how to make the most effective use of whatever passes or tickets you have, it will help if you know what to expect of Australian trains. This chapter tells you where they go, how often they run, and what they are like.

Australian express trains are only about half to two thirds as fast as their counterparts in Europe or some other areas. There is nothing comparable to the French TGV or Japanese Shinkansen. The mean speed of all country and intercity trains in Australia is less than 64 km/h (40mph) for whole journeys, but some – like the XPTs (an abbreviation for Express Passenger Train) and *Xplorer* of New South Wales and Westrail's *Prospector* – maintain over twice that speed for considerable distances.

Since the mid 1980s, when Australia briefly joined the world speed league with advertised trains that achieved start-to-stop runs between two successive stations at over 120 km/h (75mph), and became the first country in the Southern Hemisphere to do so, Australian railway systems have suffered many ups and downs. At the time of writing Australia's fastest train, the XPT of New South Wales (a train based on the well-known and successful HST125 of British Rail), limited to a line speed of 160 km/h (100mph), achieves no more than 92.6 km/h (57.5mph) overall on its fastest run between Sydney and Melbourne overnight, while in the west the non-stop *Prospector* – though limited to only 120 km/h (75mph) maximum, maintains nearly 109 km/h (67.5mph) overall for the 655 km (407 miles) between Western Australia's capital city of Perth and the goldfield centre of Kalgoorlie. On this basis, the *Prospector* lays claim to be Australia's fastest train in spite of the higher maximum of the XPT.

All Australian interstate trains are air conditioned and require seat or berth reservations. Most of them, as well as many other long distance interstate trains, do not carry passengers between all intermediate stations, especially those within an hour or two's journey of major terminals. These places with "restricted" stops (either for picking up only or setting down only) or "conditional" stops (where the train only stops on prior request for confirmed bookings) are indicated in the timetables.

Where the letter (c) follows a place name given in this guide, it means there are some such restrictions, about which intending passengers should always enquire before attempting to travel to or from those places.

As a general principle it can be expected that a long distance train will not take passengers from its city of origin to somewhere in the outer suburbs, but may well pick up passengers there to go a longer distance.

All interstate and most other long distance trains have catering of some sort, though not always for the entire journey, and with a few exceptions, non-smoking is the rule (as it is on coaches and internal air line services).

INTERSTATE TRAINS

The Indian Pacific
Sydney–Adelaide–Perth

Departs Sydney westbound Mondays and Thursdays 14.40 and Adelaide a day later at 18.00. Departs East Perth eastbound Mondays and Fridays 13.30 and Adelaide two days later at 07.45. A 67-hour transcontinental trip, of 4,348km (2,700 miles), the longest in Australia, with three nights on the train.

Stops at Lithgow (c), Bathurst (c), Blayney (c), Orange East Fork (c), Parkes, Condobolin (c), Ivanhoe (c), Menindee, Broken Hill, Peterborough, Gladstone (c), Adelaide, Port Pirie (Coonamia), Port Augusta, Pimba (c), Kingoonya (c), Tarcoola, Barton, Cook, Rawlinna, Zanthus (c), Kalgoorlie, Southern Cross (c), Merredin (c), Kellerberrin (c), Northam (c), East Perth.

Carries first class roomettes (single sleepers with toilet), twinettes (double sleepers with toilet and shower), limited family sleepers (interconnecting twinettes), also one luxury bedroom/drawing room compartment for two. Holiday class sleepers (twin) are also available, plus economy sitting cars with reclining seats.

The *Indian* has a 48-seat restaurant car and lounge bar car for first class passengers, with complimentary 24-hour tea and coffee service. The "Matilda" restaurant offers holiday class passengers main courses ordered at the counter, with quality self-serve salad bar. Bar and buffet service is also available for all coach class passengers. Video films are shown in the holiday class club car and at overhead display units in coach class. There are separate smoking "capsules" in both the first class and the holiday class club cars.

First class sleeping cabins have seats with armrests converting into beds, visitor's seat, wash basin and toilet, wardrobe, reading lights, venetian blinds, luggage rack and electric razor socket. Holiday class sleepers are less spacious, consisting virtually of two berths (upper and lower) in the space of a first class roomette. Economy sitting cars and all sleeping cars, have showers at the end of each carriage; first class twinettes have showers in every sleeping compartment.

Meals are paid in advance with the fare when booking first class sleepers. Typical menus include: breakfast of fruit juice, cereal, scrambled eggs or omelette with bacon and sausages, toast and coffee or tea; lunch of soup, lamb and rosemary pie, beef lasagne, or avocado and prawn salad, dessert, coffee or tea; dinner consisting of soup, entrée, choice of main course and dessert, cheese platter, coffee or tea and after dinner mints. Typical main dinner courses include beef Stroganoff, rack of lamb, ocean trout, and grilled porterhouse steak. Fine quality local wines are available with lunch and dinner and in the lounge and club cars, as well as beer, spirits and soft drinks.

Leaflets giving full details of the route and all the services are provided, and sleeping compartments have conductor call buttons, complimentary toilet packs and stationery.

The *Indian* carries motor vehicles between Sydney, Adelaide and Perth. Charges vary from $175 (accompanied) Sydney–Adelaide, up to $930 for a vehicle over 5.5m but not more than 7m long Sydney–Perth. Charges for unaccompanied vehicles are approximately 50% higher.

The Ghan
Adelaide–Alice Springs

The Ghan, current flagship and pride of Australian National, is Australia's oldest named train, though now very different from the old narrow gauge train which first acquired that appellation as a nickname and which took over 31 hours to cover the 869km (540 miles) from Marree, near Lake Eyre, to Alice Springs (27 km/h or 16.7mph when it was on time), but like its predecessor it has already become a legend and, in 1991 won the Australian Tourist Industry Association's award for the best tourist transport service.

The new *Ghan* runs from Adelaide north to the "red centre" at Alice Springs, 1557km (967 miles) in 20 hours with one night on board. It runs once weekly in each direction all year round, leaving

Adelaide at 14.00 on Thursday and Alice Springs at 14.00 on Friday.

A regular additional "relief" service has traditionally operated from May through October on Mondays, returning on Tuesdays, with another relief possibly running on Saturdays returning Sundays. However, shortly before this book went to press it was announced that these services would not operate until further notice.

Intermediate stations are Port Pirie (Coonamia), Port Augusta, Pimba, Kingoonya, Tarcoola, Marla (c) and Kulgera.

Named after the Afghan camel drivers who pioneered this south-north trade route, the *Ghan* is a far cry from the primitive travel standards of those pioneer days, with luxurious first class twinette and roomette sleepers, holiday sleepers and economy recliner seats. These last could well be called first class on other railway systems, being 59cm (23in) wide, in 2+1 formation, with a generous pitch of 1.17m (3ft 10in).

For first class passengers there is the "Stuart" Restaurant with silver service and tantalising dishes like venison and juniper pie entrée, baked barramundi or roast Scotch fillet, while economy and holiday passengers have a separate family-style restaurant (the "Matilda") serving excellent freshly prepared food at reasonable prices.

There are two first class lounge cars, the "Dreamtime" lounge with electronic piano/organ and the "Oasis" bar, which is available for smokers (but not excluding other passengers). Video films, showers and a ladies' retiring room are available in the economy and holiday cars, while first class passengers have showers in their compartment or at the end of the coach. Souvenir folders and toilet packs are provided to sleeping car passengers and souvenirs featuring the *Ghan* motif, a black on red camel on a buff background, are obtainable from the bar.

The *Ghan* carries motor vehicles between Adelaide and Alice Springs.

The *Alice*, a former direct Sydney–Alice Springs weekly service has been withdrawn and is unlikely to return. However, the concept of through carriages between the eastern seaboard and central or western Australian destinations is not altogether dead. Medium term plans envisage a network of interconnecting services which could link Sydney, Melbourne and perhaps even Brisbane with both Alice Springs and Perth through Adelaide. It is always worth enquiring when planning your itinerary.

The Overland
Adelaide–Melbourne

The Overland recently celebrated its one hundredth anniversary, although it had different names in its early years and followed a different route until very recently. An overnight train noted for its comfort, it now runs daily between Adelaide and Melbourne on the standard gauge line opened in 1995; 828km (514 miles) in 12½ or 13 hours. Departs Melbourne 20.20, Adelaide 19.00.

Intermediate stations are Geelong North Shore (at a date yet to be announced), then Ararat, Stawell, Murtoa, Horsham, Dimboola, Nhill (c), Wolseley, Bordertown, Coonalpyn, Tailem Bend, Murray Bridge and Mount Lofty (c).

Carries first class roomette and twinette sleepers and first and economy seats, with first class lounge bar (including a smoking "capsule") serving drinks and light snacks with complimentary tea and coffee. The coach class buffet serves only non-alcoholic drinks and snacks.

There is no dining car, but first class sleeping berth passengers are served a continental breakfast in bed, along with complimentary newspaper. First class sitting passengers also receive a breakfast tray and have video entertainment.

Motor vehicles are conveyed in both directions. The *Overland* connects at Adelaide with the *Ghan* on Thursdays.

The Olympic Spirit
Melbourne–Sydney

This is an XPT service replacing the *Intercapital Daylight Express* which was withdrawn in 1991. The 962km (597 miles) is covered in approximately 10½ hours, departing Sydney 08.10 and Melbourne 08.30 daily, calling at Benalla, Wangaratta, Albury, Henty, Wagga Wagga, Junee, Cootamundra, Harden, Yass Junction, Goulburn, Moss Vale, and Campbelltown (c) and connecting in both directions with the *Overland* to and from Adelaide.

The XPT is a sleek, modern diesel train based on the British InterCity 125 HST. It carries a take-away buffet including bar. Numerous Countrylink coach connections serve places in southern New South Wales formerly connected by train.

The Southern Cross
Melbourne–Sydney

This is the night-time counterpart of the *Olympic Spirit*; also an XPT, but with limited first class sleeping accommodation (18 berths in twinette compartments), as well as first class and economy seating. Take-away buffet with restricted bar service. Daily service, departing Melbourne 20.05 and Sydney 20.43.

Brisbane XPT
Brisbane–Sydney

Daily sitting car service. Departs Brisbane 07.30 with return overnight at 16.25; 990km (615 miles) in 14 hours. The night service carries one 18-berth sleeping car consisting of first class twinette compartments with one bathroom (toilet & shower) cubicle to each two twinettes. On the day service this car is available as first class 3-seat compartment stock. First and economy passengers have a take-away grill buffet (at seat refreshments for the aged or infirm) and very limited bar service (light beer only and no wine except with a full meal).

The seating, in common with all the XPT services, is in the 2+2 formation in both first class and economy and, although Countrylink boasts that it is based on top European designs, many passengers regard it as uncomfortable – especially on the longer journeys (such as the Brisbane and north coast services).

Calls at Strathfield (c), Hornsby (c), Gosford (c), Broadmeadow, Maitland, Dungog, Taree, Kendall (c), Wauchope, Kempsey, Macksville (c), Nambucca Heads (c), Urunga (c), Sawtell (c), Coffs Harbour, Grafton, Casino and Kyogle. The day train (southbound) calls additionally at Eungai, Gloucester and Wyong (c). Countrylink coach connections to NSW north coast centres and the Gold Coast.

Murwillumbah XPT
Sydney–Murwillumbah

This is an identical train to the *Brisbane XPT*, running Sydney–Murwillumbah daily at 07.05, returning from Murwillumbah nightly at 21.15; 935km (580 miles) in 13 hours 20 minutes. This train calls at Strathfield (c), Hornsby (c), Gosford (c), Wyong (c), Broadmeadow, Maitland, Dungog, Taree, Kendall (c), Wauchope, Kempsey, Nambucca Heads (c), Urunga (c), Sawtell (c), Coffs Harbour, Grafton, Casino, Lismore, Byron Bay and Mullumbimby. The northbound (day service) calls additionally at Gloucester, Wingham, Eungai (c), and Macksville. There are Countrylink coach connections to Coolangatta, Gold Coast, Helensvale and Brisbane to and from Murwillumbah.

Grafton XPT

The third daily XPT train on the NSW North Coast Line, and has similar facilities. It leaves Sydney at 11.35 and Grafton at 06.45;

695km (431 miles) in 9 hours, 50 minutes. Calls at all the above
stations plus Glenreagh (c).

OTHER LONG DISTANCE TRAINS

Except where specifically stated, the following trains are all air
conditioned and require seat reservations.

New South Wales

Northern Tablelands Xplorer
Sydney–Armidale & Sydney–Moree
Daily service. Departs Sydney 11.05, Moree 08.20 and Armidale
0910. Armidale 579km (360 miles) in 7¾ hours; Moree 666km
(413 miles) in 8 hours 40 minutes.

Intermediate stops at Strathfield (c), Hornsby (c), Gosford (c),
Broadmeadow, Maitland, Singleton, Muswellbrook, Aberdeen (c),
Scone, Murrundi (c), Willow Tree (c), Quirindi and Werris Creek,
where the train divides. The Armidale portion then calls at all stations
to Armidale (West Tamworth, Tamworth, Kootingal, Walcha Road
and Uralla), while the Moree portion calls at Gunnedah, Boggabri,
Narrabri, and Bellata (c). Countrylink bus connections to Burren
Junction, Inverell and Tenterfield.

First and economy seating with grill buffet bar.

The Central West XPT
This is a daily express linking Sydney with Lithgow, Bathurst,
Blayney, Orange, Stuart Town, Wellington, Geurie and Dubbo,
462km (287 miles), with conditional stops at Strathfield, Paramatta,
Penrith, Katoomba, Rydal, and Newbridge. There are numerous
coach connections for this train.

Departs Sydney 07.10, Dubbo 14.10. Journey time is 6½ hours.
First and economy class seating with grill buffet bar.

Countrylink Griffith & Broken Hill services
Newly introduced in 1996 to fulfil an election promise to restore
regional services provided by the former *Riverina Express* and
Silver City Comet, two loco-hauled weekly trains supplement the
XPT and associated coach connections serving these areas. The
service may be subject to alteration, depending on the degree of
support.

The **Griffith** train leaves Sydney at 08.15 on Saturdays, calling
at Campbelltown, Moss Vale, Goulburn, Yass Junction,
Cootamundra, Junee, Coolamon, Narranderra, Yanco and Leeton,

arriving at Griffith at 17.30; 661km (410 miles) in 9¼ hours; returning from Griffith at 08.00 Sunday.

The **Broken Hill** train commences from Sydney at 15.53 on a Tuesday and runs to Orange, calling at Strathfield, Parramatta, Penrith, Lithgow, Bathurst and Blayney. The following afternoon it continues to Broken Hill shortly after the arrival of the *Central West XPT* from Sydney, and reaches Broken Hill at 21.30, calling en route at Parkes, Condobolin, Eubalong West, Ivanhoe and Menindee. The return journey is overnight on the Thursday, leaving Broken Hill at 20.00 and arriving in Sydney the next morning at 11.33; 1,125km (699 miles) in 15½ hours.

There is no sleeping car and at Orange the seats are turned around at six o'clock in the morning to keep passengers awake.

A buffet car is included in each of the above trains.

The Canberra Xplorer
Sydney–Goulburn and Canberra

Thrice daily round trip service, departing Sydney 07.43, 11.43 and 18.14, and Canberra 06.50, 12.20 and 17.20; 327km (283 miles) in just over 4 hours.

All trains call regularly at Moss Vale, Goulburn, Tarago, Bungendore and Queenbeyan and conditionally at Strathfield, Campbelltown, Mittagong and Bowral. All except the last "up" train from Canberra also call conditionally at Bundanoon.

Diesel trainset with first class and economy seating and grill buffet/bar. Connects with railway bus services to Cooma, Bega, Eden, and Bombola in the southern highlands of New South Wales.

The Newcastle Flyer
Newcastle to Sydney

Mondays to Fridays only, departing Newcastle 06.25, Sydney 17.12; 169km (105 miles) in 2 hours 20 minutes. An inter-urban double-deck electric train with no special facilities (other than toilets), but faster than the regular Cityrail services on this route. Connects at Hamilton for Maitland and Telarah.

Endeavour is a generic name given to diesel railcar sets operating on the outer urban sections of the Sydney Cityrail network, including Dapto–Nowra, Campbelltown–Goulburn and Newcastle–Maitland, Dungog and Scone. They all have comfortable one class air conditioned carriages with 3+2 seating, and schedules connecting with Cityrail electric trains to and from Sydney. Seat reservations are not required.

Queensland

The Queenslander
Brisbane–Cairns

This service runs once weekly, departing Brisbane on Sundays at 09.55 and returning Tuesdays from Cairns at 08.00; 1,680km (1,043 miles) journey; 34 hours northbound, 31 hours return, with one night aboard. The *Queenslander* may not run mid-January to early April: dates should be checked locally.

Carries first class sleeping car passengers to and from the intermediate North Queensland stations of Mackay, Proserpine, New Bowen, Home Hill, Ayr, Townsville, Ingham, Tully and Innisfail. Also picks up northbound and sets down southbound at Caboolture, Nambour, Gympie North, Maryborough West, Bundaberg, Gladstone, Rockhampton, St Lawrence and Sarina.

Motor vehicles are carried between Brisbane and Townsville or Cairns.

Comprises roomettes with toilet and wash basin, twinette sleepers (without toilet), the "Coral Cay" restaurant, "Daintree" piano lounge, and "Canecutter's" bar. Showers and toilets are at the end of every sleeping car.

Special fares apply (first class plus supplement payable by all passengers including rail pass holders) and include berths, meals, self-serve tea and coffee, bar snacks and complimentary toilet and stationery packs and newspapers.

Breakfasts include tropical fruit, cereals, fruit juice, coffee or tea, bacon, eggs, omelette, lamb cutlet, croissant or toast with marmalade, jam, honey or Vegemite (a favourite Australian savoury spread). A typical lunch menu has choice of soup, appetiser or entrée, choice of four main courses and two or three sweets, while dinner is similar but with the addition of sorbet and the option of cheese platter in place of sweet.

Favourite dishes include chicken and shiitake mushroom terrine with smoked salmon rose, ham cornette and garden salad, Whitsunday platter of crab or Moreton Bay bug, banana prawns, oysters and salad, lamb in filo pastry, fresh steamed barramundi and prime fillet of beef or porterhouse steaks, with sweets such as Black Forest gâteau, rum-flavoured Bundaberg bombe, crêpe Calvados, and strawberry ice with fresh mango coulis. The bar serves various cocktails and quality vintage wines or wines by the glass in addition to the usual range of drinks.

The *Queenslander* is claimed to be Australia's top luxury train and is, as far as first class service is concerned. Queensland Rail (QR) is the only rail system in the world to have received the Royal Doulton Award for excellence in service and cuisine, in recognition of the standards achieved on the *Queenslander,* although in terms of accommodation the *Ghan* of Australian National just has the edge.

The Spirit of the Tropics
Brisbane–Prosperine

Introduced first in July 1992 as a mid-week service, and known unofficially as the "Whitsunday Queenslander", this train links Brisbane with Mackay and Proserpine, gateway to the Whitsunday Islands, and follows a different schedule to that of the *Queenslander* and *Sunlander*, giving views of parts of the "sunshine route" not otherwise seen by travellers.

Now an economy only train, the mid-week service departs Brisbane at 15.40 on Thursday, returning from Proserpine at 12.15 on Friday; 1,085km (674 miles) in 19 hours. It carries economy sitting and sleeping cars, as well as a buffet bar in the Club Loco, reputedly the world's only disco on rails, with videos and all-night dancing. Showers are at the end of most cars. The buffet menu includes microwaved fork-type dishes such as spaghetti bolognaise and chicken à la king with pasta, as well as meat pies, sandwiches, and drinks including wine by the glass.

On Sundays the *Spirit of the Tropics*, minus the economy sleeping cars, is attached to the *Queenslander* to and from Cairns as an economy section, making what is a probably unique formation of two separately named trains running throughout as one. Intermediate stops on the *Spirit of the Tropics* are the same as on the *Queenslander* without restriction on distance travelled.

The Sunlander
Brisbane–Cairns

The Sunlander follows the same route as the *Queenslander*, running three days a week (Tuesday, Thursday and Saturday from Brisbane and Monday, Thursday and Saturday from Cairns) but taking an hour longer southbound. Departs 09.55 from Brisbane, 08.00 from Cairns, calling at the same stations as the *Spirit of the Tropics* as well as Northgate (c), Cooroy (c), Miriam Vale, Mount Larcom, Carmila, Calen, Giru, Cardwell, Babinda and Gordonvale, as well as several other places on request.

Accommodation includes first class and economy sleeping cars and economy sitting cars, with 24-seat restaurant car, the first class

"Macrossan's" lounge and the "Tropics" club car open to all passengers. Meals are not as elaborate as on the *Queenslander* either in choice or quality but there is still a wide range from snacks and fork dishes for a few dollars in the buffet lounge cars to table d'hôte 3-course meals, or à la carte in the dining car. Although the dinner and buffet service is not available during some periods of night travel, tea, coffee and soup can be obtained at all hours from a self-serve machine in the lounge. A public telephone is available in one of the cars. There is no car carrying facility.

A relief or additional *Sunlander*, commonly called the "**Reeflander**", may link Rockhampton and Cairns at peak demand periods, connecting with the Brisbane–Rockhampton *Spirit of Capricorn* described below. Departs Rockhampton and Cairns as locally advertised.

The Spirit of Capricorn
Brisbane–Rockhampton

The *Spirit of Capricorn* is an air conditioned all-electric express service between Brisbane and Rockhampton; 639km (397 miles) in about 9½ hours. Departs 08.25 daily from Brisbane, 08.25 from Rockhampton. One class only with economy fares for first class standard. Refreshments and drinks served at seats from trolleys brought round at regular intervals throughout the journey. Contoured seating (2+1 layout throughout) with individual reading lights and background music (not all the time!).

An overnight version of this train operates on Wednesdays and Sundays from Brisbane and Wednesdays only from Rockhampton, but with limited refreshment facilities.

From late 1997, or soon after, the rolling stock will be replaced by 160km/h (100mph) tilting trainsets now under construction at Maryborough in Queensland.

The Spirit of the Outback
Brisbane–Longreach

Loco-hauled through train twice weekly between Brisbane and Longreach, the "Gateway to the Outback" in central Queensland. Departs Brisbane (Roma Street) 18.55 Tuesdays and Fridays. and Longreach 06.30 Thursdays and Sundays; 1,325km (823 miles) journey in 24 hours outward and 20 minutes longer homeward. Carries first and economy sleepers and economy sitting cars, with the "Tucker Box" restaurant car, the "Stockman's" bar (1st class) and the "Captain Starlight" club car for all passengers. A public telephone is carried.

Accompanied motor vehicles are conveyed from Brisbane–
Longreach at $208.

Calls at Caboolture, Nambour, Cooroy, Gympie North,
Maryborough West, Bundaberg, Miriam Vale, Gladstone,
Rockhampton, and 15 other stations between there and Longreach,
the major stops being at Blackwater, Emerald, Alpha, Jericho,
Barcaldine and Ilfracombe. A QR contracted road coach connects
at Longreach for Winton (a two-hour trip).

The Inlander
Townsville–Mount Isa

Runs Sunday and Wednesday from Townsville, departing 18.00;
returning Monday and Friday from Mount Isa, at 17.00; 977km
(607 miles) in 19 hours outbound, 18 hours return.

Serves Reid River, Charters Towers, Homestead, Torrens Creek,
Hughenden, Richmond, Nonda, Julia Creek, Cloncurry and Duchess,
as well as many smaller intermediate stations on request. First and
economy class sleepers, plus economy coach cars. There is a 24-
seat dining car with at-seat service for meals ordered at the
counter.

The Westlander
Brisbane–Charleville

The *Westlander* is another similar train, linking Brisbane with
Charleville in western Queensland, from where connecting QR
coaches serve Cooladdi, Cheepie, Quilpie, Wyandra and
Cunnamulla. Runs Tuesdays and Thursdays at 19.15 from
Brisbane, returning from the west on Wednesdays and Fridays at
17.45. The overnight journey takes 16 hours.

Intermediate stations are Corinda (c), Ipswich (c), Rosewood (c),
Toowoomba (Willowburn), Dalby, Chinchilla, Roma, Mitchell,
Morven and numerous smaller places (west of the Citytrain terminus
of Rosewood) on request. First and economy sleepers plus economy
class seating, with grill buffet car.

The *Gulflander* is a unique railmotor service on the remote
Normanton Railway in North Queensland's Gulf Country. Details
are given in Chapter Six (*see* pages 103-4).

The *Savannahlander*, at the time of writing, is a two-car railmotor set linking Mount Surprise and Forsayth in the rangeland
country of north Queensland. Introduced in 1995 it replaced the
former "Last Great Train Ride" (the "Forsayth Mixed", train 7A90)
which ran from Cairns. Indications are that a Cairns–Forsayth service

will soon be restored. For up-to-date details of progress on this, see the *Thomas Cook Overseas Timetable*, or contact Queensland Rail.

The *Yaraka Mixed* is one of a dwindling number of unofficially named, non-air-conditioned, long distance Queensland trains. These, with the *Gulflander* and the *Savannahlander* are discussed in later chapters. They are trains which should be experienced rather than described. They are not for the faint-hearted!

Victoria

The popular *Vinelander* overnight sleeping car train between Melbourne and Mildura in northwestern Victoria was withdrawn in 1993 and up to the time of writing has been replaced only by a bus. To avoid such an ordeal, train travellers might instead opt for the Melbourne–Swan Hill service, with bus connection from there on, described in Chapter Eight.

In Victoria the appellation "**InterCity**" has been adopted by V/Line for its principal country expresses which are air-conditioned, usually of 3 or more coaches and diesel hauled, with first and economy class seats and limited buffet service. These operate on the routes between Melbourne and Albury, Shepparton, Swan Hill, and the East Gippsland towns of Moe, Morwell, Traralgon and Sale and some carry names; for example the *Goulburn Valley Limited* (Shepparton–Melbourne), the *Twin City Limited* (Albury–Melbourne and the *Northerner* (Swan Hill–Melbourne). The former *Wimmera Limited* (Melbourne–Horsham–Dimboola) has been replaced by a bus.

The Gippslander
Melbourne–Sale

The *Gippslander* is the principal day service linking Melbourne (Spencer Street) and Sale in eastern Victoria. Departs Melbourne 07.51 returning from Sale at 13.35 Mondays to Fridays, with later times also at weekends (C 9029); 206km (128 miles) in 2 hours 40 minutes.

Stations served are Flinders Street (c), Caulfield (c), Dandenong (c), Pakenham, Warragul, Moe, Morwell, Traralgon and Rosedale. Air-conditioned non smoking train with first class (2+2 layout) and economy (2+3) seating. Limited take-away buffet service.

V/Line makes the unusual boast in its promotional literature that "Most services are alcohol free". The Gippslander buffet offers beer but no wine or spirits. V/Line coaches connect to other places in East Gippsland and over the border into New South Wales.

The Twin City Limited
Albury–Melbourne

The *Twin City Limited* is the modern, faster replacement of the mis-named former *Albury Express*, leaving Albury at 06.20 daily except Sunday, and returning from Melbourne at 17.10 Mondays to Fridays, 17.50 Saturdays. There is also a northbound only Sunday service, leaving Melbourne at 18.10. The 307km (191 miles) journey takes an average of 3 hours 45 minutes, calling at Seymour and all stations between Seymour and Albury. The Sunday service calls to take up only at Broadmeadows in Melbourne's northern suburbs. First and economy seating similar to the *Gippslander* and buffet (which has traditionally been "dry" since the days of the *Albury Express*, sometimes dubbed the travelling "pub with no beer".

There is a faster, un-named Albury service leaving Melbourne at noon on Mondays to Fridays and Albury at 12.25, while the XPT run by Countrylink of NSW on the standard gauge line is faster still (and carries full buffet facilities).

The Goulburn Valley Limited
Shepparton–Melbourne

The *Goulburn Valley Limited* links Shepparton with Melbourne, leaving at 07.10, arriving Melbourne 09.27, returning at 18.15, arriving 20.35 on Mondays to Fridays, calling at Broadmeadows (c), Seymour, Nagambie, Murchison East and Mooroopna. Times differ at weekends. This is also matched by a Melbourne-based service leaving at 08.10 and returning from Shepparton at 14.55. Accommodation and facilities are similar to other V/Line InterCity trains. Coach connections serve Cobram, Tocumwal and (connecting at Murchison East) the historic town of Echuca.

The Northerner
Melbourne and Swan Hill

The *Northerner* is the name attached to V/Line InterCity trains between Melbourne and Swan Hill, the timetable for which varies with the day of the week. The train runs daily. On Fridays it leaves Swan Hill at 16.00, on Sundays at 17.05, and on other days at 07.10, while from Melbourne the departure times are 15.50 Fridays, 18.10 Saturdays, 17.05 Sundays and 15.50 Mondays to Thursdays; the most complicated train schedule in Australia.

All *Northerner* trains call at Kyneton, Castlemaine, Bendigo, Eaglehawk, Dingee, Pyramid and Kerang; while the Friday and Sunday trains also call at St Albans (c), Sunbury (except Friday northbound) and Woodend. Additionally the northbound Sunday train calls to take up only at Footscray, while the southbound trains on Friday and Sunday call to set down only at Sunshine. V/Line coaches connect with trains at Swan Hill to serve Mildura.

The West Coaster
Melbourne–Warrnambool

The *West Coaster* is the name given to trains between Melbourne and Warrnambool, jointly run by V/Line and the privately operated West Coast Railway. The trains are loco-hauled and mostly consist of older Victorian Railways rolling stock, including first class and economy compartments. A "dry" buffet is attached. As with most country trains in Victoria, the service at weekends differs markedly from that on normal weekdays (a Victorian Sunday has long perpetuated some of the characteristics of the era so named in Britain).

There are three services each way on weekdays, two on Saturdays, and only one, in the evening, on Sundays. The 267km (166 miles) journey takes just over three hours, calling at Geelong, Winchelsea, Colac, Camperdown and Terang. Additionally the Sunday trains call at Werribee and the last weekday return train from Warrnambool at 17.35 calls at North Geelong, Corio, Lara and Werribee, reaching Melbourne at 21.00. V/Line coaches serve places further west on the Victorian coast, and Mount Gambier in South Australia.

South Australia

Regional services in South Australia, comprising the *Silver City Limited* (Adelaide–Broken Hill), the *Iron Triangle Limited* (Adelaide–Whyalla) and the *Blue Lake* (Adelaide–Mount Gambier), were all suspended in 1991 and, despite local agitation, independent inquiry, solemn agreement and careful estimates of replacement costs, they remain victims of misplaced government policy. With the standardisation of the Adelaide–Melbourne route, Mount Gambier in particular, on the 1600mm broad gauge system, has been isolated. For the foreseeable future, buses appear the only alternative for places not served by the main interstate trains.

Western Australia

The Prospector
Perth–Kalgoorlie

The *Prospector*'s route is some 655km (407 miles), normally run in 7½ to 8 hours (the schedule differs almost every day). The service runs daily in both directions, with an extra Merredin–Perth morning run on Fridays, and limited stop runs on Mondays and Wednesdays (also Fridays ex-Kalgoorlie). Normal intermediate stops are at Midland, Toodyay, Meckering, Cunderdin, Merredin, Bodallin, Southern Cross, and Koolyanobbing. First class seats only. Meals (included in the normal fare but extra to Austrailpass holders) and refreshments are served at every seat. Connects at Kalgoorlie with Westrail buses to and from Esperance.

SHORTER DISTANCE SERVICES

Australian railways also have some shorter distance trains bearing names, which generally (but not always) offer something above the average. These include the quaintly named *Fish* and *Chips* (electric inter-urban expresses between the Blue Mountains and Sydney) in New South Wales. These have a long history. In Western Australia there is the *Australind* (Perth–Bunbury) and the *Avon Link* (East Perth–Northam).

Suburban and inter-urban trains in Australia vary tremendously. **Sydney** has some ultra-modern suburban trains called the *Tangara*, continuing the pioneering spirit which gave it the honour of being the first city in the world to have double deck suburban electric multiple unit trains. Cityrail's inter-urban electric multiple unit trains are also double deck, air-conditioned, and have toilets.

Melbourne too has some modern suburban sets and a version of the *Tangara* has recently been given trials.

Brisbane has probably the best suburban trains overall; smooth, quiet, air-conditioned and well furnished; they suffer less vandalism than the older trains in the larger cities. The new Inter-Urban (IMU) sets serving the Gold Coast hinterland boast toilet and rest room accommodation, as well as luggage racks, not normally found on suburban trains, and are capable of speeds up to 140 km/h (87mph).

Adelaide and, most recently, **Perth**, also have some modern suburban trainsets, but all the capitals have some older trains which can still be pressed into service at the busiest peak periods.

Generally, wooden carriages are almost a thing of the past except for special nostalgic excursions.

Electricity is becoming the standard means of locomotion in suburban and outer urban areas and on Queensland main lines. No Australian suburban trains have any first class accommodation or buffet service.

Chapter Four

Around Australia in Fourteen Days

Yes! You can actually travel by train right round the country in only a fortnight. But if you want to make the most of an Austrailpass in a limited time it is imperative that you make advance reservations for all the trains on which you will need them. Your first decisions must therefore be the cities from which your great rail tour will begin and end.

In planning your itinerary it is important to realise, in case you had overlooked my earlier comparisons, that Australia is nearly as big as the United States of America, and three-quarters the size of Europe. Texas would fit into a corner of Queensland – and is in fact the name of a little town on a former freight branch (the trains used to carry a passenger van) in Queensland's southwest.

In the old days a trans-Australian journey by rail was not for the faint-hearted. Breaks of gauge, changes of train, intense heat, dust and flies made it something to be contemplated with misgiving and remembered with mingled horror and amazement. Many are the tales that have been told and the books that have been written. As recently as 1970 it was still not possible to go from Sydney to Perth without four changes of train – at Melbourne, Adelaide, Port Pirie, and Kalgoorlie.

It still takes three days to cross the whole continent. The round trip takes six days if you start from Perth, seven if you start from Sydney, and this without spending much more time at the other end than it takes for the train to be turned around, cleaned out and re-provisioned (five hours in Sydney, just over 24 in Perth). It is therefore sensible, if you have only a 14-day Austrailpass, to plan your arrival at one port and your departure from another. This can easily be arranged when making your airline bookings.

Many international flights regularly serve Perth, Sydney, Melbourne and Brisbane. Sydney is the base with the greatest concentration of rail as well as external air routes, but starting your rail trip in Perth and finishing in the east or starting in Queensland

(some airlines serve Cairns as well as Brisbane) and finishing in
the west can give better options for the holder of a short term
Austrailpass.

Many airline package deals to and from Australia also allow
one or more internal flights without extra charge. This sort of
concession can be useful for bridging some of the gaps in the rail
network, such as Perth–Darwin–Cairns or Alice Springs–Mount
Isa (as recommended in Itineraries 7, 9 & 10 later in this chapter),
or for travelling direct between Canberra and Melbourne, without
having to change trains at Goulburn or use the bus between
Canberra and somewhere further along the main south line.

A boon to travellers introduced in recent years is the Austrail
Flexipass, ideal for those who wish to spin out a tour by spending
several days in one place before going on to another.

THE BASIC TRIANGLE

With almost any itinerary at all, some retracing of the route is
necessary because there is no real rail "network" in the sense of a
web of intersecting routes as in Europe. Basically, Australia has a
fundamental triangle of passenger main lines – Adelaide, Sydney,
Melbourne. Every other route, however long or short, is a dead-end
system branching from this triangle, with here and there a minor
loop on one of the branches. A 14-day Austrailpass, wherever you
start, will still allow you to visit all the capital cities, but you may
well wish to include places like Cairns and Alice Springs as well,
or instead.

To give some idea of the time-scale of things, the basic southeastern capital city triangle circuit takes a minimum of from 2 days
4½ hours (anti-clockwise from Sydney starting on a Monday or
Thursday) to 3½ days (starting from Melbourne anti-clockwise on
a Monday or Friday or clockwise on a Sunday or Wednesday). This
is shown on the following summary table of interstate trains on the
basic southeastern triangle.

Sydney–Melbourne–Adelaide–Sydney
C 9020, 9026 & 9035

All trains have refreshments, must be booked, and have sleeping accommodation
on overnight journeys. Daily except as stated.

	Dep	Arr
Sydney–Adelaide	14.40 Mon & Thu	16.25 Tue & Fri
Sydney–Melbourne	08.10	18.35
	20.43	07.05

	Dep	**Arr**
Adelaide–Melbourne	19.00	07.55
Adelaide–Sydney	07.45 Wed & Sun	09.15 Thu & Mon
Melbourne–Adelaide	20.20	08.45
Melbourne–Sydney	08.30	19.13
	20.05	06.45

Alice Springs is a three-day round trip from Adelaide (more from Sydney or Melbourne) while Cairns is a five-day round trip from Sydney. You can just go from Perth to Cairns and back, or vice versa, in 14 days, but you would not have much more than a night there or anywhere in between. The nearest thing to a complete round trip of Australia by train is by spanning the gap between Alice Springs and Mount Isa in western Queensland with a one hour plane hop, and this book shows you how.

Time zones
On many interstate trips you will cross time zones, which may vary with the season. Summer time operates in the eastern states except Queensland. As a general rule, travelling west between the eastern states and South Australia, you put watches back by 30 minutes and between South and Western Australia 90 minutes; watches go forward when travelling in the other direction.

Be careful at Broken Hill, which is in New South Wales but observes South Australian time. The train conductor will clear up any doubts for you, and in fact west of Adelaide the train operates on its own sweet time, so you need not worry unless you need to telephone somebody.

Major stations
All Australian state capital cities have more than one railway station. Unless otherwise stated, all trains described in this book arrive and depart from the main interstate stations, which are as follows:

Sydney Central station (also called Sydney Terminal).

Melbourne Spencer Street station.

Brisbane Roma Street station (also called Brisbane Transit Centre); not to be confused with Brisbane Central station.

Adelaide AN Terminal, Keswick; which is 3.5km (2.2 miles) from the city centre and ten minutes walk from a suburban station of the same name, from which there is a frequent service to the central city station in North Terrace.

Perth Perth Terminal station, West Parade, East Perth; just over

1.7km (1 mile) from the town centre. The Terminal adjoins the suburban station of East Perth, from which there is a frequent service to City station in the town centre.

Canberra The railway station in Canberra is at Fyshwick, about 5km (3 miles) from the city centre at Civic or the bus station at Jolimont. Local bus services and taxis are available, while Countrylink coaches to destinations like Cooma and Yass connect with trains.

At **Port Pirie** in South Australia, at **Bunbury** in Western Australia, and at **Toowoomba**, **Gympie**, **Maryborough**, **Mackay** and **Bowen** in Queensland, new stations have been built which are anything up to 8km (5 miles) out of town. At **Toowoomba** (Willowburn), **Mackay** and **New Bowen** passengers are left to their own devices (taxi or lift from someone with a private car), while at **Port Pirie** (Coonamia station), **Maryborough West** and **Gympie North** the railways provide a coach or taxi. **Orange East Fork** station is 1.8km from the main Orange station in the town centre. There is no public transport between the two, so if descending at Orange East Fork from the *Indian Pacific* it could be worth asking the train manager to arrange something for you (such as a taxi) before arrival (you might be offered a lift in a railway van).

Using the itineraries

Later in this chapter are some ideas on how to make the best use of the Austrailpass if you are staying for a month or more, but if you are limited to an ultra-short stay, then the most you can pack into it in the way of rail travel is set out in the following 11 itineraries numbered 1, 1A, 2, 3, 4, 4A, 5, 5A, 6, 7 & 8. These 14-day packages are essentially quick reconnaissance tours – seeing on the move. Most visitors would probably prefer to spread these itineraries over a longer period, which can now readily be done by obtaining an Austrail Flexipass covering 14 days of travel in one month, but if you really are pushed you can see an astonishing amount of the country in a very short time – and at little cost. You may need to carry your belongings with you and must make sure that you have sufficient funds on the long parts of the trip where there is rarely time to seek out a bank between changing trains.

It is not difficult in 14 days to visit all the mainland state capital cities as well as the national capital of Canberra, as the first four itineraries show (1, 1A, 2 and 3). You can spend a day or more in each and still have time for side trips or variations to your itinerary.

Special departure and "getting back" advice for base cities is given later in this book to assist you in making your own plans, if the itineraries here do not suit your taste. But be warned. None of these 14-day "maximum mileage" itineraries is for geriatrics or the faint-hearted, but will be something to talk about for years afterwards – and few people will believe you did it all by train!

Itineraries 1 to 5 (14 days)

The first five itineraries are based on Sydney, but can be followed, with some adjustment and slightly less convenience, if based on Melbourne or even Perth. Variations are possible for those who, instead of sightseeing in major cities, wish to make side trips to other places of interest. These are described in Chapter Eight (*see* pages 129-154).

Itineraries 1 to 3 cover capital cities only, but capital cities are not what everyone wants to see. To many visitors, an Australian trip would not be fulfilled without seeing romantic places like the "Town called Alice" or the railway station at Kuranda. Itineraries 4 and 5 show how easy it is to fit in a trip either to the red centre of the continent or to tropical north Queensland.

Caution! If you insist on staying for a night in the middle of the Nullarbor, climbing to the top of Ayers Rock or scuba-diving on the Barrier Reef, you are not going to manage it with a 14-day rail pass. But you can come close to such achievements if you plan your itinerary carefully, following the advice given in this book.

Itinerary 4 takes you straight to north Queensland and back. The train north from Brisbane will be your home for the two days to Cairns, where you have a brief nightstop, enough to see the night life and experience the warm extrovert feeling of the tropics, and then you are back in your travelling hotel for two more days before another nightstop in Brisbane. After a day in Sydney to re-charge batteries you continue right across the continent and back. This and other itineraries are arranged so that where possible whichever way you go between Sydney and Adelaide you come back by a different route.

Itinerary 5, the final Sydney-based 14-day itinerary, includes Alice Springs instead of Cairns. It starts on Saturday. First stop is Melbourne for the day; then overnight to Adelaide with just time to see the city centre before catching the famous *Ghan* to Alice Springs. Unless you have also pre-booked a cab and a chartered helicopter you would unfortunately not have time for an out-and-back flight to Ayers Rock. But there is plenty to see in town before returning to the train to take you on across the "plain with no trees" to Perth. There you have time to spare. You return east to Sydney on the *Indian Pacific*, still with time to visit Canberra.

Itinerary 1

Fourteen-day Austrailpass based on Sydney, commencing Sunday or Wednesday. Visiting all capital cities. Nightstops in Melbourne (or night on train), Perth and Brisbane with seven or eight nights on trains (all with sleeping cars available) and a return to Sydney half way through. Maximum continuous time away from base eight days. If based on Perth, commence as on Day 6, ending as on Day 5.

Day		Programme		
Day 1	Sun or Wed	Dep Sydney	08.10[a]	*Olympic Spirit*
		Arr Melbourne	18.35	nightstop
Day 2	Mon or Thu	Dep Melbourne	20.20	*Overland*
Day 3	Tue or Fri	Arr Adelaide	08.45	9 hours free
		Dep Adelaide	18.00	*Indian Pacific*
Day 4	Wed or Sat	en route		
		Nullarbor plain and Kalgoorlie		
Day 5	Thu or Sun	Arr Perth	07.00	nightstop
Day 6	Fri or Mon	Dep Perth	13.30	*Indian Pacific*
Day 7	Sat or Tue	en route		
		Nullarbor plain		
Day 8	Sun or Wed	en route		
		Spencer Gulf to central west NSW		
Day 9	Mon or Thu	Arr Sydney	09.15	two night stopover
Day 10	Tue or Fri	In Sydney		
		Local journeys if desired		
Day 11	Wed or Sat	Dep Sydney	16.24[b]	*Brisbane XPT*
Day 12	Thu or Sun	Arr Brisbane	06.00#	nightstop
Day 13	Fri or Mon	Dep Brisbane	07.30#	*Brisbane XPT*
		Arr Sydney	21.35	nightstop
Day 14	Sat or Tue	Dep Sydney	07.43	*Canberra Xplorer*
		Arr Canberra	11.50	5½ hours free
		Dep Canberra	17.20	*Canberra Xplorer*
		Arr Sydney	21.26	

[a] Alternatively Dep Sydney 20.43 by Southern Cross, arriving Melbourne 07.05 on Day 2; sleeper recommended if available.

[b] If unable to secure a sleeper, take the daytime *Murwillumbah XPT* instead (*see* Chapter Eleven, page 193).

One hour earlier during Eastern Summer Time.

Itinerary 1A

Virtually the same as Itinerary 1 but based on Melbourne, commencing Monday or Thursday. Nightstops in Perth, Brisbane, Sydney (two nights) and Canberra, but without a mid-itinerary return to base.

Day		Programme		
Day 1	Mon or Thu	Dep Melbourne	20.20	*Overland*
Day 2	Tue or Fri	Arr Adelaide	08.45	9 hours free
		Dep Adelaide	18.00	*Indian Pacific*
Day 3	Wed or Sat	en route		
		Nullarbor plain and Kalgoorlie		
Day 4	Thu or Sun	Arr Perth	07.00	nightstop
Day 5	Fri or Mon	Dep Perth	13.30	*Indian Pacific*
Day 6	Sat or Tue	en route		
		Nullarbor plain		
Day 7	Sun or Wed	en route		
		Spencer Gulf to central west NSW		
Day 8	Mon or Thu	Arr Sydney	09.15	two night stopover
Day 9	Tue or Fri	In Sydney		
		local journeys		
Day 10	Wed or Sat	Dep Sydney	16.24a	*Brisbane XPT*
Day 11	Thu or Sun	Arr Brisbane#	06.00a	nightstop
Day 12	Fri or Mon	Dep Brisbane#	07.30	*Brisbane XPT*
		Arr Sydney	21.35	nightstop
Day 13	Sat or Tue	Dep Sydney	07.43	*Canberra Xplorer*
		Arr Canberra	11.50	nightstop
Day 14	Sun or Wed	Dep Canberra	06.50b	*Canberra Xplorer*
		Arr Goulburn	08.17b	change trains
		Dep Goulburn	10.50b	*Olympic Spirit*
		Arr Melbourne	18.35	

a If unable to secure a sleeper, take the daytime *Murwillumbah XPT* instead (*see* Chapter Eleven, page 193).

b An alternative is the Countrylink Transborder coach connection leaving Canberra 10.40 and connecting with the *Olympic Spirit* at Yass Junction, arriving 11.28, departing 11.55.

One hour earlier during Eastern Summer Time.

Itinerary 2

Fourteen-day Austrailpass commencing Monday or Thursday. Based on Sydney, with other nightstops in Perth, Melbourne, Canberra and Brisbane, and eight nights on the train. Visiting all capital cities. Maximum of nine consecutive nights away from base. If based on Perth, commence as on Day 5, ending as on Day 4.

Day		Programme		
Day 1	Mon or Thu	Dep Sydney	14.40	*Indian Pacific*
Day 2	Tue or Fri	en route		
		Broken Hill and Spencer Gulf		
Day 3	Wed or Sat	en route		
		Nullarbor plain and Kalgoorlie		
Day 4	Thu or Sun	Arr Perth	07.00	nightstop
Day 5	Fri or Mon	Dep Perth	13.30	*Indian Pacific*
Day 6	Sat or Tue	en route		
		Nullarbor plain		
Day 7	Sun or Wed	Arr Adelaide	06.15	12 hours free
		Dep Adelaide	19.00	*Overland*
Day 8	Mon or Thu	Arr Melbourne	07.55	nightstop
Day 9	Tue or Fri	Dep Melbourne	20.05	*Southern Cross*
Day 10	Wed or Sat	Arr Sydney	06.45	nightstop
Day 11	Thu or Sun	Dep Sydney	07.43[a]	*Canberra Xplorer*
		Arr Canberra	11.50[a]	nightstop
Day 12	Fri or Mon	Dep Canberra	12.20	*Canberra Xplorer*
		Arr Strathfield	16.13	change trains
		Dep Strathfield	16.36[b]	*Brisbane XPT*
Day 13	Sat or Tue	Arr Brisbane	06.00[#b]	nightstop
Day 14	Sun or Wed	Dep Brisbane	07.30[#]	*Brisbane XPT*
		Arr Sydney	21.35	

[a] Option of later train departing Sydney 11.43, arriving Canberra 15.50.

[b] If unable to book a sleeper in advance for this sector, return from Canberra the previous evening and take the daytime *Murwillumbah XPT* from Sydney in the morning instead (*see* Chapter Eleven, page 193).

[#] One hour earlier during Eastern Summer Time.

Itinerary 3

A variation of Itinerary 2, commencing Saturday or Wednesday, with a brief return to base on Day 5. The same itinerary could be commenced from Melbourne as Day 14 below, ending on Day 13. If based on Perth, commence as on Day 10, ending as on Day 9.

Day		Programme		
Day 1	Sat or Wed	Dep Sydney	11.43	*Canberra Xplorer*
		Arr Canberra	15.50	nightstop
Day 2	Sun or Thu	Dep Canberra	17.20	*Canberra Xplorer*
		Arr Sydney	21.26	nightstop
Day 3	Mon or Fri	Dep Sydney	16.24a	*Brisbane XPT*
Day 4	Tue or Sat	Arr Brisbane	06.00#a	nightstop
Day 5	Wed or Sun	Dep Brisbane	07.30#	*Brisbane XPT*
		Arr Sydney	21.35	nightstop
Day 6	Thu or Mon	Dep Sydney	14.40	*Indian Pacific*
Day 7	Fri or Tue	en route		
		Broken Hill and Spencer Gulf		
Day 8	Sat or Wed	en route		
		Nullarbor plain and Kalgoorlie		
Day 9	Sun or Thu	Arr Perth	07.00	nightstop
Day 10	Mon or Fri	Dep Perth	13.30	*Indian Pacific*
Day 11	Tue or Sat	en route		
		Nullarbor plain		
Day 12	Wed or Sun	Arr Adelaide	06.15	12 hours free
		Dep Adelaide	19.00	*Overland*
Day 13	Thu or Mon	Arr Melbourne	07.55	nightstop
Day 14	Fri or Tue	Dep Melbourne	08.30	*Olympic Spirit*
		Arr Sydney	19.13	

a If unable to book a sleeper in advance for this sector, return from Canberra the previous evening and take the daytime *Murwillumbah XPT* from Sydney in the morning instead (*see* Chapter Eleven, pages 193).

One hour earlier during Eastern Summer Time.

Itinerary 4

Fourteen-day Austrailpass. Travelling to north Queensland, South Australia, Western Australia and Victoria. Involves nightstops in Cairns, Brisbane and Perth with nine nights on trains. Sleeping berths are available on night trains. Maximum continuous time away from base seven days. Commencing on a Friday from Sydney. This itinerary must be varied if based on Melbourne (see Itinerary 4A) but can be commenced in Perth as on Day 11, ending as on Day 10.

Day		Programme			
Day 1	Friday	Dep	Sydney	16.24	*Brisbane XPT*
Day 2	Saturday	Arr	Brisbane	06.00#	5½ hours free
		Dep	Brisbane	09.55	*Sunlander*
Day 3	Sunday	Arr	Cairns	18.00	nightstop
Day 4	Monday	Dep	Cairns	08.00	*Sunlander*
Day 5	Tuesday	Arr	Brisbane	16.10	nightstop
Day 6	Wednesday	Dep	Brisbane	07.30#	*Brisbane XPT*
		Arr	Sydney	21.35	nightstop
Day 7	Thursday	Dep	Sydney	14.40	*Indian Pacific*
Day 8	Friday	en route			
		Broken Hill to Spencer Gulf			
Day 9	Saturday	en route			
		Nullarbor plain and Kalgoorlie			
Day 10	Sunday	Arr	Perth	07.00	nightstop
Day 11	Monday	Dep	Perth	13.30	*Indian Pacific*
Day 12	Tuesday	en route			
		Nullarbor plain			
Day 13	Wednesday	Arr	Adelaide	06.15	12 hours free
		Dep	Adelaide	19.00	*Overland*
Day 14	Thursday	Arr	Melbourne	07.55	change trains
		Dep	Melbourne	08.30	*Olympic Spirit*
		Arr	Sydney	19.13	

#One hour earlier during Eastern Summer Time.

Itinerary 4A

The foregoing itinerary modified for a Melbourne base.

Day		Programme		
Day 1	Tuesday	Dep Melbourne	08.30	*Olympic Spirit*
		Arr Sydney	19.13	nightstop
Day 2	Wednesday	Dep Sydney	16.24	*Brisbane XPT*
Day 3	Thursday	Arr Brisbane	06.00[#]	5½ hours free
		Dep Brisbane	09.55	*Sunlander*
Day 4	Friday	Arr Cairns	18.00	nightstop
Day 5	Saturday	Dep Cairns	08.00	*Sunlander*
Day 6	Sunday	Arr Brisbane	16.10	2½ hours free
		Dep Brisbane	19.00[a]	Countrylink coach
		Arr Murwillumbah	20.50[#a]	change to train
		Dep Murwillumbah	21.15	*Murwillumbah XPT*
Day 7	Monday	Arr Sydney	10.30	4 hours free
		Dep Sydney	14.40	*Indian Pacific*
Day 8	Tuesday	en route		
		Broken Hill to Spencer Gulf		
Day 9	Wednesday	en route		
		Nullarbor plain and Kalgoorlie		
Day 10	Thursday	Arr Perth	07.00	nightstop
Day 11	Friday	Dep Perth	13.30	*Indian Pacific*
Day 12	Saturday	en route		
		Nullarbor plain		
Day 13	Sunday	Arr Adelaide	06.15	12 hours free
		Dep Adelaide	19.00	*Overland*
Day 14	Monday	Arr Melbourne	07.55	

[a] For alternatives to Brisbane–Murwillumbah coach *see* Chapter Eleven, pages 193-4.

[#] One hour earlier during Eastern Summer Time.

Itinerary 5

Fourteen-day Austrailpass based on Sydney. Commencing Saturday. Visiting
Brisbane, Melbourne, Adelaide, Alice Springs, Perth and Canberra. Involves
eight nights on the train (sleepers available) and one brief night out in the
Nullarbor at Tarcoola. Other nights away in Brisbane, Adelaide, Perth and
(optionally) Canberra. Maximum continuous time away from base 9½ days. Not
one for the faint-hearted. If based on Perth, commence as on Day 10, ending as
on Day 9.

Day		Programme		
Day 1 Saturday	Dep Sydney	16.24[a]	*Brisbane XPT*
Day 2 Sunday	Arr Brisbane	06.00[#a]	nightstop
Day 3 Monday	Dep Brisbane	07.30[#]	*Brisbane XPT*
	Arr Sydney	21.35	nightstop
Day 4 Tuesday	Dep Sydney	20.43	*Southern Cross*
Day 5 Wednesday	Arr Melbourne	07.05	over 13 hours free
	Dep Melbourne	20.20	*Overland*
Day 6 Thursday	Arr Adelaide	08.45	5 hours free
	Dep Adelaide	14.00	*Ghan*
Day 7 Friday	Arr Alice Springs	10.30[#]	3½ hours free
	Dep Alice Springs	14.00[#]	*Ghan*
	Arr Tarcoola	23.25	nightstop[b]
Day 8 Saturday	Dep Tarcoola	05.29	*Indian Pacific*
Day 9 Sunday	Arr Perth	07.00	nightstop
Day 10 Monday	Dep Perth	13.30	*Indian Pacific*
Day 11 Tuesday	en route		
	Nullarbor plain		
Day 12 Wednesday	en route		
	Spencer Gulf and western NSW		
Day 13 Thursday	Arr Sydney	09.15	nightstop
	Dep Sydney	11.43[c]	*Canberra Xplorer*
	Arr Canberra	15.50[c]	nightstop
Day 14 Friday	Dep Canberra	17.20	*Canberra Xplorer*
	Arr Sydney	21.26	

[a] If unable to secure a sleeper, take the daytime *Murwillumbah XPT* instead (*see* Chapter Eleven, page 193).

[b] Hotel reservation essential. The hotel is near the station, but prior arrangement must be made for meeting the train, since arrival and departure times may vary and should be checked on day of travel.

[c] If preferred, an option is a nightstop in Sydney followed by a day trip to Canberra on the last day (as Day 14 of Itinerary 1).

[#] One hour earlier during Eastern Summer Time.

Itinerary 5A

Covering the same places as Itinerary 5 but based on Melbourne.

Day		Programme		
Day 1 Saturday	Dep Melbourne	08.30	*Olympic Spirit*
	Arr Sydney	19.13	nightstop
Day 2 Sunday	Dep Sydney	16.24a	*Brisbane XPT*
Day 3 Monday	Arr Brisbane	06.00#a	nightstop
Day 4 Tuesday	Dep Brisbane	07.30#	*Brisbane XPT*
	Arr Sydney	21.35	nightstop
Day 5 Wednesday	Dep Sydney	08.10	*Olympic Spirit*
	Arr Melbourne	18.35	change trains
	Dep Melbourne	20.20	*Overland*
Day 6 Thursday	Arr Adelaide	08.45	nightstop
	Dep Adelaide	14.00	*Ghan*
Day 7 Friday	Arr Alice Springs	10.30#	3½ hours free
	Dep Alice Springs	14.00#	*Ghan*
	Arr Tarcoola	23.25	nightstopb
Day 8 Saturday	Dep Tarcoola	05.29	*Indian Pacific*
Day 9 Sunday	Arr Perth	07.00	nightstop
Day 10 Monday	Dep Perth	13.30	*Indian Pacific*
Day 11 Tuesday	en route		
	Nullarbor plain		
Day 12 Wednesday	en route		
	Spencer Gulf and western NSW		
Day 13 Thursday	Arr Sydney	09.15	change trains
	Dep Sydney	11.43	*Canberra Xplorer*
	Arr Canberra	15.50	nightstop
Day 14 Friday	Dep Canberra	06.50c	*Canberra Xplorer*
	Arr Goulburn	08.17c	change trains
	Dep Goulburn	10.50c	*Olympic Spirit*
	Arr Melbourne	18.35	

a If unable to secure a sleeper, take the daytime *Murwillumbah XPT* instead (*see* Chapter Eleven, page 193).

b Hotel reservation essential. The hotel is near the station, but prior arrangement must be made for meeting the train, since arrival and departure times may vary and should be checked on day of travel.

c An alternative is the Countrylink Transborder coach connection leaving Canberra 10.40 and connecting with the *Olympic Spirit* at Yass Junction, arriving 11.28, departing 11.55.

One hour earlier during Eastern Summer Time.

Itineraries 6 to 8 (14 days)

Even more interesting use can be made of the 14-day Austrailpass if you start your journey on one side of Australia and finish it on the other. Three itineraries are given, all covering the mainland state capitals plus Alice Springs and north Queensland, and all starting in Perth and finishing in the east. Itinerary 7 allows time to see Ayers Rock by including an air hop from Alice Springs to Mount Isa. The Ayers Rock – Mount Olga National Park is now more often known by the aboriginal name, Uluru. There is no accommodation within the national park but it is served by the resort township, Yulara. For those who prefer coastal scenes, Itinerary 6 offers time to visit Kuranda or the Great Barrier Reef.

Note that an Austrailpass does NOT cover air or boat trips, nor are discounts on other transport offered to Austrailpass holders to the extent often found in Europe.

Itinerary 6

Fourteen-day Austrailpass, starting in Perth on a Sunday and ending in Cairns. Nine nights on the train and briefly visiting all the eastern state capital cities plus Alice Springs before ending the tour in North Queensland. Nightstops in Sydney (two), Melbourne and Cairns.

Day		Programme		
Day 1 Friday	Dep Perth	13.30	*Indian Pacific*
Day 2 Saturday	en route		
	Nullarbor plain		
Day 3 Sunday	en route		
	Spencer Gulf and western NSW		
Day 4 Monday	Arr Sydney	09.15	nightstop
Day 5 Tuesday	Dep Sydney	08.10	*Olympic Spirit*
	Arr Melbourne	18.35	nightstop
Day 6 Wednesday	Dep Melbourne	20.20	*Overland*
Day 7 Thursday	Arr Adelaide	08.45	5 hours free
	Dep Adelaide	14.00	*Ghan*
Day 8 Friday	Arr Alice Springs	10.30#	3½ hours free
	Dep Alice Springs	14.00#	*Ghan*
Day 9 Saturday	Arr Adelaide	11.30	7½ hours free
	Dep Adelaide	19.00	*Overland*
Day 10 Sunday	Arr Melbourne	07.55	change trains
	Dep Melbourne	08.30	*Olympic Spirit*
	Arr Sydney	19.13	nightstop
Day 11 Monday	Dep Sydney	16.24	*Brisbane XPT*
Day 12 Tuesday	Arr Brisbane	06.00#	3½ hours free
	Dep Brisbane	09.55	*Sunlander*

Day	Programme		
Day 13 Wednesday	Arr Cairns	18.00	nightstop
Day 14 Thursday	Dep Cairns	09.15	Kuranda Tourist Train*
	Arr Kuranda	10.55	4½ hours free
	Dep Kuranda	15.30	Kuranda Tourist Train
	Arr Cairns	17.10	

* For details *see* pages 64 and 144.
# One hour earlier during Eastern Summer Time.

Itinerary 7

On this itinerary you can experience travel on Australia's three top trains; the *Indian Pacific*, the *Ghan* and Queensland Rail's *Queenslander*. Fourteen-day Austrailpass, starting in Perth on a Friday and ending in Sydney. Briefly visiting all the eastern state capital cities plus Alice Springs. Includes time for a quick flight to Ayers Rock and back and involves an air hop between Alice Springs and Mount Isa (air fares and *Queenslander* supplement not covered by Austrailpass). Nightstops in Sydney, Melbourne, Alice Springs, Mount Isa (two) and Brisbane with seven nights on trains (all with sleeping accommodation).

Day	Programme		
Day 1 Friday	Dep Perth	13.30	*Indian Pacific*
Day 2 Saturday	en route		
	Nullarbor plain		
Day 3 Sunday	en route		
	Spencer Gulf and western NSW		
Day 4 Monday	Arr Sydney	09.15	nightstop
Day 5 Tuesday	Dep Sydney	08.10	*Olympic Spirit*
	Arr Melbourne	18.35	nightstop
Day 6 Wednesday	Dep Melbourne	20.20	*Overland*
Day 7 Thursday	Arr Adelaide	08.45	5 hours free
	Dep Adelaide	14.00	*Ghan*
Day 8 Friday	Arr Alice Springs	10.30	nightstopª
Day 9 Saturday	Dep Alice Springs	11.50	by air, flight 462
	Arr Mount Isa	13.25	2 night stopover
Day 11 Monday	Dep Mount Isa	17.00	*Inlander*
Day 12 Tuesday	Arr Townsville	11.00	4½ hours free
	Dep Townsville	15.30	*Queenslander*
Day 13 Wednesday	Arr Brisbane	14.25	nightstop
Day 14 Thursday	Dep Brisbane	07.30#	*Brisbane XPT*
	Arr Sydney	21.35	

ª For details of Ayers Rock option, see Itinerary 9.
One hour earlier during Eastern Summer Time.

Visiting Alice Springs

A former long distance train, the *Alice*, considerably widened the options for anyone wishing to make the most of a fortnight (or any) Austrailpass. This went direct between Sydney and Alice Springs, via Broken Hill, Port Pirie, and Tarcoola. It started as a seasonal service in 1983, became weekly throughout the year until 1986, then was stopped. It reappeared in February 1987, and looked like settling down to regular operation until it went for good in 1988. Australian National and State Rail of NSW never seemed to be able to agree about it, and its reappearance is unlikely, although the possibility of through services to Alice Springs from Sydney or even Melbourne or Brisbane in future cannot entirely be ruled out.

When the *Alice* ran, it doubled the service to and from Alice Springs, allowing a three or four-day stay there and making possible a more complete itinerary in a fortnight. A relief *Ghan*, running variously from April or May to October, November, or even January, later filled this gap. Reports in late 1996 that this service would not continue were denied as this book went to press, and it is expected to resume in April 1997. The relief *Ghan* makes possible a three or four-day stop in the "red centre", as shown in Itinerary 8.

However, a three-day wait in one place takes rather a large slice of your time with only a 14 day Austrailpass. The Flexipass would be a better investment, but an exyended pass is another option.

Itinerary 8

Fourteen-day Austrailpass starting in Perth on a Friday and ending in Brisbane, visiting Adelaide, Alice Springs, Melbourne, Canberra and Sydney, with ample time to visit Uluru (Ayers Rock). Six nights on trains, all with sleeping berths available. This itinerary is valid only if the relief *Ghan* is operating.

Day		Programme		
Day 1 Friday	Dep Perth		13.30	*Indian Pacific*
Day 2 Saturday	en route			
	Nullarbor plain			
Day 3 Sunday	Arr Adelaide		06.15	2 night stopover
Day 4 Monday	Dep Adelaide		14.00	relief *Ghan*
Day 5 Tuesday	Arr Alice Springs		10.30[#]	3 night stopover[a]
Day 8 Friday	Dep Alice Springs		14.00	*Ghan*
Day 9 Saturday	Arr Adelaide		11.30	6 hours free
	Dep Adelaide		19.00	*Overland*
Day 10 Sunday	Arr Melbourne		07.55	12 hours free
	Dep Melbourne		20.05	*Southern Cross*
Day 11 Monday	Arr Sydney		06.45	nightstop
Day 12 Tuesday	Dep Sydney		11.43[b]	*Canberra Xplorer*
	Arr Canberra		15.50[b]	nightstop

Day		Programme		
Day 13 Wednesday	Dep Canberra	12.20c	*Canberra Xplorer*
	Arr Strathfield	16.13c	change trains
	Dep Strathfield	16.36c	*Brisbane XPT*
Day 14 Thursday	Arr Brisbane	06.00#	

a Option of one or more nightstops at Yulara Resort (for Uluru/Ayers Rock).

b Option of earlier train to Canberra at 07.43, arriving 11.50.

c Option of earlier train from Canberra at 05.50 arriving Sydney 10.56 departing 16.24 (no change at Strathfield) or departing Sydney 11.35 on *Grafton XPT* and break journey on NSW north coast for several hours before joining *Brisbane XPT* in the early hours of the morning. *See* Chapter Eleven, pages 192-4, for alternatives for this part of the itinerary.

One hour earlier during Eastern Summer Time.

Itineraries 9 and 10 (21 days)

On any of the foregoing itineraries, much of your time will be spent on trains of high quality, which will become your travelling hotel. You will need to take enough clean clothes and money to last most of the time because the itineraries allow limited opportunity for shopping or bank transactions after leaving your starting point.

When you have a ticket for a longer period, or a Flexipass, not only will you have more time to look around, you will be able to do your banking and have laundry attended to. You can plan your excursions from selected bases, leaving your luggage at a hotel to be called for later. You need not rent a room for this; it is usually possible to come to an arrangement with the management. Luggage can also be left at station depositories and laundry can be left at laundries where it belongs. Remember to keep a note of where you've left everything; it is annoying to have to make a special trip back somewhere just to collect a suitcase you had forgotten about.

Whatever you do, watch the days of the week! Saturday afternoons and Sundays must be counted as dead periods for attending to necessities. On a Sunday it is almost impossible, even in Sydney, to obtain cash unless you have a card with PIN number and can find the right autobank. American Express offices may be useful but you will find them only in larger cities. It is easy to forget the day of the week when travelling on long distance trains. Time zone changes are enough to contend with as it is!

By extending your pass to 21 days (or by buying a 21-day pass before you leave home), a fairly leisurely trip using the Alice Springs–Mount Isa air hop is possible, with more time in most places visited. Itineraries 9 and 10 show the possibilities. This route is not viable in the other direction, because the connections are unsuitable.

Itinerary 9 shows how the air hop can allow a visit to Ayers Rock plus time to explore Cairns and north Queensland. Itinerary 10 shows how the relief *Ghan* (if running) can be combined with a longer tour and the chance to enjoy some of north Queensland.

Itinerary 9

Twenty-one-day tour commencing in Perth on a Monday and ending in Melbourne with two or more night stopovers in Mount Isa, Cairns, Brisbane and Sydney and other nightstops in Adelaide, Alice Springs and Townsville. Six nights on the train. Includes air hop Alice Springs to Mount Isa. Could equally end in Sydney preceded by a return Sydney-Melbourne trip.

Day		Programme		
Day 1 Monday	Dep	Perth	13.30	*Indian Pacific*
Day 2 Tuesday	en route			
	Kalgoorlie and the Nullarbor plain			
Day 3 Wednesday	Arr	Adelaide	06.15	nightstop
Day 5 Thursday	Dep	Adelaide	14.00	*Ghan*
Day 6 Friday	Arr	Alice Springs	10.30#	nightstop[a]
Day 7 Saturday	Dep	Alice Springs	11.50	by air, flight 462[b]
	Arr	Mount Isa	13.25	2 night stopover
Day 9 Monday	Dep	Mount Isa	17.00	*Inlander*
Day 10 Tuesday	Arr	Townsville	11.00	nightstop
Day 11 Wednesday	Dep	Townsville	10.35	*Sunlander*
	Arr	Cairns	18.00	3 night stopover
Day 13 Friday[c]	Dep	Cairns	09.15[c]	Kuranda Tourist Train*
	Arr	Kuranda	10.55	4½ hours free
	Dep	Kuranda	15.30[c]	Kuranda Tourist Train
	Arr	Cairns	17.10	
Day 14 Saturday	Dep	Cairns	08.00[d]	*Sunlander*
Day 15 Sunday	Arr	Brisbane	16.10	3 night stopover
Day 18 Wednesday	Dep	Brisbane	07.30#	*Brisbane XPT*
	Arr	Sydney	21.35	3 night stopover
Day 20 Saturday	Dep	Sydney	20.43[e]	*Southern Cross*
Day 21 Sunday	Arr	Melbourne	07.05	

[a] Option of nightstop at Yulara Resort instead. There are flights to Ayers Rock at 11.50 and 14.00 and a connecting return flight at 11.50 next morning, but times should be checked and bookings made in advance.

[b] Times subject to change and must be checked and booked in advance.

[c] Day round trip may be taken to Kuranda on either of the free days. Additional trains available between Cairns and Kuranda.

[d] *See* Chapter Eight, pages 129-154, for alternative ideas for the southbound journey which may be broken almost anywhere between Cairns and Melbourne.

[e] Overnight journey could be replaced by day train *Olympic Spirit* leaving Sydney 08.10, arriving Melbourne 18.35.

One hour earlier during Eastern Summer Time.

* For details *see* pages 64 and 144.

Itinerary 10

A variation of the foregoing possible if the relief *Ghan* is running, allowing much more time to explore Australia's red centre from Alice Springs. Commencing in Perth on a Thursday and visiting all state capital cities as well as Mount Isa, Cairns and Townsville to end in Melbourne. Five nights on the train. Includes air hop Alice Springs–Mount Isa.

Day		Programme		
Day 1 Thursday	Dep	Perth	13.30	*Indian Pacific*
Day 2 Friday	en route			
	Kalgoorlie and the Nullarbor plain			
Day 3 Saturday	Arr	Adelaide	06.15	2 night stopover
Day 5 Monday	Dep	Adelaide	14.00	relief *Ghan*
Day 6 Tuesday	Arr	Alice Springs	10.30[#]	4 night stopover[a]
Day 10 Saturday	Dep	Alice Springs	11.50	by air, flight 462[b]
	Arr	Mount Isa	13.25	2 night stopover
Day 12 Monday	Dep	Mount Isa	17.00	*Inlander*
Day 13 Tuesday	Arr	Townsville	11.00	nightstop
Day 14 Wednesday	Dep	Townsville	10.35	*Sunlander*
	Arr	Cairns	18.00	3 night stopover
Day 16 Friday[c]	Dep	Cairns	09.15[c]	Kuranda Tourist Train[*]
	Arr	Kuranda	10.55	4½ hours free
	Dep	Kuranda	15.30[c]	Kuranda Tourist Train
	Arr	Cairns	17.10	
Day 17 Saturday	Dep	Cairns	08.00	*Sunlander*
Day 18 Sunday	Arr	Brisbane	16.10	nightstop
Day 19 Monday	Dep	Brisbane	07.30[#]	*Brisbane XPT*
	Arr	Sydney	21.35	2 night stopover
Day 21 Wednesday	Dep	Sydney	08.10	*Olympic Spirit*
	Arr	Melbourne	18.35	

[a] Option of one or more nightstops at Yulara (for Uluru/Ayers Rock) and/or Kings Canyon, travelling either by coach or by air. There are flights to Ayers Rock at 12.30 and 14.00 on the day of arrival at Alice Springs and a connecting return flight at 11.50 the morning of departure for Mount Isa, but times should be checked and bookings made in advance.

[b] Times subject to change and must be checked and booked in advance.

[c] Day round trip may be taken to Kuranda on either of the free days. Additional trains available between Cairns and Kuranda.

[#] One hour earlier during Eastern Summer Time.

[*] For details *see* pages 64 and 144.

Using a longer pass

The ultimate in travel value is the 30-day Austrailpass (and even more so, a 29-day Flexipass). These can allow a fairly leisurely to extremely leisurely exploration of at least the main Australian rail routes, but they also enable the more energetic visitor to pack in a tremendous variety, if full advantage is taken of the possible overnight journeys.

Assuming that among other things you will want to spend a day or two in most, if not all, capital cities; to cross the Nullarbor, visit Alice Springs and Ayers Rock, north Queensland and the Barrier Reef, and other places of scenic, cultural, or historic interest – even if only so that you can say you have been there – the following out-line itinerary allows a full day or more in most major centres and a return to base part way through for laundry or other "domestic" purposes. Three successive nights are allowed in Sydney, and this gives your hotel a chance to deal with all your laundry of the previous week and a half. You can miss out any of the side trips (for example Days 11 and 25-26) if you want a complete break.

Some readers of the first edition of this book protested that this itinerary was too exhausting. It is a revised and updated version of an itinerary that was first published in my earlier book *Great Rail Non-journeys of Australia*. It packs in about the maximum it is reasonably possible to achieve in a short time. Certainly it is not for the easily discouraged. I class it as "moderate to intensive", but for those who seek a more leisurely month on the railways of Australia, the answer is to omit some parts.

The itinerary is capable of many variations, which are discussed in Chapter Eight, "Planning Your Own Itinerary", *see* pages 129-154. However, the days of travel for the principal journeys cannot be altered without disrupting the schedule. These are marked by the symbol † in the table overleaf.

Itinerary 11

One month Austrailpass comprehensive itinerary based on Sydney, with return to base at Day 10. Could be based on Melbourne by starting a day earlier, taking the day train to Sydney and, later, on the return journey from the west, changing from the *Indian Pacific* to the *Overland* at Adelaide and thence returning to Melbourne. Many other variations and side trips are possible but the symbol † indicates a key section of the itinerary which cannot be varied, except as above.

Day				Programme	
Day 1	Wednesday	†Dep	Sydney	07.05	*Murwillumbah XPT*
		Arr	Byron Bay	19.27	nightstop
Day 2	Thursday	Dep	Byron Bay	19.27	*Murwillumbah XPT*
		Arr	Murwillumbah	20.30	change to bus
		Dep	Murwillumbah	20.55	Countrylink coach
		Arr	Gold Coastᵃ	21.50#	2 night stopover
Day 4	Saturday	Dep	Gold Coast	07.11	Surfside buslines
		Arr	Helensvale	07.45	change to train
		Dep	Helensvale	08.21	Interurban electric
		Arr	Brisbane	09.22	Roma St station
		†Dep	Brisbane	09.55	*Sunlander*
Day 5	Sunday	Arr	Cairns	18.00	nightstop
Day 6	Monday	Dep	Cairns	09.15	Kuranda Tourist Train*
		Arr	Kuranda	10.55	4½ hours free
		Dep	Kuranda	15.30	Kuranda Tourist Train
		Arr	Cairns	17.05	nightstop
Day 7	Tuesday	†Dep	Cairns	08.00	*Queenslander*
Day 8	Wednesday	Arr	Brisbane	14.55	2 night stopover
Day 10	Friday	†Dep	Brisbane	07.30#	*Brisbane XPT*
		Arr	Sydney	21.35	nightstop
Day 11	Saturday	Dep	Sydney	09.38ᵇ	local train
		Arr	Dapto	11.16	change trains
		Dep	Dapto	11.28	*Endeavour*
		Arr	Nowra	12.30	5 hours free
		Dep	Nowra	17.36ᶜ	*Endeavour*
		Arr	Dapto	18.35	change trains
		Dep	Dapto	18.41	local train
		Arr	Sydney	20.16	nightstop
Day 12	Sunday	Dep	Sydney	11.43ᵈ	*Canberra Xplorer*
		Arr	Canberra	15.50ᵈ	nightstop
Day 13	Monday	Dep	Canberra	06.50ᵉ	*Canberra Xplorer*
		Arr	Goulburn	08.17	2½ hours free
		Dep	Goulburn	10.50ᵉ	*Olympic Spirit*
		Arr	Albury	15.30	nightstop
Day 14	Tuesday	Dep	Albury	12.25	V/Line InterCity
		Arr	Melbourne	16.07	nightstop
Day 15	Wednesday	†Dep	Melbourne	20.20	*Overland*
Day 16	Thursday	Arr	Adelaide	08.45	5 hours free
		†Dep	Adelaide	14.00	*Ghan*

Day		Programme		
Day 17 Friday	Arr	Alice Springs	10.30[#]	3½ hours free[f]
	[†]Dep	Alice Springs	14.00[#]	*Ghan*
Day 18 Saturday	Arr	Adelaide	11.30	3 night stopover
Day 21 Tuesday	[†]Dep	Adelaide	18.00	*Indian Pacific*
Day 22 Wednesday	Arr	Kalgoorlie	20.15	nightstop
Day 23 Thursday	Dep	Kalgoorlie	08.35	*Prospector*
	Arr	Perth Terminal	15.50	2 night stopover
Day 25 Saturday	Dep	Perth City	09.30	*Australind*
	Arr	Bunbury	11.45	nightstop
Day 26 Sunday	Dep	Bunbury	16.15	*Australind*
	Arr	Perth City	18.30	nightstop[g]
Day 27 Monday	[†]Dep	Perth Terminal	13.30	*Indian Pacific*
Day 28 Tuesday	en route			
	Kalgoorlie and the Nullarbor			
Day 29 Wednesday	en route			
	Adelaide[h] and Broken Hill			
Day 30 Thursday	Arr	Sydney	09.15	

[a] Surfers Paradise. One hour earlier during Eastern Summer Time.

[b] Other trains at 07.44 and 11.38, arriving Nowra 10.30 and 14.38 respectively, changing at Dapto.

[c] Other trains at 15.36 and 19.32, arriving Sydney 18.16 and 22.16 respectively, changing at Dapto, and at 20.48, arriving 23.46, changing at Wollongong.

[d] Option of earlier train to Canberra at 07.43, arriving 11.50.

[e] An alternative is the Countrylink Transborder coach connection leaving Canberra 10.40 and connecting with the *Olympic Spirit* at Yass Junction, arriving 11.28, departing11.55.

[f] A round trip flight to see Ayers Rock could just be possible during this break, but only if pre-booked by charter.

[g] A nightstop in historic Fremantle is another option. See "Perth" in Chapter Five, page 87.

[h] A major alternative is to break the return journey in Adelaide and take the *Overland* direct to Melbourne for a nightstop there.

[*] For details *see* pages 64 and 144.

[#] One hour earlier during Eastern Summer Time.

Itinerary highlights

The highlights of these journeys are mostly described in the order in which the places are reached in the foregoing itineraries, but the extra timetables in this and other chapters show alternative trains as well as return services on the same routes for the benefit of those who prefer to devise their own itineraries. Services shown in this book are daily unless otherwise stated. Things to do and see in and around the capital cities from which you may start or finish your itinerary, or in which you may have time to spare en route, appear in Chapter Five, pages 73-88.

North from Sydney

Climbing north out of Strathfield in Sydney's western suburbs, and once clear of the northern suburbs beyond Hornsby (30 minutes after leaving Sydney) the trains follow the edge of Ku-ring-gai Chase National Park (on the right) through Berowra and Cowan, then descend steeply through the Boronia tunnels until the waters of the Hawkesbury River come into view (left and right as you cross the bridge). Look out for the oyster farming in these waters.

The delightful forest and lake scenery of Brisbane Water National Park flanks the line (mostly on the right) from Hawkesbury River to Gosford, a useful turning point for a day trip. The Woy Woy tunnel 13km (eight miles) south of Gosford in this area will be of interest to rail fans. Some surprisingly fast running will be experienced on the far from straight track north of Gosford through Wyong and Morisset.

Broadmeadow (2 hours from Sydney) is the junction for Newcastle, a coal port and birthplace of Australia's railways – a wagonway of 1827 was the first. This is the gateway to the Hunter Valley, one of Australia's premier wine regions, west of Maitland. Perhaps incongruously, coal is also a feature of the Hunter Valley, particularly around Newcastle and Maitland, and heavy coal trains can be observed on the freight lines paralleling the route between Broadmeadow and Maitland. Here also is one of the straightest and fastest parts of the main north coast line, on which the XPT will quickly achieve and maintain its permitted maximum of 160 km/h, which at one time the train conductor would proudly announce: "The train is now travelling at 100 miles an hour". Slow to adapt fully to metric measurement, everyone on board understood, but the news appeared to frighten some older passengers.

After **Maitland** (a good place to break the journey for a night-stop) the north coast line swings away from the valley and curves northward among bush covered hills between Dungog and Taree, connecting point for a Countrylink bus service on an alternative route from Newcastle via the coast and Great Lakes district. On the right you should sight coastal lakes north of Johns River, and of the Tasman Sea itself between Macksville and Coffs Harbour, especially at Urunga. The scenery on this part of the line is pleasant, with numerous creeks, plantations and small settlements.

Coffs Harbour itself, self-named capital of "the Banana Republic" (from the many plantations in the locality) is noted for the beauty of its coastal scenery, its rich hinterland and magnificent beaches. It is well worth breaking a journey here or at the nearby stations of Nambucca Heads, Urunga, Raleigh, or Sawtell. North of Coffs Harbour the track climbs at a steady 1-in-80 through numerous curves and a series of short tunnels to a minor summit (just over 100m/330ft) at Landrigan's Loop. Rail buffs should watch out a little further on for the historic Dorrigo branch at Glenreagh, on the left about 35 minutes north of Coffs Harbour.

Grafton City, terminus of the *Grafton XPT*, is noted for its colourful jacaranda trees, smothering the roads and footpaths in season with their beautiful blue-purple blossoms.

Byron Bay is the farthest point east on Australian railways and is a popular surfing resort. You will see the surfies with their multi-coloured boards, sun-bleached hair and bronzed skin. This part of northern New South Wales is noted for its lush green pastures.

While Itinerary 11 envisions a nightstop in Byron Bay, followed by rail and bus connections via the Gold Coast to Brisbane, a determined rail addict can avoid the bus by returning on the XPT to Grafton and then taking the *Brisbane XPT* north, with nightstops in Byron Bay, Grafton, or elsewhere within the time available, the deadline being Saturday morning in Brisbane. Even with only a couple of hours in Byron Bay you have time to walk to the beach and back, or have a good meal, or enjoy the nightlife with the locals at the swinging bar lounge (the Railway Friendly Bar – phone [066] 85 7662) which now occupies most of the former station refreshment and waiting rooms. This should steel you for the tedious midnight wait you will later endure at Grafton for your connection north to Brisbane at two o'clock in the morning.

The sensible alternative to a Byron Bay–Grafton–Brisbane overnight journey is to continue on the train to **Murwillumbah**, railhead for Queensland's Gold Coast, and from thence by bus to Helensvale with a Gold Coast nightstop en route as shown in the suggested itinerary and discussed in Chapter Eleven, *see* page 193.

The following timetable summarises the alternatives north-bound. The options southbound from Brisbane are similar but at easier times of day – without middle of the night transfers.

Sydney–Grafton, the Pacific coast of northern NSW, the Gold Coast and Brisbane–northbound options.

C 9015, 9017; T 194 & local

Buses between Surfers and Helensvale except 21.50 (20.55 ex-Murwillumbah) operated by Surfside Buslines – not covered by rail tickets or passes. All trains in this table are air-conditioned and all except the Queensland Rail Helensvale–Brisbane services require reservations.

Dep	Sydney	07.05ᵃ	11.35ᵃ	16.24ᵃ
Arr	Grafton City	16.45	21.25	01.59
Dep	Grafton City	16.50	—	02.01
Arr	Casino	18.14	—	03.20ᵇ
Dep	Casino	18.16	—	03.35ᶜ
Arr	Byron Bay	19.27	—	05.14
Arr	Murwillumbah	20.30ᵇ	—	06.12
Dep	Murwillumbah	20.55ᵈ	—	—
Arr	Surfers Paradise	21.50#	—	06.26#
Dep	Surfers Paradise	21.50#	—	07.29ᶠ
Arr	Helensvale	22.05	—	07.59ᶠ
	Change to train			
Dep	Helensvale	22.51#	—	08.21ᶠ
Arr	Brisbane	23.52#	—	09.22ᶠ
	Alternatives from Murwillumbah			
Dep	Murwillumbah	07.43ᵈ	—	21.15ᵃ
Dep	Byron Bay	—	—	22.06
Arr	Casino	09.53ᵉ	—	23.27
Dep	Casino	10.12ᵃ	—	23.29
Arr	Grafton City	11.31	—	00.48ᵍ
Dep	Grafton City	—	—	02.01
Dep	Casino	—	—	03.26
Arr	Brisbane	—	—	06.00#

ᵃ XPT train with buffet.

ᵇ Change to air conditioned State Rail Countrylink bus.

ᶜ 03.35 departure is for Byron Bay and Murwillumbah.. There is a separate Countrylink bus R63N, which departs Casino at 03.36 for Surfers Paradise direct but does not call at Byron Bay or Murwillumbah.

ᵈ Air conditioned Countrylink bus (State Rail operated).

ᵉ Change to train.

ᶠ Frequent service, approximately every 30 minutes.

ᵍ Change trains.

One hour earlier during Eastern Summer Time.

The **Gold Coast**, of which Surfers Paradise is the heart, is noted for its surf beaches, its mountainous hinterland, sailing on the Broadwater, the many islands, the famous "meter maids" in the main shopping area, its casino, and its excellent restaurants. Queensland seafoods are a speciality. Try Queensland mud crab or Moreton Bay bugs. A word of warning, however: in Australia "lobster" always means crayfish, "trout" may mean coral trout, a choice white-fleshed reef fish but nothing at all like brown or rainbow trout or sea trout, and "salmon", unless specified as red, can mean a very unexciting greyish fish called Australian salmon and bearing no relationship to the tasty varieties well-known in North America and Europe.

The current terminus of the Queensland Rail Gold Coast Railway is at Helensvale, but it is being extended 17km (11 miles) further south to Robina, near Mudgeeraba in the Gold Coast hinterland 7km (4 miles) west of Mermaid Beach. The Interurban Multiple Unit trains of the Gold Coast line are capable of 140 km/h (87mph), currently the fastest in Queensland, although average speeds are substantially lower. Helensvale and the intermediate stations on the line between Helensvale and Beenleigh are served by connecting buses to local attractions such as Dreamworld, a major entertainment park.

Rail enthusiasts may note the dual and combined gauge track on the right between Rocklea (after the branch joins the standard gauge New South Wales line which comes in from the left) and the city. At Yeerongpilly, 8km (5 miles) from Roma Street, the Gold Coast train is likely to swing over onto combined gauge track west of the suburban lines.

Approaching **Brisbane** you will see the city centre on the right as you pass South Brisbane to cross the Merivale Bridge. In the foreground just before South Brisbane are the South Bank Parklands, developed on the site of the 1988 World Expo while on the other side of the track is Brisbane Convention Centre.

Going north from Brisbane, look out for the **Glasshouse Mountains**, so named by Captain Cook, on the left ahead after leaving Caboolture; and then the long slow climb up the Eumundi Ranges to the old gold mining town of Gympie. Gympie itself is by-passed by the realigned north coast line but glimpses of the town may be seen on the left before Gympie North. **Maryborough West**, station for Fraser Island, is the next stop. Then follows some fast running, with possibly a conditional stop at Howard, before reaching **Bundaberg**, famous for rum and sugar, where the track swings over the wide Burnett river to run for a short distance along the street in North Bundaberg.

Gladstone, reached on most northbound services in the evening, is an industrial town in a beautiful natural setting of tree clothed hills. It bustles with railway activity, especially evident when passing Callemondah yard shortly after leaving the station travelling north.

The thrice weekly *Sunlander* and the daily *Spirit of Capricorn* also reach **Rockhampton** in the evening. This is the first major stop north of the tropic of Capricorn. If new to Queensland, this is a place to get out of the train and stretch your legs. You will feel the warmth even at night.

North of Rockhampton, Mackay and Proserpine are good places from which to visit parts of the Barrier Reef and tropical islands, but unfortunately these towns are visited by most passenger trains only in the very early hours (or late in the evening southbound). To see by day the parts of the coast route normally traversed by night necessitates taking the Sunshine Daylight Rail Experience (*see* pages 145-6) or the mid-week *Spirit of the Tropics* to Proserpine.

Further north, **Bowen**, a centre for fruit and famous for its mangoes, is reached next, and from there on you are in sugar cane country most of the way. Between Home Hill and Ayr the train crosses the Burdekin River, mightiest of the Queensland rivers east of the Great Dividing Range. Wild birds including the dancing brolga or native companion are a feature of the marshy flats around **Giru** between Ayr and Cromarty, just before the train starts its slow crawl alongside the main road into Townsville. Here you have time to look briefly around town and get used to the tropic heat.

Townsville, Queensland's fourth city, features Flinders Mall, to your right on leaving the station, where you first cross a small park and look up towards Castle Hill, a pink granite peak which towers over the city. Then turn round and observe the station building itself, historically the main station of the former Great Northern Railway, and looking very much the part.

Once past Townsville's northern industrial suburbs, the next stop is **Ingham**, famous as the original home of the "Pub with No Beer", made famous the world over in Gordon Parsons' ballad. This was reputed to be a local hotel which American servicemen drank dry during World War II. There is a rival claim; at Taylors Arm, 26km (16 miles) from Macksville on the NSW North Coast main line there is a pub with this name but Ingham is right on the railway and an easier place to visit – if you go for pubs with no beer. In general, Australians don't.

The pub just over the road from the southern end of Ingham railway station is cool and more convenient, serving excellent homemade pies if you decide to stop there for lunch. Here, as at many places on this route, narrow gauge cane lines cross the roads and the railway, and you may see cane trains even longer than the *Sunlander* on their way to the mill.

There is a brief glimpse of the coast at **Cardwell**. You should also see some of the many islands on parts of this route. Hinchinbrook, north of Cardwell, is particularly prominent, appearing as a mountain range on the seaward side. The scenery is excellent on both sides; the coast is on the right.

North from Tully the train passes slowly through lush sugar cane fields amid tree-clothed mountains, including Mount Bartle Frere on the left, Queensland's highest peak, in the Bellenden Ker Range north of Innisfail near the little town of Babinda.

Cairns The essence and heart of north Queensland. Warm and extrovert, it is a thriving town of close on 60,000 population, a major centre of game fishing and the gateway to the Barrier Reef and the Atherton Tableland. The visitor information centre is just opposite the station on McLeod Street. Attractions of Cairns include the harbour with its marlin jetty and the sailing club, the surrounding cane fields and the exciting hinterland of misty mountains and tropical rain forest. There are many excellent restaurants and eating places ranging from the really cheap to the very expensive, particularly noted for seafood. And, of course, there are always the easily accessible islands of the Barrier Reef, including Green Island with its underwater observatory. Cairns has many fine hotels, but within easy reach by rail service are smaller places where accommodation is cheaper: Freshwater, Redlynch, Kuranda, Gordonvale and Babinda.

Despite all the attractions of Cairns itself, it would be almost unforgivable to visit this area and fail to make the rail trip to **Kuranda**, the "village in the rainforest". The *Kuranda Tourist Train* has become one of Australia's most popular train rides and not without reason. Only 33km (20.5 miles) long, the line first runs for 12km (7.5 miles) along the flat coastal strip north of Cairns to Redlynch, when the climb up the coastal ranges really begins. In the next 19km (12 miles) the line rises 318m (1,040ft) up the side of the Barron River Gorge, first negotiating a horseshoe bend, then a series of tight curves and fifteen tunnels. Mostly clinging to the edge of a 45-degree slope it then crosses a trestle bridge on another tight bend almost in the spray of a waterfall before coming out above the wide amphitheatre above Barron Falls. The round trip takes three hours, not counting time spent in Kuranda.

The station itself is like a tropical garden. Nearby is the river, and on the other side the Bottom Pub where you can not only get a good counter lunch, you can meet some of the locals and buy a souvenir bottle of their specially made claret. Ask for "Saviour Wine". Depending on which train you join for the return trip, there will be time to visit the markets – 100 metres or so up the main street, or the butterfly house just beyond.

Other ideas on what to do and see in and around Cairns, and the trips you can make from there, are given in later chapters.

Itinerary 11 (and Itinerary 7) include a trip on the *Queenslander*, Queensland Rail's premier train at the time of writing. A "heritage train" is soon to be added to the fleet, which will surpass even the *Queenslander* in Orient Express-style luxury and possibly Orient Express-style prices! But the *Queenslander* is a travel experience not to be missed, even though the supplementary fare (including meals and sleeping berth) may cost a third as much as your Austrailpass. After all, even going by ordinary train you would still need to eat and sleep, and you could spend just as much money sitting in a lonely motel room for the day and a half it takes you to travel through entrancing scenery in comfort and style!

After a break in Brisbane, you can return south by daylight on the *Brisbane XPT*. After leaving Bromelton (a former whistle stop about 45 minutes out of Brisbane), the railway passes through the magnificent border ranges, timber and mist covered with small waterfalls, bridges and rivers between Tamrookum and Kyogle. This scenery was one of the highlights of especially the north-bound run of the former *Brisbane Limited*, but the timing of the XPT is such that it can now only be enjoyed on the southbound run. Look out for the Border Loop with viaduct and spiral tunnel about half an hour before the train is due in Kyogle. First sight of it is on the right but ask your conductor to make sure you don't miss it.

South from Sydney

From Sydney to the south there are two routes, one inland and the other along the coast. The branch line connecting Unanderra on the south coast line and Moss Vale on the main south route is a detour worth making but, being privately operated, is not included in this itinerary. Details are given in Chapter Six, *see* pages 91-94.

The suggested itinerary, however, includes a trip down the coast line to Nowra and back. The coast both north and south of Wollongong is fascinating. Not much of Australia's coast is visible from its railways, but the Illawarra line is an exception, taking the passenger right to the water's edge or along the cliff tops. North of Wollongong the scenery is marred by coal mining, but the natural features still predominate.

At **Nowra**, there is time for lunch, a walk round town, and a choice of trains for your return, or even for a break of journey on the homeward trip. See Chapter Eight, page 137, for some ideas.

The inland route south goes past Campbelltown, a modern planned "new town", and climbs into the Southern Highlands through Moss Vale, a pleasant little destination for a day trip, and Goulburn, whose jail is one of the most conspicuous features on the approach by rail. Here the line for Canberra and the Southern Highlands branches from the main south line. A feature of the Canberra route is the scenic Molonglo Gorge, on the right after Bungendore.

Canberra, Australia's Federal Capital, is famed for its layout and civic buildings, pedestrian ways, and surrounding new towns which distinguish it from unplanned city growth elsewhere. See Lake Burley Griffin (named after the United States architect who won the original design for this national capital), and its 140m (450ft) water jet (operates 10.00–12.00 and 14.00–16.00), plus the Sunday afternoon concerts of the 53-bell carillon on Aspen Island.

The Sydney–Melbourne main line southwest from Goulburn passes Yass Junction, from where there is an alternative link to Canberra by Countrylink bus, then Harden, from where State bus services have replaced trains on the former branch through the fruit country of Young and Cowra to the western main line at Blayney. Between Cootamundra and Junee watch out for the Bethungra loop, where the northbound line describes a complete circle to overcome the gradient while the line south follows a deviation. Between Wagga Wagga and Albury is the racetrack straight where the XPT twice broke the Australian train speed record in 1981 at 183 km/h (114mph) and again in 1992 at 193 km/h (120mph). Normal speeds on this section are more usually 110-160 km/h (68-100mph).

Albury is where the NSW State Railway meets up with the Victorian system and where, in years past, passengers had to change trains, usually in the early hours of the morning. All trains on the standard gauge now run right through, but you can break the journey here and take a V/Line InterCity service for the Albury–Melbourne section. At Albury the train crosses the river Murray, Australia's mightiest, to its twin town Wodonga on the Victorian side. Wodonga has its own railway station and so has Chiltern, a quiet remnant of a once thriving gold rush town. Further south are Wangaratta, Benalla, and Seymour, gateways to the Goulburn Valley on the west and the mountains (the Victorian Alps) on the east. The valley can be reached by train from Seymour (*see* Chapter Eight, page 148) or bus from Benalla but the Alps only by bus or hired transport. Between Wangaratta and Benalla the train passes **Glenrowan**, famous in Australian history as the haunt of bushranger Ned Kelly.

For information on **Melbourne** *see* Chapter Five, page 79.

Melbourne to Adelaide

The standard gauge line from Melbourne–Adelaide follows the Victorian broad gauge route to Geelong North Shore, where a new station may be constructed by the time this book is published. (The various authorities have been arguing about who should pay for it since the interstate line was standardised in 1995.) Although much of the new route is rather interesting, it is traversed mostly during the hours of darkness by the *Overland* train. There are no other passenger trains between Geelong and Ararat where the new route joins the old interstate line 211km (131 miles) from Melbourne.

En route to Adelaide, you may wake to an early morning crossing of the 576m (628 yard) long Murray Bridge just 40km (25 miles) from the entry of Australia's greatest river into **Lake Alexandrina** from which it flows into the Southern Ocean. After climbing again from the Murray up to Mount Barker Junction, the rail route winds down through the National Park area of the Mount Lofty ranges between Bridgewater and Adelaide, giving views on the final approach over Gulf Saint Vincent.

Adelaide to the west

After leaving Adelaide's Keswick terminal note on the right the lines to the original station, now the suburban terminal. See the way the edge of the city stands out behind a "green wedge" on the right as you continue north to the planned suburb of Salisbury and past the Royal Australian Air Force base. Look out for camels in enclosed paddocks. These were the form of transportation used on the north–south route across central Australia before the railway. Driven by Afghan riders, their memory is perpetuated in *The Ghan* today.

Once clear of Adelaide's outer northern suburbs the line passes through rich South Australian farming country with the Spencer Gulf to the left and the Mount Lofty Ranges to the right. At Crystal Brook the line joins the Sydney–Perth route. **Coonamia** is now the station for **Port Pirie**, reached by railway bus (about 3km). Port Pirie is worth visiting to see the original long railway station platform and, down the main street, the historic early station preserved as a museum. Port Pirie boasts the largest lead smelting plant in the world. Little tubes of smelter slag containing traces of lead, silver, zinc and gold can be purchased in town. Port Pirie was formerly a compulsory stop on the Trans–Australian route where three rail gauges met.

Between Port Pirie and **Port Augusta** the Spencer Gulf is close on the left and the attractive Flinders Ranges on the right. Port Augusta is still an important railway centre worth a visit even though most trains now call only in the early hours or late at night.

West of Port Augusta the train winds its way at night through numerous sand hills and past salt pans and scrub forests, an eerie scene by moonlight if you happen to be awake. The train calls at **Tarcoola** in the early hours. Here is the only pub between Port Augusta and Kalgoorlie. There is reputed to be an annual horse race on which there are no bets and no one ever remembers the winner. To get the real feel of the middle of nowhere, step down from the train and breathe the pure air of the outback. The sky will be brilliant with stars. Before sunset you may already have seen the stars shining against the brilliant red sky. The dawn will be similar, golden red above the brown earth all around.

Highlights of the line between Tarcoola and Alice Springs are the crossing of the Northern Territory border just south of Kulgera, the Iron Man monument to the railway workers who built the line, and the bridge over the Finke River, where the *Alice* used to stop for photographs. Approaching Alice Springs the train passes through a gap in the MacDonnell ranges, outcrops of special interest to geologists.

Alice Springs itself, capital of the "red centre" is the current railhead and gateway to the Northern Territory. With only a few hours to spare there is still time to mooch around town. You can do a walking tour of the town centre in an hour or so; see the Aviation Museum, the School of the Air, the Panorama "Guth" and the Old Gaol, or walk up to Anzac Hill Lookout to view the surroundings. You have time for a couple of beers or a counter lunch in one of the excellent restaurants, where you may sample some of the more unusual meats found in the Northern Territory, like camel, buffalo, crocodile, emu and kangaroo. Eye fillet of camel is superb, while roo steaks are fat free, as tasty as venison, and low in cholesterol. Try Alice's Restaurant in Todd Mall for lunch.

If you are fortunate enough to be in Alice Springs at the right time of year, you may have an opportunity to witness its unique boat race, the Henley-on-Todd Regatta. Run in the dry bed of the Todd River, with contestants carrying their boats, this had to be cancelled in 1994. The reason it couldn't be run? The river was full of water!

On the return from Alice Springs by *The Ghan*, the sun may be up in time for you to catch a glimpse of Pimba, where the train stops briefly. On your left is the disused rail branch to Woomera, 6km (3.7 miles) north, site of the former rocket testing range.

Westwards from Tarcoola features the vast Nullarbor plain with the longest straight line of railway in the world, Cook and its jail cells and the remote and little known railway settlement of Rawlinna. Rawlinna is noted for its club, which boasts the largest car park in the world. There is space for a million cars at least; north, east and west from the club the empty "car park" reaches to the horizon and beyond – the Nullarbor plain. Not a tree and not a house are in sight, except the few around the station, which, with the club itself, make up all there is to Rawlinna.

Next comes **Kalgoorlie**, rich in history and present day interest too. The evening stop of the *Indian Pacific* there allows plenty of time to look around – there is much to see, and if you are following the suggested one month Austrailpass itinerary you will be staying the night.

While waiting in Kalgoorlie for your train to depart next morning you may see a freight train thundering by on an outside track. These mostly ignore Kalgoorlie, having their own stations at Parkeston (Australian National) 5km to the east, and at West Kalgoorlie (Westrail) on the other side. Kalgoorlie station has other features of interest. Notice the standpipes for watering the passenger trains. There are enough for a train of around 20 coaches. Some of the longest passenger trains ever put together ran on this route, when floods caused delays which resulted in the running of combined *Indian Pacific/Trans Australian* sets. There are historical notes about the railways of this area in the booking hall and you might be interested to learn that Kalgoorlie has the longest railway platform in Australia, which you will know about if you try walking its length with your heavy luggage!

If continuing west on the *Indian Pacific*, you will probably be asleep for most of the rest of the journey, but look out for the picturesque Avon valley near Perth, some of which you may see if you awake an hour or two before the final approach to Western Australia's capital city. The views are similar on both sides of the train, but with slightly more of interest on the north. A fuller description of this part of the route is given for the return trip, which is commenced during daylight, but you can see it all in daylight either way travelling on Westrail's *Prospector*.

Notes on **Perth** appear in Chapter Five, *see* page 87.

Instead of staying in or around Perth, a pleasant day trip by rail takes you down south to **Bunbury**, as suggested in the itinerary. Bunbury is now the most southerly terminus of the passenger rail system in Western Australia, although the line through Donnybrook to Bridgetown, some 102km (63 miles) further south was briefly re-opened in 1995 for an experimental weekend extension to the *Australind* service (ask if it still runs – you never know!). Bunbury is on the Indian Ocean. Worth seeing are the basalt rock formations on the beach, the many historic buildings like the Rose Inn near the old station (try a counter meal there). Commercial redevelopment unfortunately displaced Bunbury station to Wollaston, about two kilometres away, but a free bus service connects with the trains. North of Bunbury the country is full of wild flowers. You can hardly miss them even without taking one of the special wildflower bus tours put on by Westrail.

Travelling between Perth and Kalgoorlie by daylight, look out for the brightly coloured parrots and the flocks of black cockatoos in the pleasantly winding Avon Valley. Rail buffs will be interested, too, in the combined gauge track from Perth to Northam (standard and 1067mm (3ft 6in) gauge together).

Returning eastwards from Kalgoorlie you should wake up somewhere near **Forrest**. The name is that of a former Australian Prime Minister; nothing to do with trees as you are already well out into the Nullarbor, the "plain with no trees". Forrest is noted for its international standard airfield, used during World War II and occasionally more recently as an emergency alternative to Perth. If you are allowed to look out of the door of the train you will see that the line is straight as far as the eye can see in both directions. You are now on the longest straight line of railway in the whole world, have been for the last hour or more, and will continue to be for the next seven! Indeed, most of the first complete day on the train you will be riding smoothly across the Nullarbor. This is the time to get your "train legs" if you have started the tour in Perth. The only walking you need to do will be backwards and forwards along the corridor to and from the lounge or dining car. You can stretch your legs a bit further when the train stops at Cook around midday.

Cook, where you put your watch forward (or back if going west) also has a club, open only in evenings, but is better known for its jail cells. These now adjoin the station; one for males and one for females, and they look very much like the little tin sheds people used to have at the bottom of the garden before the advent of piped sewage disposal. Cook also has a hospital, but with so small a population (a few dozen at most) finds it hard to keep it in patients (let alone doctors and nurses, one would imagine). Travellers are therefore invited to "go crook at Cook" – the Australian colloquial for getting sick. The locals will ply you with souvenirs when the train stops there for about half an hour, as it usually does. Not all the souvenirs will have been made in Cook, like souvenirs everywhere.

The Cook interlude is a good time to get out and stretch your legs, but don't forget to look along the track. You won't see a longer stretch of straight line anywhere. When you look along the straight at night towards the headlights of an oncoming train, it is an unbelievably long time before it reaches you – but you will only be able to do this if your train is running extremely late, or you are travelling on the "Tea and Sugar" or a goods train.

After the train reaches Adelaide (the AN terminal at Keswick), where it spends three-quarters of an hour, it returns north through the farming lands of South Australia to Crystal Brook, where it turns east for Broken Hill. Look out on the right after Crystal Brook for remnants of the formation of the former narrow gauge South Australian railway between there and Gladstone.

At **Gladstone**, rail buffs have a rare treat; in the yards on the left are triple gauge tracks of four parallel rails, and a complicated system of points and crossings. Three gauges – standard, Irish (1600mm) and narrow (1067mm) – meet here. Gladstone is a centre for the wheat trade in this area, and a request stop on the *Indian Pacific*. Next is Peterborough, where again three rail gauges meet and passengers from Adelaide formerly joined the train to Broken Hill.

By the time you wake up in the morning you should be up in the Great Dividing Range around Wallerawang (not a scheduled stopping place), where you may see Australia's largest power station off to the left.

After Lithgow, the next and last stop before Sydney, electric traction takes the train smoothly through the ten tunnels of the Blue Mountains. Look out, ahead left and then right, for the Zigzag railway, the original route by which the trains crossed the range. Now a tourist line, with steam, it can be reached by road or by local train from Lithgow or Sydney. The scenery through the Blue Mountains as you climb and then descend between Lithgow and Katoomba is interesting on both sides but the best panoramas – which you will glimpse rather quickly – are on the right.

By morning rush hour the *Indian Pacific* is nearing Sydney's western suburbs, a strange contrast from the environment of the last three days. You may feel you have been on the move for ever, but even if this is your last day, your pass may still allow a local trip before you say farewell to the railways of Australia.

Other Bradt Rail Guides

Eastern Europe by Rail
   Rob Dodson

Greece by Rail and Ferry
   Zane Katsikis

India by Rail
   Royston Ellis

Russia by Rail
   Athol Yates

Spain and Portugal by Rail
   Norman Renouf

Sri Lanka by Rail
   Royston Ellis

Switzerland by Rail
   Anthony Lambert

USA by Rail
   John Pitt

Available from good bookshops or direct from
Bradt Publications, 41 Nortoft Road,
Chalfont St Peter, Bucks SL9 0LA
Tel/fax 01494 873478

Chapter Five

Capital City Itineraries

This chapter is for those who wish to base their tour on the state capital cities. It summarises the train services between them, tells you how to use the local trains when you are there, and gives suggestions on what to see. The following alphabetically arranged timetable summary should enable the visitor to devise an itinerary to taste. Full details of the trains are given elsewhere in this book.

Note that in summer time (late October to early March) times at Brisbane are an hour different from the other eastern states and both arrivals and departures of trains to and from other states should therefore be checked locally.

Intercapital summary

Some of the connections to and from Canberra marked "*via* Goulburn" involve a long wait there. Where this occurs, marked with an asterisk * below, pass holders have the option of changing later in the day at Moss Vale or Campbelltown instead. There are also some alternative connections between Canberra and the south and west using Countrylink road coaches. These and other bus services operated by the railways are not included in this table.

Change of train is required at all the places named *via* on each route.

From Adelaide	Schedule		Route
to Brisbane	Dep 07.45	Wed and Sun	*via* Sydney
	Arr 06.00	two days later	
	Dep 19.00	daily	*via* Melbourne and Sydney
	Arr 06.00	three days later	
to Canberra	Dep 07.45	Wed and Sun	*via* Sydney
	Arr 15.50	next day	
	Dep 19.00	daily	*via* Melbourne and Goulburn*
	Arr 22.20	next day	
to Melbourne	Dep 19.00	daily	
	Arr 07.55	next day	
to Perth	Dep 18.00	Tue and Fri	
	Arr 07.00	two days later	
to Sydney	Dep 07.45	Wed and Sun	
	Arr 09.15	next day	
	Dep 19.00	daily	*via* Melbourne
	Arr 19.13	next day	

From Brisbane	**Schedule**		**Route**
to Adelaide	Dep 07.30	Wed and Sun	*via* Sydney
	Arr 16.25	two days later	
	Dep 07.30	daily	*via* Sydney and Melbourne
	Arr 08.45	two days later	
to Canberra	Dep 07.30	daily	*via* Sydney
	Arr 11.50	next day.	
to Melbourne	Dep 07.30	daily	*via* Sydney
	Arr 18.35	next day	
to Perth	Dep 07.30	Wed and Sun	*via* Sydney
	Arr 07.00	four days later	
to Sydney	Dep 07.30	daily	
	Arr 21.35		

From Canberra	**Schedule**		**Route**
to Adelaide	Dep 06.50	Mon and Thu	*via* Sydney
	Arr 16.25	next day	
	Dep 06.50	daily	*via* Goulburn and Melbourne
	Arr 08.45	next day.	
to Brisbane	Dep 12.20	daily	*via* Strathfield
	Arr 06.00	next day	
to Melbourne	Dep 06.50	daily	*via* Goulburn
	Arr 18.35		
	Dep 17.20	daily	*via* Goulburn*
	Arr 07.05	next day	
to Perth	Dep 06.50	Mon and Thu	*via* Sydney,
			or: *via* Goulburn, Melbourne and Adelaide
	Arr 07.00	three days later	
to Sydney	Dep 06.50	daily	
	Arr 10.56		
	Dep 12.20	daily	
	Arr 16.28		
	Dep 17.20	daily	
	Arr 21.26		

From Melbourne	**Schedule**		**Route**
to Adelaide	Dep 20.20	daily	
	Arr 08.45	next day	
to Brisbane	Dep 20.05	daily	*via* Sydney
	Arr 06.00	two days later	
to Canberra	Dep 08.30	daily	*via* Goulburn*
	Arr 22.20		
	Dep 20.05	daily	*via* Goulburn*
	Arr 11.50	next day	
to Perth	Dep 20.20	Wed and Sun	*via* Adelaide
	Arr 07.00	three days later	

From Melbourne	Schedule		Route
to Sydney	Dep 08.30	daily	
	Arr 19.13		
	Dep 20.05	daily	
	Arr 06.45	next day	

From Perth	Schedule		Route
to Adelaide	Dep 13.35	Mon and Fri	
	Arr 06.15	two days later	
to Brisbane	Dep 13.35	Mon and Fri	*via* Sydney
	Arr 06.00	four days later	
to Canberra	Dep 13.35	Mon and Fri	*via* Sydney
	Arr 15.50	three days later	
to Melbourne	Dep 13.35	Mon and Fri	*via* Adelaide
	Arr 07.55	three days later	
to Sydney	Dep 13.35	Mon and Fri	direct
	Arr 09.15	three days later	

From Sydney	Schedule		Route
to Adelaide	Dep 08.10	daily	*via* Melbourne
	Arr 08.45	next day	
	Dep 14.40	Mon and Thu	direct
	Arr 16.55	next day	
to Brisbane	Dep 16.24	daily	
	Arr 06.00	next day	
to Canberra	Dep 07.43	daily	
	Arr 11.50		
	Dep 11.43	daily	
	Arr 15.50		
	Dep 18.14	daily	
	Arr 22.20		
to Melbourne	Dep 08.10	daily	
	Arr 18.35		
	Dep 20.43	daily	
	Arr 07.05	next day	
to Perth	Dep 14.40	Mon and Thu	direct
	Arr 07.00	three days later	

Local services and sightseeing

Within all the state capitals there are suburban rail services giving
access to the city centre and other points of interest. Canberra has
an intensive bus service. Suburban rail services operate usually at
least every half hour during daytime and at least hourly in late
evening and on Sundays. Between central city stations the
frequency is often every few minutes. Some ideas and outline
itineraries are given to allow the visitor to make the most of even
one day in each capital. They assume a start from the main station,

but remember that suburban locations are often very convenient and generally offer cheaper accommodation.

Sydney

Australia's largest city has enough to keep you sightseeing for days. Sydney's extensive suburban railway system can take you to many of the principal attractions and right into the heart of the city. St James, Town Hall, and Wynyard are the best stations for the central business district, but the main terminal itself is close to Chinatown, where you can enjoy Oriental cuisine equal to any in Hong Kong (and some pretty awful stuff as well). Quality does not always vary in proportion to price and since proprietors and menus frequently change it would be potentially misleading to suggest specific establishments in a book of this sort. Local advice is worth seeking. Another good indicator (apart from the obvious one of looking at the menu and the appearance of the place) is to note how well a restaurant is patronised. Plenty of Chinese in a Chinese restaurant is usually a fair indication of authenticity and quality.

A fine collection of traditional and modern Australian and European art may be seen at the Art Gallery of New South Wales, open daily. Take the Art Gallery Road from nearby St James station. You can carry on from there into the Royal Botanic Gardens, open daily until sunset, and see the lush tropical plants and exotic trees.

North of the gardens at Bennelong Point is the famous Opera House, of which visitors can enjoy a guided tour. Circular Quay station is nearby, also convenient for a walking tour around The Rocks, the oldest part of Sydney and well supplied with quality eating places. The Rocks Visitor Centre is at 104 George Street, west of Circular Quay. The Geological and Mining Museum, 36-64 George Street, and the craft, gift and curio shops at Argyle Arts Centre, open daily are all within walking distance of Circular Quay station. From there you can also take a harbour cruise, a ferry to one of the many coves or to Manly for Marineland or the beach, or take a hydrofoil to Taronga Park Zoo. Coach tours also depart from here. The state government runs an *Explorer* bus to 20 places of interest.

Museum station will bring you to the ANZAC War Memorial in Hyde Park where they change the guard every Thursday at 13.30, and also to the Australian Museum, open Tuesday to Saturday from ten in the morning and Sunday and Monday from midday, for Australia's largest natural history collection and a display of aboriginal artifacts and relics. You can enjoy panoramic 360-degree views of the city, the harbour and the Pacific Ocean from

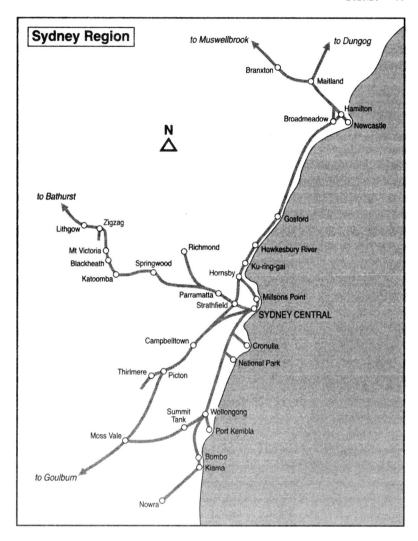

the top of Australia Square or of Sydney Post Office Tower, highest
in the Southern Hemisphere. Both also feature a revolving restaurant
and are near Wynyard station.

Should the revolving meal turn you "crook", Martin Place station
is next door to Sydney Hospital, but also adjoins the Martin Place
mall, where you can listen to a free lunchtime concert. It is also
convenient for visiting the Library of New South Wales and seeing
Parliament House. The Town Hall (at the station of the same name)
features a magnificent pipe organ and rich internal decoration.
There are many hotels between here and Sydney Central. Town

Hall is a good place to transfer to the Darling Harbour Monorail circuit which is a must for every Sydney visitor. The monorail will take you across Pyrmont Bridge to the Maritime Museum and the Exhibition Centre. At the city end of the bridge is the Sydney Aquarium where you can stroll through underwater tunnels past live sharks and other denizens of the sea.

One stop away from Central station on the suburban lines is Redfern, now the location of Paddy's Market Entertainment Centre. Slightly further afield, the Sydney–Wollongong rail route skirts Sydney airport at Sydenham and passes close to famous Botany Bay. Rail buffs will note the XPT depot at Tempe. The route then skirts the first of Australia's National Parks, the Royal, just south of Sutherland (27min; C 9014). A branch to the park ranger's office, where the traveller is in the heart of the "bush", has closed but has been reopened as a tramway. You can spend a whole day exploring the park's walking tracks and enjoying its excellent views.

With even a half day in Sydney, several interesting rail tours can be made. You can go over the Sydney Harbour Bridge and see the commuters on their daily rat race. Take the round trip via Hornsby and Strathfield (85-105min; C 9014 and local timetables) but go first on Cityrail to Circular Quay (8min) to view Sydney Harbour and the Opera House. You can go on to colourful Kings Cross or to Bondi Junction (7 & 10min), though the latter might prove to be a disappointment if you are expecting Bondi Beach. Bondi Junction has a mall, with plenty of interesting shops, market stalls, and restaurants. Bondi Beach, with many more restaurants, is but a short bus ride or a 20 minute walk from the station. If you want to go all the way to a beach in the Sydney area by train, take the Cronulla service (47min); you may find it full of bronzed, golden haired kids out for a day of sunshine and surf.

Nearby Parramatta is packed full of Australian history. See the birthplace of Batman. No, not the Gotham City "caped crusader" but John Batman, the surveyor who went over the Bass Strait from Launceston in Tasmania in 1835 (not accompanied by Robin) and, on the banks of the River Yarra in Victoria, said "Here is the place for a city" and thus founded Melbourne. Within walking distance of Parramatta station (25min from Central) you can also find the 1802 Lennox Bridge, the old Government House, the remains of Australia's first observatory, and other historic buildings that are maintained by the National Trust.

In a day tour of Sydney area by rail you could start at Central station, visit Town Hall or Wynyard for the city shopping centre, then Circular Quay for the harbour and Opera House, go over the Harbour Bridge to Millsons Point (for Luna Park amusement centre); then return to Central for the train to Cronulla for a spell at the beach before returning to the City centre for dinner. Or you could go at night perhaps to Kings Cross, home of Sydney's annual Gay Mardi Gras and noted for alternative lifestyles. If that is your scene you can certainly find good budget priced accommodation at the Cross but unless you are the partying type you may find it too noisy.

An alternative (or another day's choice) might take you to Campbelltown New Town (49min via East Hills, 68 or 78min via Liverpool), Parramatta (23-30min) for its history, Richmond (80min), to see the air base or just for a quiet suburban retreat (a good place to stay), or to Warwick Farm (45-50min) for the races if they are on.

Sydney's Cityrail has recently reintroduced a day pass for the suburban system. Passes for selected parts of the system, covering longer periods, are also obtainable at reasonable prices, but an Austrailpass covers them all.

Melbourne

Melbourne has long been Sydney's arch rival, and was Australia's administrative capital before the creation of Canberra. The 64 regular street blocks of its central business district are ringed by the railway, serving the main stations at Spencer Street (interstate), Flinders Street (for all local lines), Parliament, Museum, and Flagstaff. No part of the city centre is more than ten minutes walk from one of these stations. An intricate network of tram routes also links the stations with city centre streets and with most of the inner suburbs. Suburban routes penetrate to the outer suburbs and rural hinterland, and go around Port Philip Bay to Geelong in the west and Frankston in the east.

Spencer Street is reportedly Australia's busiest railway station, and is also the terminal for V/Line coach services operating from Melbourne, but Flinders Street is in the very heart of the city, adjoining Princes Bridge which crosses the Yarra, linking the south end of Swanston Street with St Kilda Road. Batman Avenue runs along the side of the Yarra south of the Flinders Street railway yards.

Just opposite Flinders Street station is Young & Jacksons Prince's Bridge Hotel, where J.J. Lefebvre's famous "Chloe" painting, which caused much controversy when first acquired in

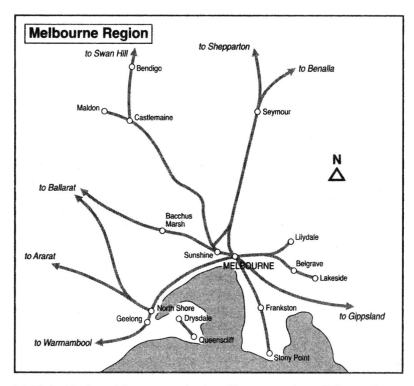

1883, is displayed in an upstairs bar. For nature in a different form, Melbourne boasts the largest plant collection in the Southern Hemisphere. This is at the Royal Botanical Gardens, open daily until sunset. Any tram down St Kilda Road from Flinders Street will take you there. Also in St Kilda Road is Australia's largest art collection at the National Gallery, open daily, and the Victorian Arts Centre, Melbourne's answer to the Sydney Opera House. Day tours or performances must be booked well in advance and are not cheap.

From the Arts Centre, go along the banks of the Yarra, walk or hire a cycle, or take a ferry boat from Princes Walk (adjoining Batman Avenue) on the northern bank. Walk or take a tram to the east end of Flinders Street for a look at Treasury Gardens. Jolimont station, a little further on, is handy for the Melbourne Cricket Ground and nearby Fitzroy Gardens where Captain Cook's Cottage, imported from Yorkshire, honours the "discoverer" of eastern Australia. In Russell Street, city centre, see the Old Melbourne Gaol and Penal Museum and the collection of Australian birds, animals, minerals and aboriginal artifacts, at the National Museum, open Monday to Saturday and on Sunday afternoons. The Institute of Applied Science Museum is in nearby Swanston Street.

Just north of Parliament station (city loop from Flinders or Spencer Street) on Nicholson Street, take in the view from the top of the ICI Building, with a guide to point out the main features of interest. Slightly further afield in Carlton, see the exhibit of Australian ceramics, weaving and hand-made jewellery in the Galaxy of Handicrafts, 99 Cardigan Street. A tram up Swanston Street will take you there. Nearby Lygon Street is famous for its ethnic restaurants, coffee bars, and boutiques.

Melbourne is a cosmopolitan city. See the Museum of Chinese Australian History at 22 Cohen Place, in the heart of Chinatown (Lonsdale and Little Bourke Streets close to Parliament station), open daily except Tuesdays. For bargain craft wares, try the Meat Market Craft Centre, 42 Courtney Street, North Melbourne (by tram along Flemington Road). Just north again is Royal Park and the Zoological Gardens, traversed by tram route, or by train to Royal Park station (Upfield Line, 13min; C 9023).

For something completely different, try the Colonial Tramcar Restaurant for a unique culinary and travel experience. To make reservations for lunch or dinner, phone (03) 9696 4000 or call at their office, 254 Bay Street, Brighton (tram or train to North Brighton station). The journey starts at National Art Gallery just south of Flinders Street station.

For those without an Austrailpass, rail/bus/tram passes on "The Met" can be obtained for parts or the whole of Melbourne area by the hour or day at very reasonable rates. Even if you are visiting Melbourne en route you have time between the arrival of overnight trains from interstate and their departure the same evening to travel all over the suburban area, around the bay to Frankston in the east (58min) or to Geelong in the west. Geelong is a 60-65 minute journey (C 9023) but is not covered by "Met" tickets.

For a pocket tour, take in Flinders Street and the underground loop (for city centre sights and shops), St Kilda (for the beach), historic Port Melbourne and Williamstown in the morning, and go out towards the Dandenong Ranges in the afternoon. If races or shows are on, you can go by train to Newmarket, the showgrounds or Flemington racecourse. The picturesque Dandenong Ranges, an hour from Melbourne by electric train to Upper Ferntree Gully or Belgrave (C 9023), are Melbourne's doorstep national park. Here you can see lyrebirds displaying their plumage, or visit the 40 hectare (98 acre) rhododendron garden at nearby Olinda.

From Belgrave, the *Puffing Billy* steam train skirts the south of the Dandenongs to Emerald. Operated by Emerald Tourist Railway Board, it runs mainly at weekends but not in seasons of high fire danger. See Chapter Seven, page 121, for more details.

North of the Dandenongs is Lilydale (a good suburban base about an hour from the city by frequent suburban train), from where connecting buses serve Healesville with its Sanctuary. Here you can watch kangaroos, koalas, emus, wombats and platypuses in a natural setting.

Brisbane

Subtropical Brisbane's warmth will greet you as you alight at this northern capital. Founded in the 1830s and now established as Australia's third city, Brisbane has seen rapid urban growth in the last two decades and its straggling suburbs cover an area equal to Greater London. Unlike Sydney and Melbourne, the city is under one administration: its budget is equal to that of the state of Tasmania.

A good view is obtainable from the observation platform of the clock tower at City Hall but the best panorama is from the viewpoint on Mount Coot-Tha, a short drive from the city centre but unfortunately not connected by public transport. You can make a day of it there, exploring the rainforest, and then calling for afternoon tea or dinner at the restaurant. There are more lookout points in Brisbane Forest Park, further into the ranges. If you are unable to reach the real thing, there is a simulated rainforest in Mount Coot-Tha Botanic Gardens, open daily from eight in the morning – and served by City Council buses. Australia's largest planetarium is also located there; viewing times should be checked locally.

Brisbane's suburban trains are mostly modern, smooth, well furnished electric units. The two main stations, Roma Street and Central, are within the city centre and within 15 minutes walk of each other. En route, climb up to the Old Windmill observatory on Wickham Terrace or go down through King George Square and Albert Street to the Queen Street Mall. From the north end of the Mall you take the walkway along the side of Anzac Square or through the square and past the Shrine of Remembrance to the old Central station façade, now the entrance to the Sheraton Hotel (as well as to the station itself).

Just over one kilometre to the north is Brunswick Street, station for colourful Fortitude Valley with its many ethnic restaurants and Brisbane's Chinatown. At the east end of Brunswick Street is New Farm Park, with up to 12,000 rose trees in bloom from September

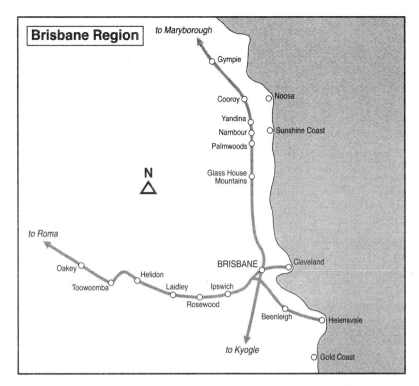

through November (and avenues of jacaranda and poinciana trees) beside the Brisbane River. Visit St John's Cathedral, open daily, where brass-rubbing workshops are held (check times locally). At nearby Spring Hill are many of Brisbane's dozens of art and craft galleries. Near here, too, is the Brisbane Exhibition site – they call it the "Ekka". If an exhibition is on, there will be frequent special trains from all city stations, and your rail pass will be honoured.

In the city itself a few blocks from Central station are the Brisbane Botanic Gardens, the 20 hectare (49 acre) site offering a profusion of sub-tropical flowers and shrubs.

A circular inner-city bus route takes the strain out of walking between city centre features (the main strain being having to wait to cross roads at traffic lights – it takes just about the same time whether you walk or wait for the bus). At the south end of the Queen Street Mall is Conrad's Casino in the old Treasury building, and a hotel where you can obtain a fairly up-market counter lunch at reasonable prices. Rather more down-market is Fihelly's Arms, a bar at the Ann Street entrance to Central station, where you can enjoy a cheap but nourishing counter lunch while looking at the railway memorabilia adorning the walls.

Brisbane city centre is well supplied with restaurants. You will find more of them at the Riverside Centre, on the northern perimeter of the central business area, also served by the city circle bus. The Brisbane Convention Centre, occupying part of the site of the former World Expo 1988, is just over the river, a five minute walk across Victoria Bridge or take the train over the Merivale A-frame bridge from Roma Street or Central to South Brisbane, the first stop after Roma Street.

Adjoining South Brisbane station on the other side is South Bank Parklands while right opposite the station is the Cultural Centre with its Performing Arts Complex, restaurants and bars. Across the road (by covered walkway) is also Queensland Art Gallery with its fine collection of paintings, sculptures, photographs and prints, and Queensland Museum where exhibits include dinosaurs and the only surviving World War I German tank.

Near Vulture Street station in Stanley Street (the next station after South Brisbane on the Beenleigh or Cleveland line) you can see many fine ship models and an old frigate at Queensland Maritime Museum, open on Wednesdays, Saturdays and Sundays from 10.00.

Within walking distance of Bowen Hills station (the next to the north after Brunswick Street) is Miegunyah, built 1884 and now a Folk Museum, open Tuesday, Wednesday, Saturday and Sunday from 10.30 hours. Less than a kilometre away is Brisbane's oldest surviving house, Newstead, at the bend of the river in Newstead Park. Look along the river to the wharves in both directions and across to Bulimba Point. Downstream the Gateway Bridge dominates the skyline beyond Hamilton Reach, while the jets loom large overhead on their approach to Brisbane airport.

Near the airport itself (there is no rail link yet and you need a taxi or the airport bus) you can see the *Southern Cross*, the aircraft in which the first solo flight to Australia was made from England in 1928. Before leaving the Newstead area, visit the famous "Brekky Creek" Hotel, north of the river, for a beer or the best steak you'll ever see, or try the seafood at the Breakfast Creek Wharf. Just behind the pub in Higgs Street is a rare Chinese Joss House, built 1884, phone (07) 3262 5588 for appointment.

For exotic animals, birds and plants visit Alma Park Zoo and 13 hectare (32 acre) Tropical Palm Gardens, open daily, just over a kilometre from Dakabin station on the Caboolture line. Some trains have special bus connections to Alma Park – ask for leaflets at Central or Roma Street.

More accessible is Brisbane's most popular tourist spot for overseas visitors, the world famous Lone Pine Sanctuary at Fig Tree Pocket. Open daily, it can be reached by City bus services from the City or from Indooroopilly Interchange (near the station) or by taking a launch from North Quay, phone (07) 3229 7055. You can hold a koala, be photographed wearing a snake, feed the kangaroos, wallabies and emus, and see wombats, dingos, sugar gliders and the elusive and unbelievable platypus.

River cruises as well as ferries will give you unrivalled views of the city and its bridges, particularly at night. Try taking a dinner cruise on the *Kookaburra Queen,* phone (07) 3352 3797 for information and reservations, a launch trip to Tangalooma on Moreton Island, or a day cruise to Stradbroke if you have a day or more to spare.

For the rail enthusiast, there is a railway shop at the end of the outbound platform at South Brisbane. The Australian Railway Historical Society operates several runs of steam trains in this area. The suburban rail system can also take you to the coast at Manly, Lota, or Raby Bay (Ormiston station on the Cleveland line, 50min; C 9015), or southeast to Beenleigh (41min by express, hourly from Roma Street or 56min by stopping train every half hour) for the rum distillery and nearby Lion Park.

Within day trip reach by coach is O'Reilly's Guest House, high in the rain forest of Lamington National Park, an unforgettable experience of mountains and gorges, breathtaking vistas, cool dense forests, waterfalls, colourful parrots and bower birds and little pademelons. These are marsupials the size of rabbits which hop around unconcerned while you feed the rosellas. Visitors can obtain lunch at the guesthouse.

If your time is more strictly limited, you can taste something of wild life even in the city. Round the corner from Central station is Koala House, with realistic bush habitat of eucalypt, rainforest and coast wetland. Live koalas are a feature of this "Wilderness Walk". Also in the city, see the giant old fig trees at the bottom end of Creek Street, and at some other road junctions in the inner suburbs.

If travelling interstate, your train leaves Roma Street's platform 1. If travelling north on a Queensland Rail traveltrain service (*Sunlander, Queenslander, Spirit of the Tropics, Spirit of Capricorn* or *Spirit of the Outback*), platform 10 is your starting point. Allow a good ten minutes to cross with your luggage from the suburban platforms or from the coach station at Brisbane Transit Centre.

Adelaide

Adelaide is the City of Light, its site being chosen and original plan drawn by surveyor Colonel William Light in 1836. See the view of Adelaide from Light's Vision on Montefiore just three kilometres (1.8 miles) north of the central station.

There is a fairly comprehensive network of suburban services, including buses, in the Adelaide area but from long distance trains you have first to get to a local station. The main city station in North Terrace is three kilometres (1.8 miles) from the interstate terminal at Keswick. You must first therefore go to the suburban platform at Keswick. The railway planners have rather overlooked the passengers' need for a direct link between platforms, and many of the local trains do not stop at Keswick. Check the times first and consider the option of taking a taxi at five times the price.

Keswick suburban platform is within sight of where you arrive from interstate but you must allow ten minutes walk and up to half an hour's wait for a local train. You have to walk just as far if you want to catch a city bus. Leave luggage in a locker at the Australian National terminal if you are only in town for one day.

Once at the old city station you are in the heart of the town. Immediately adjoining is the new Festival Centre with its concert halls and drama theatre, restaurants, and plaza. There are hourly guided tours on Mondays to Saturdays from 10.00. Take a cruise on the nearby River Torrens to the zoo, noted for its birds, or try a ride on the O-bahn busway, Australia's first, which runs through some of the parklands of Adelaide's "green belt". It passes close to the station, as does a local city centre bus.

At the east end of North Terrace the Botanic Gardens features spectacular water lilies. Near the station see the collection of prints, drawings, sculpture, graphic arts, coins and paintings at the Art Gallery of South Australia, and the Australian birds and animals in the South Australian Museum, which also holds the largest collection of aboriginal artifacts in the world.

Among the many interesting day or half day tours from Adelaide is the tram ride to **Glenelg**, about a 20 minute journey from Victoria Square in the city or from Goodwood, the next station south of Keswick (C 9030, T 550). The fare is not covered by the Austrailpass but will not break you. A local day pass for a few dollars covers all suburban buses and trains as well as the trams and O-bahn. The Glenelg tram is the only inter-urban tram ride left in Australia and Glenelg, at the seaside on the Spencer Gulf, is well worth a visit. At Glenelg North you can watch the sea life at

Symbols of some of Australia's leading long-distance trains

Top: *The* Ghan *Adelaide–Alice Springs* (AN)

Above: *The* Explorer, *Sydney–Canberra* (HB)

Left: *The* Indian Pacific, *Sydney–Perth* (HB)

Top: *An aerial view of downtown Melbourne. Flinders Street Station is at the bottom left of the picture.* (HB)

Above: *The* Ghan *rolls by in the background but the lizard is more concerned to see the photographer off its territory.* (AN)

Left: *They really seem to mean it when they say "Go crook in Cook!"* (HB)

Above: *Fitroy Falls in Morton National Park, New South Wales* (PB)

Right: *Queensland Rail's Mount Surprise–Forsayth* Savannahlander, *described by the rail company as a "safari into the sunburnt country".* (QR)

Giants of earth and sea
Above: *The Pinnacles in Namburg National Park, Western Australia, are fossilised remains of an ancient forest.* (PB)
Below: *The 12 apostles dominate this area of the Great Ocean Road in Victoria.* (GS)

Marineland, then stroll along the beach, or take a bus, to the pier at Grange. Try the nearby Grange Hotel for an evening meal or nightstop, cheaper than in the city which is only 22 minutes away by train.

Much of the Adelaide area, including the beach suburbs of Brighton, Seacliffe, Marino, Largs and Outer Harbour, is served by both bus and train. Trains also go up to the Mount Lofty ranges, locally known as the Adelaide Hills to Belair (36min, T 550). The view of Adelaide's lights from this railway is particularly good, and may be enjoyed by travellers on the *Overland* as well as on the local services.

The South Australian Tourist Bureau (diagonally opposite the city centre station at 18 King William Street) has details and prices for state-run tours to city sights such as Cleland Conservation Park (where you can hold koalas and feed kangaroos), the National Park and beaches, Torrens Gorge, Morialta Falls and the wineries of the Barossa Valley and the Southern Vales. At Barossa Junction, a collection of old railway carriages makes up an unusual hotel and restaurant complex.

Your deadline departures from Keswick AN terminal are 07.45 on the *Indian Pacific* to the east, 14.00 if going on the *Ghan,* 18.00 if going west and 19.00 if bound for Melbourne.

Perth

Perth is Australia's most isolated state capital, with 3,000km (almost 2,000 miles) and more of ocean to the west and about the same amount of desert to the east. Other Australians refer to the residents of this area as "sandgropers". As Saltzman's *Eurail Guide* points out, (despite its name the *Eurail Guide* has some coverage of railways worldwide) Perth is known for its "wide sandy beaches on the Indian Ocean, with good surfing", an apt description. Take the suburban train from Perth City to Cottesloe or Leighton on the Fremantle line (C 9037), the latter actually in sight of the beach, reached by footbridge over the incongruous railway yards. Choicer beaches are found north and south, reached by city transport.

Perth Terminal station is not in the town centre, but adjoins the suburban station from where local trains will take you to City, right in the heart and adjoining the bus terminal. A free city circle bus runs from here, but many of the sights and places you will want to visit are within easy walking distance. See the Hay Street Mall, with London Court, a shopping area re-created as a 16th century English street. The red London double-deck bus parked in the street is your signpost. Round the corner in St. George's Terrace see the historic cloisters and archway.

Walk over the freeway bridge and up to the 400 hectare (980 acre) Kings Park for the marvellous display of wild flowers and the view over Perth Water. Look for the old windmill at the south end of Narrows Bridge, then stroll back past Parliament House to see the markets at West Perth, from where the train will take you back to City.

North of City station in Beaufort Street see the exhibit of large Blue Whale skeletons, meteorites, aboriginal culture and paintings in the Western Australian Art Gallery, and the old Gaol and Barracks Museum. On the other side of the railway, Barrack Street leads down to Perth Water and the ferry terminal. Look out for the lovely Georgian-style Old Court House, in nearby Stirling Gardens.

Hire a car for the day to visit El Caballo Blanco, 60km (37 miles) to the east, where Andalusian dancing horses are bred, or go a similar distance north to the 2500 hectare (6200 acre) Yanchep Park, with its koalas, black swans, limestone caves and profusion of wild flowers. Try skin-diving at the popular Rottnest Island resort, 18km (11 miles) offshore. Ferries operate five days a week, daily in summer (C 9059).

You can also go further afield by train. The suburban system can take you north to Whitfords, Joondalup or Currambine on Perth's newest suburban railway (17 or 26min; C 9037) or west to Midland, where you are near the Swan valley and you can take river cruises or visit the vineyards near Middle Swan. Transperth buses serve most districts and supplement the rail system. For local transport information phone 132 213 from within Western Australia; (09) 325 1633 from elsewhere.

The railway line also goes down the coast to the port of Fremantle (27min) where the station itself, built 1906, is designated a historic building. Here you can wander down to the harbour, and on to the yacht club, home of the boat which took the *America*'s Cup away from America in 1983 for the first time in its history.

Visit the Maritime Museum and Art Centre and see the great views of the city and harbour from the Round House. Have some fish and chips at Cicerello's on the waterside before you return to the station for the trip back to Perth.

Deadline for trains back east is 13.35 from the East Perth Terminal. Allow a good hour to return from Fremantle.

Chapter Six

Scenic and Outback Touring

In the *Eurail Guide* a list is given of the most scenic rail journeys in Europe, based mainly on research by John Price, the then Managing Editor of Cooks Timetables. Scenic appreciation is partly an individual matter but not entirely so; there is a consensus about what is attractive, as evidenced by calendars, picture postcards, colour slide sales and the facts of where people go, where they stay, and what they gasp about and take photographs of. My own list of the most scenically interesting or unusual routes served by regular (and in some cases irregular) passenger services in Australia may help tourists plan their own itinerary, but two sample itineraries are presented to make it easy.

Timetable changes and bus substitutions in recent years in nearly all states have deprived rail travellers of the opportunity of enjoying scenery such as Glen Innes–Armidale, the Brisbane Valley, Mareeba–Ravenshoe, Toowoomba–Warwick, Ballarat–Ararat and Wolseley–Mount Gambier. Even the scenic NSW-Queensland border ranges north of Kyogle can only now be enjoyed on the south-bound journey and the NSW North Coast between Byron Bay and Murwillumbah is traversed in darkness most of the year.

The hash sign # indicates those scenic routes which are traversed by day, in at least one direction in either of the itineraries which follow. Some of the scenic routes are covered by other itineraries elsewhere in this book. In particular, it should be noted that the scenic Sydney suburban sections North Sydney–Wynyard, Sutherland–Cronulla and the Blue Mountains (Penrith–Lithgow) are readily accessible and are either included in all or most of the itineraries in this book or can easily be included in virtually any itinerary by using one or more of the spare periods of Sydney stopovers.

An asterisk * indicates a scenic route on which regular services no longer operate but which could in future be restored or on which some special excursions might well be advertised from time to time.

Selected Scenic Journeys

Scenic sections	Route	Itineraries
New South Wales		
Kyogle–Tamrookum (Qld)#	NSW North Coast	13
Murwillumbah–Lismore#	Murwillumbah branch.	13 (part)
Glenreagh–Nambucca Heads#	NSW North Coast	13
Glenreagh–Dorrigo*	*See* pages 108-9	
Gloucester–Taree#	NSW North Coast	13
Glen Innes–Armidale*	Main North NSW	
Willow Tree–Muswellbrook#	Main North NSW	12
Gosford–Cowan#	Main North NSW	12, 13
North Sydney–Wynyard	NSW North Shore	
Penrith–Lithgow#	Main West NSW	12
Lithgow–Mudgee*	Wallerawang–Gwabegar	
Manildra–Parkes	Main West NSW	
Sutherland–Cronulla	Sutherland–Cronulla	
Sutherland–Nowra#	Illawarra	13 (part)
Wollongong–Moss Vale#	Unanderra–Moss Vale	13
Bungendore–Cooma*	Joppa Junction–Bombala	
Victoria		
Ballan–Bacchus Marsh#	Main Western	12
Gisborne–Malmsbury#	Bendigo line	12
Belgrave–Lakeside	Emerald Tourist Railway	
South Australia		
Bridgewater–Adelaide#	Melbourne-Adelaide	12
Port Pirie–Port Augusta	Main East-West line	
Quorn–Woolshed Flat	Pichi Richi Railway	
West and central Australia		
Kulgera–Alice Springs	Central Australia Railway	
Nullarbor Plain#	Trans-Australian Railway	12
Northam–Perth#	Kalgoorlie–Perth	12
Queensland		
Rosewood–Laidley#	QR Western line	13
Helidon–Toowoomba#	QR Western line	13
Warwick–Stanthorpe*	QR Southwestern line	
Caboolture–Gympie#	QR North Coast	13
Kilkivan–Murgon	Kingaroy branch	
Gladstone–Monto*	Gladstone–Monto	
Gladstone–Mount Larcom	QR North Coast	
Gladstone–Mt Rainbow*	Moura Short Line	
Sarina–Bloomsbury	QR North Coast	
Kabra–Mt Morgan*	Mount Morgan branch	
Anakie–Alpha	QR Midland	
Home Hill–Townsville#	QR North Coast	13

Scenic sections	Route	Itineraries
Ingham–Tully#	QR North Coast	13
Innisfail–Cairns#	QR North Coast	13
Cairns–Kuranda#	Cairns–Mareeba	13
Atherton–Ravenshoe	Atherton Railway	
Dimbulah–Lappa*	Cairns Railway	
Almaden–Chillagoe*	Cairns Railway	
Almaden–Forsayth	Etheridge branch	
Stuart–Charters Towers	QR Northern Railway	
Cloncurry–Mount Isa	QR Northern Railway	

Itineraries 12 and 13 (14 days)

Here is the first ready made scenic itinerary. It is for 14 days based on Sydney and covers eight of the most scenic or dramatic stretches of railways. With a Saturday start, it offers contrasting scenery, commencing with the Hawkesbury and Brisbane Water region north of Sydney, on to the tablelands of Northern New South Wales, the western end of the Great Dividing Range in Victoria, South Australia's Mount Lofty Ranges, then the wide open spaces of the Nullarbor, and finally the escarpments and canyons of the Blue Mountains.

The second 14 day scenic itinerary based on Sydney covers even more scenic routes, though confined more to the eastern seaboard. By omitting the long trek across the Nullarbor and back, there is time to experience the scenery of Queensland's coastal ranges. It commences on Sunday with a break on the NSW north coast, a Brisbane nightstop, then a trip up the ranges to Toowoomba on the Darling Downs. This is followed by a trip up the Queensland north coast line to Cairns, with an excursion up the ranges on the Kuranda Tourist Train.

A diversion on the southbound return trip to Byron Bay, the most easterly point on Australia's rail system, is followed by an exciting run down the NSW south coast to Unanderra to return via Moss Vale to Sydney. This line, operated at weekends by State Rail until only a few years ago, is now known as the *Cockatoo Run*, operated by a private company, 3801 Limited (named after one of Australia's most famous locomotives). From Unanderra, junction with the South Coast Line, it ascends at a steady 1-in-30 gradient to Summit Tank, opening out to magnificent panoramic views over Lake Illawarra and the coast. It then passes through dense rainforest before quietly curving into the junction at Moss Vale, itself an attractive station and in the heart of the small town of that name. Moss Vale would be quite a good base for excursions; all trains passing through stop there, whether Cityrail or Countrylink, including express services to and from Melbourne.

Special Scenic Itinerary 12

NSW Tablelands, the Great Dividing Range west of Melbourne (old gold mining country), the Mount Lofty Ranges, the Nullarbor, the Avon Valley, and the Blue Mountains. Fourteen days based on Sydney. Can be adapted to Melbourne base by starting as at Day 4 and ending as at Day 3.

Day		Programme		
Day 1	Saturday	Dep Sydney	11.05	*N Tableland Xplorer*
		Arr Armidale	18.50	nightstop
Day 2	Sunday	Dep Tamworth	09.10	*N Tableland Xplorer*
		Arr Sydney	17.00	local nightstop
Day 3	Monday	Dep Sydney	08.10	*Olympic Spirit*
		Arr Melbourne	18.35	nightstop
Day 4	Tuesday	Dep Melbourne	09.35	V/Line
		Arr Ballarat	11.10	4½ hours free
		Dep Ballarat	16.00	*via* North Shore line
		Arr Melbourne	17.45	nightstop
Day 5	Wednesday	Dep Melbourne	08.35	InterCity
		Arr Bendigo	10.35	4½ hours free
		Dep Bendigo	15.20	InterCity
		Arr Melbourne	17.08	nightstop
Day 6	Thursday	Dep Melbourne	20.20	*Overland*
Day 7	Friday	Arr Adelaide	08.45	9 hours free
		Dep Adelaide	18.00	*Indian Pacific*
Day 9	Sunday	Arr Perth	07.00	9 hours free[a]
		Dep Perth	16.15	*Prospector*
		Arr Northam	17.58	nightstop
Day 10	Monday	Dep Northam	15.25	*Indian Pacific*
Day 13	Thursday	Arr Lithgow	06.15	change trains
		Dep Lithgow	06.39	local train
		Arr Katoomba	07.24	nightstop
Day 14	Friday	Katoomba to Sydney at leisure		

[a] Optional round trip to Fremantle – allow 2 hours minimum.

Special Scenic Itinerary 13

Northern NSW coast, Toowoomba, Queensland's north coast line, northern Queensland including the Kuranda Ranges, and Illawarra. Fourteen days based on Sydney. Could be based on Brisbane commencing as Day 3 or Day 11.

Day		Programme		
Day 1	Sunday	Dep Sydney	11.35	*Grafton XPT*
		Arr Kempsey[a]	18.36	4½ hours free
		Dep Kempsey[a]	23.19	*Brisbane XPT*
Day 2	Monday	Arr Brisbane	06.00#	nightstop

Day		Programme		
Day 3	Tuesday	Dep Brisbane	19.15	*Westlander*
		Arr Toowoomba[b]	21.26	2 night stopover
Day 5	Thursday	Dep Toowoomba[b]	05.45	*Westlander*
		Arr Brisbane	09.35	change trains
		Dep Brisbane	09.55	*Sunlander*
Day 6	Friday	Arr Cairns	18.00	2 night stopover
Day 8	Sunday[c]	Dep Cairns	09.15	Kuranda Tourist Train
		Arr Kuranda	10.55	4½ hours free
		Dep Kuranda	15.30	Kuranda Tourist Train
		Arr Cairns	17.05	nightstop
Day 9	Monday	Dep Cairns	08.00	*Sunlander*
Day 10	Tuesday	Arr Brisbane[d]	16.10	nightstop[d]
Day 11	Wednesday	Dep Brisbane	07.30[#]	*Brisbane XPT*
		Arr Urunga	13.10[e]	2 hours free
		Dep Urunga	15.10[e]	*Murwillumbah XPT*
		Arr Byron Bay	19.27	nightstop
Day 12	Thursday	Dep Byron Bay	22.02	*Murwillumbah XPT*
		Arr Casino	23.27	Nightstop
Day 13	Friday	Dep Casino	10.09	*Brisbane XPT*
		Arr Sydney	21.35	nightstop
Day 14	Saturday	Dep Sydney	07.44	local train
		Arr Unanderra	09.21	change trains
		Dep Unanderra	10.00	*Cockatoo Run*[f]
		Arr Moss Vale	12.40	change trains
		Dep Moss Vale[g]	14.34	*Canberra Xplorer*[r]
		Arr Sydney	16.26	

Alternative for Day 14

Day	Programme		
Day 14	Dep Sydney	09.38	local train
	Arr Nowra[h]	12.23	4½ hours free
	Dep Nowra[j]	16.53[h]	local train
	Arr Sydney	19.46[j]	

[a] This break could be made at other places en route – see text.

[b] Willowburn station.

[c] Kuranda side trip could equally be taken on the Saturday.

[d] Option of nightstop at Surfers Paradise instead. See next page.

[e] Request stop – advance booking required.

[f] Privately run train by 3801 Limited. Austrailpass not valid. Fare $11 one way, $20 round trip. Buffet car on train.

[g] Other trains back to Sydney at 16.02, 17.11[r], 17.20, 19.02, 19.35[r], 20.32, taking 2-2½ hours, the last arriving Sydney 22.56.

[h] Change at Dapto.

[j] Later trains from Nowra at 17.32, 18.50 and 19.56, arriving Sydney 20.46, 21.46 and 22.46, all changing at Dapto.

[r] Refreshments available on train.

[#] One hour earlier during Eastern Summer Time.

Alternative for Days 10 & 11

With Surfers Paradise Nightstop.

Day 10	Tuesday	Arr	Brisbane	16.10	change trains
		Dep	Brisbane	17.39	Interurban MU
		Arr	Helensvale	18.04	change to bus
		Dep	Helensvale	19.00#	Countrylink coach
		Arr	Surfers Paradise	19.15	nightstop
Day 11	Wednesday	Dep	Surfers Paradise	07.00#	Countrylink coach
		Arr	Casino	09.56	change to train
		Dep	Casino	10.09	*Brisbane XPT*
		Arr	Urunga	13.10k	2 hours free

One hour earlier during Eastern Summer Time.

k Request stop – advance booking required.

The real outback

While the experience of crossing the Nullarbor by train gives a vivid impression of the vast expanse of near nothingness that is a feature of inland Australia, and you can understand the remoteness and heat experienced by workers in the railway camps along the track, this is not really the true outback of the cattle and sheep stations, or of the tiny towns with their verandahed pubs and dusty roads. To see some of these you have to leave the main routes (but not necessarily the air-conditioned trains) and you have to allow plenty of time. Rather than present an itinerary (which might well cover two months or more), this chapter describes a series of rail safaris from major centres, leaving the traveller to select one or more as time and inclination dictate.

These journeys are all in Queensland, the only state which still has rail services to small inland settlements. This is not to say there are not some delightful small towns to come upon in other states, but you will usually see these on your way through to somewhere else, and if the place attracts your attention you can break your journey there, depending on the time.

The base cities for these outback safaris are Brisbane, Rockhampton, Townsville and Cairns. With all of them the climbing of the ranges – the northern spurs of the Great Dividing Range – is always of scenic interest, though unfortunately done at night by some of the main air-conditioned trains. Once beyond the ranges, the countryside becomes fairly flat, semi-bushland, brigalow scrub, with occasional hills and rocky outcrops, numerous small creeks, dry for most of the year, but with here and there a deep ravine and, on the Mount Isa line, a major bridge over the Burdekin River. Soil gives way to sand and the bush to flat plains the further west you travel. On some routes the rails may be very lightweight, reducing speed to 40km/h (25mph) or less. The towns bask in the hot glare of the sun, and the locals seek the cool shade of the verandah or bar. Some will sit on the station platform for hours and it is a good idea to wave to them. The arrival of the train, usually only twice weekly, is still something of an event.

The first trip is by the *Westlander*, possibly the most threatened of all the major inland air-conditioned services of Queensland Rail, but which has survived in spite of all the worst efforts of government commissions, economic rationalists, Treasury "razor gangs" and the efforts of rival transport operators, not to mention inconvenient timing, general apathy and falling patronage. The *Westlander*'s non-air-conditioned cousin, the *Dirranbandi Mail* described in earlier editions of this book, was the first victim of the branch line closure mania when it hit Queensland in earnest in the early 1990s. That the *Westlander* still survives, despite truncation of its route, relocation of a major station, alterations to timetable and days of running, and withdrawal of booking facilities from country stations, is something of a testimony to the determination of country people to survive and hold fiercely onto their tangible links with the rest of the world, of which the railway is one of the most symbolic and well-loved. By travelling on a train like the *Westlander* you become part of a clan, identifying yourself with local interests and learning about a way of life that is a far cry from the suburban rat race that is now all too typical of the Australia most people know.

At Roma Street the *Westlander*, alone among Queensland Rail's "Traveltrain" fleet, leaves not from the main long distance platform number 10, but from a platform at the other side of the station, closer to the interstate platform, since the western line exits in the same direction as the line going south. The latter swings away across the Brisbane River, while the western line of four tracks, the main western "up" and "down" lines and the adjacent suburban lines, follows the north bank of the river past the Castlemaine XXXX brewery at Milton, through Toowong to cross the river seven or eight minutes after leaving Brisbane at Indooroopilly. Toowong is the modal interchange for Queensland University. Shuttle buses operate from just over the road from the station, and opposite the station is the Royal Exchange Hotel, favourite watering place of students after lectures and exams. At Indooroopilly the river is crossed by three bridges together, two double track rail and one for road traffic, the last-named noted for its entry towers and a

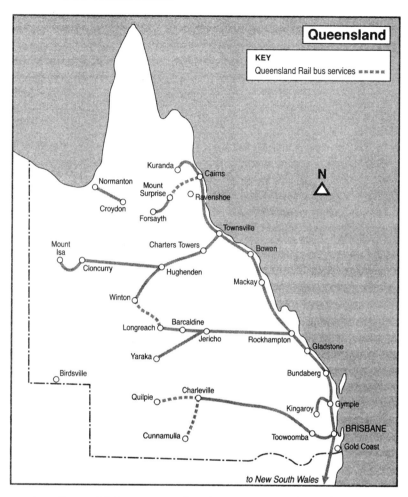

road surface which seems to be almost constantly under repair.

The river is seen again on the right approaching Ipswich, some 45 minutes after leaving Brisbane. From here the first railway in Queensland ran to **Grandchester**, or Bigge's Camp as it was then called, some 31km (19 miles) further on, and just past the end of the electrified suburban system recently extended to Rosewood. Rosewood station and Grandchester are request stops for the *Westlander*. West of Grandchester the train climbs the ranges towards Toowoomba, a long, winding deviation while the highway climbs much more steeply on a shorter but less scenic route. In the Little Liverpool ranges is one of the oldest tunnels and the longest single bore tunnel on Australian railways. There are good views to the south and east, and the best side for viewing is the left going west, although on the westbound journey it will be dark and you will probably be concentrating on having a meal in the quaintly named "food bar car" (a grill buffet with tables). You can see this part of the ranges by day from the eastbound *Westlander*.

Helidon, at the foot of the main range, is a pleasant little town famous for its spa waters, and a good place to break the journey. **Spring Bluff**, right in the middle of the ranges (left side going west) is always winning the competition for the best kept station, and is worthy of a look on the return trip when its profusion of flower beds is evident on both sides of the track. **Toowoomba**, Queensland's third city and on the top of the range, is well worth a break of journey. Not only has it excellent restaurants and a pleasant climate, it is a colourful town, proud of its trees and flowers. On the edge of the escarpment, looking out towards Brisbane, is a lookout tower with a camera obscura, like the one pioneer town planner Patrick Geddes established in Edinburgh, Scotland. The station refreshment room is a relic of gracious living of the past. You will still get silver service, a tablecloth, and a very substantial meal for a ridiculously reasonable price, but unfortunately in the most recent change to the *Westlander*'s itinerary, the Toowoomba stop has been relocated to Willowburn, some 3km (2 miles) to the north and the old station is no longer visited.

Warwick, once gateway to the south by rail and still on what Queensland Rail calls the "main line", is the outlet for the fruit growing area of Queensland's "Granite Belt", which can be reached by going further south either on an excursion or by freight train. The *Sydney Express* used to follow the NSW Tableland route as far north as Wallangarra, where the station still stands, junction of the Queensland and New South Wales systems, about five hours south of Warwick by freight train. The orchards, wineries, and scenic lookouts in these granite ranges are all worth visiting.

Inglewood, which the Dirranbandi passenger train used to reach in the early hours, was junction for Queensland's own Texas, a small border town once served by regular freight trains but an early victim of the closures of the last decade. **Dirranbandi** was the end of the southwestern line, served now only by twice weekly freight trains. There are not even any substitute buses offered in place of the former mail train.

En route to Charleville, current terminus of the *Westlander*, is **Roma**, a flourishing western Queensland grazing town, centre for gemstones and home of Bassetts winery, long well known for its rich Sauternes-style white wines. Further on are Mitchell and

Morven, both worth a visit and linked by bus as well as the rail services. (C 9012)

Charleville, heart of Queensland's "mulga country" and second largest outback town in the state, is where the train now turns around but formerly divided in two, one part continuing west to Quilpie. Passengers on the Quilpie portion of the train, for many years consisting of a single coach and known locally and with affection as the "Flying Flea", faced five hours rolling uncertainly along the slender track which itself almost disappears – they call it "two wires in the grass". In the main street of Quilpie a road sign tells you how far it is to places further west.

If you are able to arrange a trip there on a goods train (or can face the long bus ride) go to the end of the line in Quilpie station yard and look out west. This is the nearest you can get on Australia's rail network to Birdsville, that remotest of all outback settlements, famous for its annual races and the four-wheel drive Birdsville Track down to South Australia. If you intend to stay the night out west, be sure to pack mosquito repellent. You'll need it.

The other branch from Charleville led to **Cunnamulla**. Both Quilpie and Cunnamulla are now served by connecting buses on charter to Queensland Rail (and covered by the Austrailpass). There is time for a quick out and back trip to either place while the train turns around and is cleaned and watered in Charleville, but you can spend a little longer and get a good taste of life out west by stopping off instead at one of the smaller places en route such as Wyandra, Cooladdi (from the aboriginal word for "black duck"), or Cheepie ("whistling duck").

You will feel the heat if wandering far from the pub or road house in the middle of the day. Don't walk too far; the ground is full of prickles anyway. Go back and have a drink before the bus arrives. On the other hand, if you wait with the train in Charleville there is much of interest to see just by taking a walk up the main street. At the Hotel Corones on the right you will find souvenirs of the major floods which inundated the town a few years ago but, although you may see thunder clouds piling up in the afternoon sky, drought is more of an experience in this sunburned outback country than floods. When there has been "good" rain, the land can be green here; at other times it is burned bronze.

Other inland long distance trips by air-conditioned train are from Rockhampton and from Townsville. The *Spirit of the Outback* from "Rocky" actually starts its journey at Brisbane's Roma Street, covering the north coast sector overnight and in the morning turning to make its leisurely way west through the Bowen Basin coalfields to Longreach, "border to the far outback".

At Rockhampton the locomotive changes ends, or a new one is attached and the train retraces its route for 5½km (3½ miles) to Rocklands, where it leaves the north coast main line for Gracemere on the electrified midland line. In times of severe flooding affecting Rockhampton and particularly the low lying parts of the track between there and Rocklands, passenger trains may use the Gracemere Diversion (as all coal trains do) to by-pass Rocky and detour inland via the central Queensland electrified coal lines. The *Spirit of the Outback*'s next major stop, after negotiating the coast ranges between Kabra and Duaringa, is Bluff, a major staging post for the coal trains which run almost hourly through this section and where three or more may often be seen together in the four passing "roads" of the station yard.

Blackwater, a tad further west, is where mine branches start to peel off the main midland route, south to Laleham and Koorilgah, north to Curragh and at Rangal south again to Boorgoon and Kinrola.

Blackwater is a mining town, somewhat famous, or notorious, in Australia's political history as the place where the locals showed a prominent politician, the then Federal Treasurer, in no uncertain terms what they thought of his bright idea to tax the miners' free housing, a move as unpopular as taking away miners' free coal in Britain or depriving sailors of their rum ration!

At Burngrove, conspicuous by a major electricity substation for the power to the overhead catenaries, the main coal line swings north through the Bowen Basin. After passing German Creek it joins other coal lines from Blair Athol, Riverside and Goonyella at Copabella, before winding back down the ranges to the loading terminal at Hay Point south of Mackay, crossing the main coast line at Yukan.

The major town between Rockhampton and Longreach is **Emerald**, noted and named for the gemstones mined in the locality. Here the station is on the south side of the main street, handy for hotels, shops and other amenities, and a place to break the journey. While the train stops (usually at least 15 minutes) there is time to nip over to one of the local pubs opposite for a quick glass of beer or to buy an ice cream at the shop opposite the railway station. This confection is highly regarded locally. But warn the conductor if leaving the train and intending to re-board. Passengers have been known to be left behind and be forced to beg a lift from the local police to catch up with the train further west.

At the brief stop of **Bogantungan**, the climb into the Drummond Ranges begins, full of sharp curves among which you can look out of the window from anywhere in the train to see either the locomotive end or the rear or both, curving one way or the other. The curves are as tight as four chain (80m) radius and the track, which has been climbing steadily for the preceding 26km (16 miles), steepens to an average 1-in-70 for the 13km (8 miles) up to Hannan's Gap from where it descends at just under 1-in-100 to the tiny station named Drummond.

Shortly after Drummond comes Alpha, a small settlement but (relative to the scale of things out west) a reasonably important railway centre, where freight trains are marshalled and train staff vans are attached or detached. Trains for the remote Yaraka branch may start or finish here, unless at Emerald further back, and they enter and leave the branch at Jericho, a slightly larger settlement 55km (34 miles) further west. Between Alpha and Jericho the only other station now operative is Beta. Presumably they ran out of letters of the Greek alphabet after that. The Yaraka branch is discussed in the next chapter, page 119.

At **Barcaldine**, "Garden City of the West", see the "Tree of Knowledge" just outside the railway station in Oak Street. Here the Australian Labor Party was founded after the Shearers' Strike of 1891, of which Barcaldine was the centre. Barcaldine also has a folk museum, and good outback town hotels where a counter tea and a bed can be obtained at very reasonable cost. If staying the night is not on your agenda, there is just time for you to see and photograph the tree while the train pauses at the station.

Between Barcaldine and Longreach you will be offered high tea in the train's dining car, otherwise known as the "Tucker Box" Restaurant, the arrival time in Longreach being rather early for dinner. This is rare in railway catering nowadays, reminiscent of pre-war days in the north of England where "dinner" was the midday meal, followed later by high tea and then supper. The *Spirit of the Outback* high tea, however, is unlikely to include succulent York ham or other typical English fare, although the menu does offer "pie floater" – beef pie in a sea of mushy peas – and hot scones with jam and cream (a typical "Devonshire tea" known all over Britain and Australia) as "afters". Somewhat atypical, but nevertheless good tucker, is the roo burger, described as "delicious kangaroo steak served on a burger bun with the works". All of the dishes in the "Tucker Box" are worth going for, from the "bushman's cackle berries" (traditional eggs and bacon) at breakfast to the

Barcaldine beef kebab and rice followed by granny's apple pie at lunch, and the traditional roast, grilled T-bone steak, or Mary River crocodile steaks served with lemon grass sauce, baked potato, pumpkin, crusty fresh damper and billy tea or coffee. The "billy tea" is perhaps a bit of advertising licence; it may be called that on the packet but I have yet to see the staff whirling a billy can around or stirring it with a eucalyptus twig!

At **Longreach**, see the early Qantas hangar, and the "Stockman's Hall of Fame". Here also, excellent meals and cheap accommodation can be obtained. There is a historic hotel (rebuilt after a disastrous fire) just one block away from the station. Longreach also has modern motels with all the amenities, and even a night club. It is a place in which to stay for more than the one night you would have if returning by the train on which you arrive.

From Longreach station, Alan and Suzie Smith's Outback Aussie Tours offer excursions to Winton and beyond. Phone toll free 1800 810510 for details. Since the withdrawal of passenger trains between Longreach and Winton, Queensland Rail has introduced charter buses which connect with the arrival and departure of trains, although allowing even less time in Winton than there is in Longreach, unless the return journey is postponed to the next of the twice-weekly services.

Winton, a major sheep and cattle centre of the west, is the birthplace both of "Waltzing Matilda", based on a story about a swagman who stole a sheep and jumped into the Combo Waterhole, 145km (90 miles) from Winton, to escape police. Written by "Banjo" Patterson, a visiting solicitor who was staying at nearby Dagworth cattle station a few years later, in 1895, the song was first publicly sung in Winton's North Gregory Hotel.

An enthralling account of events connected with this origin of the song, Australia's own folk anthem, is given in the book *Matilda my Darling* by Nigel Kranth in which, incredibly, the publishers were not allowed to include the words, known by heart and loved by all Australians, because some American person or body has apparently acquired the copyright.

Winton is also the birthplace of Australia's own airline, Qantas (Queensland and Northern Territory Air Service). See the "Qantilda" museum in the main street (about ten minutes from the station) for a journey into history, or with $80 and time to spare hire a car to see the dinosaur tracks 111km (69 miles) south of town at Lark's Quarry Environmental Park on the Jundah road. Winton's water supply comes from boreholes over one kilometre deep and has a temperature close to boiling point. The original rail link to Winton was from Hughenden on the QR Great Northern line, and this is now the only way it can be reached by passenger train, though not without difficulty. (See next chapter, pages 119-121).

The *Inlander* train links Townsville and Mount Isa, through Hughenden and such romantic places as Charters Towers, Julia Creek, and Cloncurry, not to mention Nonda. At **Charters Towers** you are back in gold rush history. Legacies of past glories include many fine buildings. From the top of Towers Hill you can see the Venus Gold Battery, a stamping mill restored by the National Trust. See also the old German church in Ann Street, or simply visit one of the remaining pubs of which there were 80 in the town's heyday.

Hughenden is a place you are only likely to visit by rail en route to or from Winton, unless joining or leaving a train at a rather isolated station in the middle of the night has irresistible appeal. Many freight trains by-pass the station, but stop for vacuum tests and crew changes on sidings on an avoiding loop to the west.

Julia Creek, described as being in the middle of nowhere, is reached either in early morning or late at night on the *Inlander*. This small outback town features in Scyld Berry's book *Train to Julia Creek*, representing to his mind "the end of a journey in search of the spirit of Australia". An hour or more before "the Creek" going west, or 40 minutes or so after midnight going east, the train will stop at **Nonda**, a depot for railway freight and mineral train crews which still boasts a station master and a waiting room with refreshments (a soft drink slot machine). Cartoon postcards, obtainable at the station, rather cynically advertise it as "Nonda by the Sea".

Cloncurry, known as "the Curry" for short, boasts the remains of the "Great Australian" copper mine of 1867. See also the Cloister of Plaques in Uhr Street, site of the Flying Doctor's first base. Tourist information is at the Council Chambers, Scarr Street. Cloncurry is the junction for the disused Kajabbi branch, and a good place to break the journey if intending to take the bus to Normanton and the Gulf Country.

Between Cloncurry and Mount Isa the scenery is particularly rugged. On your left you may see wandering camels, one of which was said to be a customer at the pub nearby at Duchess, where a brief stop may be made by the *Inlander*.

Mount Isa, largest city in the world – by area (40,977km^2 or 15,822 square miles) is roughly twice the size of Wales but with only a fraction of the population, about 25,000 people. This is an industrial complex which looks almost incongruous in the middle of nowhere. You will be acutely aware of the giant chimneys, but don't miss the Underground Museum in Shackleton Street. A nearby lookout offers a good view of city and mine.

Probably the nearest places on the railway to the real Gulf Country of "Crocodile Dundee" fame are **Mount Surprise**, **Einasleigh** and **Forsayth** in Etheridge Shire, and **Croydon** and **Normanton** in the Shire of Carpentaria. The last two are isolated from the rest of the system, while the others are at the end of a long inland branch from Mareeba, currently served by a twice weekly railcar, the *Savannahlander*, with only a bus connection to or from Mareeba or Cairns. Until early 1995 a weekly freight train carrying passenger cars, marketed as "The Last Great Train Ride", covered the whole route. Reinstatement of a through service has been promised in 1996, though what form this will take and when it will run is yet to be resolved. This long journey is unique.

Normanton–Croydon Railway   This totally isolated 152km (94 miles) branch of Queensland Rail is now quite well-known and frequented by many tourists other than rail enthusiasts. The once weekly regular passenger service (sometimes with non-passenger wagons attached) is by the *Gulflander* railmotor. It also carries motor vehicles.

If you want to ride the *Gulflander* on the Normanton Railway or the *Savannahlander* between Mount Surprise and Forsayth, various coach firms operate services offering some form of connection. One recommended itinerary is to take the Karumba coach leaving Cairns at 06.45 on Mondays, reaching Normanton at 17.15 the same day, returning at 08.00 on Fridays (C 9070). There is also a coach from Mount Isa on Tuesdays (T 125). From Croydon, a coach connection to Forsayth on Thursdays is an alternative to a Normanton return by train, but like most services in the outback, schedules are prone to change according to tourist demand and the weather.

Alternatives are to take in part of the *Gulflander* trip with a package tour or you can fly to Normanton, take the train to Croydon and back, then fly back to Cairns. Either way, it will take the best part of a week. Hiring a car in Cairns might be quicker, but Croydon is over 560km (350 miles) from Cairns and much of the road is rough. The trip is one you will never forget. One tourist told the *Gulflander* driver "Thanks for the wonderful ride. It's taken all the kinks out of my back".

Normanton–Croydon
The Gulflander C 9010

Wednesday		**Thursday**	
Dep Normanton	08.30	Dep Croydon	08.30
Arr Croydon	12.30	Arr Normanton	12.30

Check on connecting coaches and accommodation by phoning Cairns QR office
(070) 526 249. Bookings may be made through Cairns Tourist Bureau, QR Travel
Centres or at Normanton station.

Alice Springs – The Red Centre

By any standards **Alice Springs**, over 650km (400 miles) as the
crow flies from any town of more than 20,000 population (and
even that is Mount Isa in far western Queensland), located in the
very centre of the continent nearly 1,000km (roughly 600 miles)
from the nearest reach of the sea, must be regarded as part of the
Australian Outback. It certainly looked like it in the film *A Town
Like Alice* although the film scenes were mostly shot in Broken
Hill and Silverton in western New South Wales. Getting to "the
Alice" by train is simple, thanks to *The Ghan* (C 9034), except that
you have to go to Adelaide first; or alternatively you can fly from
Mount Isa, Darwin, Brisbane, Sydney, or Perth.

Coach tours and regular flights from Alice Springs serve all the
surrounding natural attractions including Ayers Rock, the Olgas,
MacDonnell ranges and Kings Canyon. In some of the itineraries
in this book you do not have long in Alice Springs, as far as seeing
much of the surrounding country is concerned. A quick out-and-
back air trip to Ayers Rock, if you needed only to say that you've
seen it, was possible before they re-timed *The Ghan*, but now you
would probably have to chase the train down the line by taxi, as it
leaves "the Alice" before the plane's return. Unless there is a relief
Ghan on another day you will have to wait a week in the red centre if you miss your train back south.

A short way north of the town is the old telegraph station, the
original Alice Springs, well worth a visit. If staying overnight you
can visit the casino, or try a buffalo steak with witchetty grub
dressing in the Overlander Steakhouse. Worth visiting also, for a
good lunch, with wine, is the Chateau Hornsby winery, a few
kilometres east of the city, the only winery in the Northern
Territory, whose waters come from artesian bores.

For something completely different, you can indulge in an
afternoon camel safari followed by a barbecue, or you can go out
on a "bush tucker" excursion, watch boomerang throwing, aboriginal

dancing and eat witchetty grubs live, but remember, this is the heart of a wide continent. Distances are very great. Ayers Rock is six hours by coach. If time permits, stay at Yulara Resort, its modern township (everything from a Sheraton hotel to camping sites). There you can listen to an aboriginal folk group and learn how not to play a didgeridoo, or you can take a three day bus pass from Ayers Rock Touring Company for conducted tours of the Rock and the Olgas. The red centre is not quite the traditional outback, but it is not to be missed.

Chapter Seven

Railways for the Enthusiast

This chapter is obviously mis-named. Of course *all* railways are of interest to enthusiasts, but some kinds are perhaps of more interest than others. This chapter therefore deals with historic, preserved and unusual railways – with which Australia abounds.

Rail travel centres and enquiry offices operated by the various rail companies at the main stations have information on private railways in their area, and also on special excursions which are run quite frequently by the Australian Railway Historical Society (ARHS) and other societies, often on lines normally used only for freight or primary produce. An excellent and comprehensive guide to private and preserved railways for the whole of Australia, is published by the ARHS, NSW Division as *Rail Scene Australia Issue 3 – the 1995 Guide to Australian Tourist Railways and Museums*. This can be obtained, price $9.95, from the ARHS or specialist railway bookshops, like The Railway Shop, South Brisbane Station, the Railfan Shop at the corner of Flinders Lane and Market Street, Melbourne, or direct from the publishers, ARHS New South Wales Division, 67 Renwick St, Redfern, NSW 2016.

Previous editions of *Australia by Rail* offered an outline itinerary for those rail buffs or any other tourists who might wish to experience some of the best of such railways without spending unnecessary time finding out what there is, where it is, when it operates, and how to get there. Most enthusiasts prefer to work out their own itinerary, so in this edition the former itinerary has been replaced by details, state by state, of the major rail museums and operating historic or unusual railways, with the name of the nearest regular station, the distance or journey time from there to the place of interest, and advice on how to get to that station (and back) from the nearest major centre.

As with preserved and private railways the world over, some are now unfortunately totally disconnected from the rest of the system and can only be reached by private transport. Particularly saddening in recent times has been the isolation of the former South Australian Railways broad gauge Mount Barker Junction–Victor Harbour branch from the broad gauge Adelaide suburban network by the conversion to standard gauge of the Adelaide–Melbourne line east of Belair. This prevents the former loco-hauled *Steam Ranger* making a full day round trip from Adelaide up over the Mount Lofty Ranges which, at 264km (164 miles) each way, was the longest tourist rail route in Australia.

New South Wales and Canberra

Border Loop This former passing place, 41km (25 miles) north of Kyogle on the Sydney–Brisbane main line, is of interest because of its spiral tunnels by which the differences in altitude crossing the NSW/Queensland border ranges are overcome. Altogether there are five tunnels on this section, spiral No. 1 and spiral No. 2 about 3km (2 miles) south of Border Loop station, the border tunnel just north of the summit of 271 metres (890ft) and two more a few kilometres further north. Throughout the border range crossing from Km 862 to Km 885 the train negotiates a series of 12-chain (241m) reverse curves on a constant 1-in-66 compensated gradient.

Set in wild country, the Border Loop area is only accessible, apart from the railway, by unsealed gravel road. Before the advent of the XPT it was best viewed in the early morning mists from the northbound *Brisbane Limited*, but may still be seen from the southbound *Brisbane XPT*. Look out for Tamrookum or Glenapp about an hour after leaving Brisbane, then look first down to the right, then to the left after the main tunnel, when you should see the track you have just been on looming on a viaduct on the mountainside up above. If in doubt, ask the passenger attendant.

Broken Hill Transport Museum, is in the former Sulphide Street station of Silverton Tramway, opposite the Tourist Information Centre at the corner of Blende and Bromide Streets. Open daily 10.00–15.00. Static display includes one of the large 4-8-2 steam locos formerly used on the Silverton Tramway and cars from the old *Silver City Comet* diesel express.

The museum is an easy walk from Broken Hill station, served by the *Indian Pacific* from Sydney or Adelaide twice weekly or train WL33/34 once weekly. On other days the only access to Broken Hill is by coach to and from the XPT at Dubbo (8½ hour bus journey connecting with a 6½ hour train journey!) or by Hazelton Air Services. Rail connections are summarised in the timetable overleaf.

Sydney–Broken Hill–Adelaide
C 9020

All trains in this table are air-conditioned, have refreshment facilities and require reservations.

	Mon & Thu	Tue	Wed
Dep Sydney	14.40a	17.10	07.10
Arr Orange	—	21.11	11.58x
Dep Orange	21.05b	—	12.10
Arr Broken Hill	08.50c	—	22.00e
Dep Broken Hill	09.00d	—	—
Arr Adelaide (Keswick)	16.25	—	—

	Wed & Sun	Thu
Dep Adelaide (Keswick)	07.45a	—
Arr Broken Hill	15.00d	—
Dep Broken Hill	15.35e	20.00e
Arr Sydney	09.15c	11.33c

a The *Indian Pacific*. Sleeping accommodation available.

b Orange East Fork station. No arrival time at Orange is given because the *Indian* calls to take up only.

c Next day.

d Central Standard Time.

e Eastern Standard Time.

x Change trains.

Canberra Railway Museum, operated by the ARHS at Geijera Place, Kingston, near Canberra station. Open weekends and public holidays; phone (062) 257 1379. Excursion trains operate to scenic Molonglo Gorge and various centres in the Southern Highlands and to Sydney.

Darling Harbour Monorail, Sydney. The Darling Harbour Monorail, of the straddle type, circles the city centre area and the Darling Harbour complex. Nearest Cityrail station is Town Hall, (three minutes from Central) just one street block away. A day pass costs $6. The complete circuit offers an excellent snapshot of Sydney attractions.

Dorrigo Steam Railway and Museum claims to have the largest collection of railway vehicles in the Southern Hemisphere, including 54 locomotives, and over 300 other rolling stock items. Steam hauled tourist trains are planned to operate on the 70km (43 mile) former State Rail branch which joins the main north coast line at Glenreagh, but at the time of writing this service is yet to commence and the museum is not open to the public.

Some vehicles may be seen at Glenreagh on the NSW main north coast line but this is not a regular stop for the *Brisbane* or *Murwillumbah XPT* services, nor is there now a feeder bus service as originally provided when the XPT first replaced the loco-hauled north coast trains. However, the southbound *Grafton XPT* calls at Glenreagh, 43km (27 miles) south of Grafton, at 07.18, while the northbound service calls on request at 20.48. The sidings at Dorrigo may also be observed on the right side of the southbound *Brisbane XPT* at 12.09 if the train is on time, or northbound on the left from the *Murwillum*bah *XPT* at 16.08.

Kings Bus Service (T 225) links Dorrigo with Coffs Harbour (70 minutes) and Armidale (1h 45m). Phone (066) 57 2176 for further information. Coffs Harbour, 608km (375 miles) and Armidale, 579km (357 miles) from Sydney respectively are both served by daily Countrylink trains.

Hunter Valley This area was the site of some of Australia's earliest railways (horse drawn tramways carried coal to Newcastle as long ago as 1827) and like England's Tyneside, after which so many of its places are named, is now a fascinating area for the industrial archeologist as well as the rail enthusiast. Places of particular note include Newcastle, Maitland, Morpeth, Hexham, East Greta, Rothbury and Kurri Kurri but, with some exceptions, the major attractions are not readily accessible by public transport.

In April, the annual Hunter Valley Steamfest is based on Maitland, from where tours by rail and road take in most places of interest. The address is PO Box 351, Maitland, NSW 2320; phone (049) 33 2611.

At other times the following locations of special interest are reasonably accessible:

Newcastle Tramway Museum, Lee Wharf Road, operates heritage trams on one kilometre (0.6 mile) of track each Sunday and public holiday from 10.00–16.30; phone (049) 55 8206. The route runs from near Merreweather St, 100m from Civic Station, to Throsby Wharf, 500m (550yd) from Wickham station, both on the Newcastle suburban system and served by frequent electric trains.

Rothbury Riot Railway at Branxton, 10km (6 miles) west of Maitland on the Great Northern Railway. The museum is sited at the former Rothbury Colliery, 5km (3 miles) from Branxton, but monthly steam-hauled trains should be operating by the time you read this book. Phone (049) 30 7758 or write to PO Box 37, Branxton, NSW 2335 for details.

Frequent electric trains link Sydney with Newcastle. A regular diesel service links Newcastle with Maitland and trains also serve Branxton. For details see C 9014 & 9016. The Branxton services are given below.

Sydney–Newcastle–Branxton

C 9014, 9016; T 232, 235a, 235b, 238

	M–F	M–F	M–F	M–F	SaSu	SaSu
Dep Sydney	—	05.41[a]	13.17[b]	15.12[b]	—	15.17[b]
Dep Newcastle	03.23	08.07	16.01	17.39	03.43	17.44
Dep Maitland	03.56	08.52	16.34	18.12	04.16	18.17
Arr Branxton	04.15	09.11	16.53	18.31	04.35	18.36
Dep Branxton	07.13	11.03	19.44	21.28	07.38	21.51
Arr Maitland	07.33	11.23	20.04	21.48	07.58	22.10
Arr Newcastle	08.03	11.55	20.36	22.20	08.30	22.42
Arr Sydney	10.21[c]	15.10[b]	23.10[b]	02.11[d]	11.10[b]	02.11[d]

[a] Change at Broadmeadow.
[b] Change at Hamilton.
[c] *Newcastle Flyer*. Change at Hamilton.
[d] Arrive next day. Change at Hamilton.

Keans Travel operates coach services between Sydney and Tamworth which serve most places in the Hunter Valley but call neither at Newcastle nor Broadmeadow nor Maitland. Buses from Muswellbrook at 05.35 (except Sunday), 12.35 (weekdays) and 13.35 (Sundays) serve Singleton (35min), Branxton (55min), Rothbury (61min), Pokolbin (70min), Cessnock (85min) and Kurri Kurri (100min), returning from there at 17.10 (except Sunday), 20.10 (weekdays) and 20.40 (Sundays). The full timetable appears in *Travel Times Australia* T 247.

At Maitland, the local Blue Ribbon buses serve North Rothbury and Greta and then continue to Branxton and Singleton (the latter being a scheduled stop for the *Northern Tablelands Xplorer*). *Travel Times* T 238 gives departure and journey times to intermediate points.

Some of these services may be useful for those wishing to explore the less accessible parts of the Hunter Valley. This is note-worthy not only for coal mines but for wine growing. Further details from Blue Ribbon Coaches; phone (049) 33 5204.

Richmond Vale Railway, Kurri Kurri, operates steam trains over 4km (2.5 miles) of line between Richmond Main and Pelaw Main collieries (a route on which steam-hauled coal trains regularly operated until as late as 1987). Enquiries to PO Box 184, Adamstown, NSW; phone (049) 36 1124.

Katoomba Scenic Railway, 1219mm gauge. Built to serve a coal mine, this 0.45km (0.25 mile) incline railway is the steepest in the world with a maximum gradient of 128% (1-in-0.78). Frequent daily service 09.00–16.50. Round trip fare $3.60. Reached by bus from opposite the Carrington Hotel outside Katoomba station, or by a good 2.5km (1.5 mile) walk. The top station adjoins the Katoomba Skyway terminal; the descent gives magnificent views of Blue Mountain scenery and the bottom station gives access to walking tracks in Jamieson Valley.

Katoomba station is some 110km (68 miles) west of Sydney and is served by frequent Inter-Urban EMUs from Sydney Central. (C 9014)

Lachlan Valley Railway, Cowra. The museum and depot at Cowra is reached by *Countrylink* XPT and coach connection via Bathurst on the western line from Sydney Central. Trains operate to various points along the 75km (47 mile) Cowra–Blayney line on weekends once or twice monthly. Phone Cowra (063) 431 1052 or Sydney (02) 9809 2021 for full information, including details of timetables and fares.

Although the trains call at Blayney, the supposedly connecting buses to or from Cowra miss the train by just a few minutes in each direction – one of those seemingly deliberate non-connections some railway systems achieve so effortlessly! But a nightstop in Blayney can avoid that extra 35 minutes of bus travel. There is also a Rail and Pioneer Museum near Cowra, making it a rewarding stopover for enthusiasts.

Sydney–Blayney–Cowra (Countrylink)
C 9020, 9104

All trains are air-conditioned and have refreshment facilities. Trains and buses require reservations. Both arrival and departure times are shown at Bathurst and Blaney when a change between bus and train is needed.

	MWF	Daily	MWF	Tue	ExSat
Dep Sydney	07.10[a]	07.10[a]	—	15.53[c]	15.53[c]
Arr Bathurst	10.41		—	—	19.50
Dep Bathurst	10.55[b]	10.41	10.55[b]	19.50	20.05[d]
Arr Blayney		11.34		20.44	—
Dep Blayney	11.30[b]	—	11.30[b]	—	20.37[d]
Arr Cowra	15.00	—	15.00	—	21.45

	Fri	Mon–Fri	MWFSun	Daily
Dep Cowra	—	06.28^f	15.10^g	—
Arr Blayney	—	07.41	16.25	—
Dep Blayney	06.40^e			16.22^a
Arr Bathurst		08.19	17.00	
Dep Bathurst	07.39^e	—	—	17.14^a
Arr Sydney	11.33	—	—	20.48

^{a} *Central West XPT.*
^{b} Countrylink bus R31W.
^{c} Train WL31.
^{d} Countrylink bus R81W.
^{e} Train WL34.
^{f} Countrylink bus R82W.
^{g} Countrylink bus R32W/R84W.

Michelago Tourist Railway, Queenbeyan. Operates on the first Sunday of each month over 50km (31 miles) of the former Queenbeyan-Cooma–Bombola branch of State Rail. A scenic route commencing with a 1-in-40 climb and affording views of Tuggeranong, one of Canberra's satellite new towns. Details and bookings from ARHS ACT Tours, Room G10, Griffin Centre, Bunda St, Canberra City or PO Box 112, Civic Square, ACT 2608; phone (06) 257 1370 or 297 1242. Queenbeyan station is reached by Countrylink's *Xplorer* services from Sydney or Canberra.

Sydney–Queenbeyan–Canberra (Countrylink)
C 9021

All trains are fully air-conditioned, have refreshment facilities, require reservations, and operate daily.

Train number	SP19	SP21	SP23
Dep Sydney	07.43	11.43	18.14
Arr Queenbeyan	11.35	15.35	22.05
Dep Queenbeyan	11.38	15.38	22.08
Arr Canberra	11.50	15.50	22.20

Train number	SP20	SP22	SP24
Dep Canberra	06.50	12.20	17.20
Arr Queenbeyan	06.58	12.28	17.28
Dep Queenbeyan	07.00	12.30	17.30
Arr Sydney	10.56	16.28	21.26

NSW Rail Transport Museum, Thirlmere. Whatever the Dorrigo museum may claim, Thirlmere Railway Museum is regarded as Australia's largest, and includes an operating steam-hauled service on the first and third Sundays of each month. These connect with Cityrail electric trains at Picton on the main south line 82km (51 miles) from Sydney, while Thirlmere itself can be reached by a connecting private bus from Picton (C 9014; T 292c, 714). Trains run from Picton to Buxton 13.8km (8.6 miles) on the route of the steeply graded original south main line (on a steady 1-in-40 most of the way from Picton–Thirlmere). The museum is open Saturdays, Sundays and public holidays (except Good Friday and Christmas Day); phone (02) 744 9999 or (046) 81 8001. Admission $6, train ride $8, with reductions for pensioners and students.

Perisher SkiTube Railway (C 9019). This is an 8.6km (5.3 miles) standard gauge line, operating on the Voll Rack system, under electric power. Journey time is 12 minutes and frequency mostly every 20 minutes (longer intervals in the off-ski season) from Thredbo (Bullocks Terminal) to Perisher Valley, 70% of the route being in tunnel. There is no service between October and December. Reputed to have the widest rail passenger vehicles in the world, it is also the world's fastest rack railway at 40 km/h (25mph) and Australia's highest railway reaching an altitude of 1900m (6,200ft). Bus connections by Greyhound twice daily from Canberra (Jolimont bus station) take 3hr 10min. SkiTube round trip fare $20. For details ring 1 800 654 681 toll free.

Powerhouse Museum, Sydney. This museum of transport and technology includes rail exhibits. Open daily from 10.00–17.00, admission $5. Located in Harris St, Ultimo, linked to the city by the Darling Harbour Monorail (Haymarket Station).

Sydney Tramway Museum, Loftus, and **Sutherland Tourist Tramway**, adjoining Loftus station. Trams operate hourly on Sundays and public holidays on the former 2km (1.2 mile) Royal National Park branch of State Rail. Frequent electric trains link Sydney Central to Loftus, 36min journey. (T 713 with 295)

Zigzag Railway, Lithgow. Steam trains on historic Blue Mountains former zigzag route, one of the engineering wonders of the 19th century; 7.5km (4.3 miles) now converted to 1067mm gauge. Operates Saturdays, Sundays and public holidays (except Christmas Day) between 10.00 and 16.00, as well as some services on weekdays. The round trip takes 1½ hours and costs $10. Zigzag is a request stop on regular Sydney–Lithgow inter-urban services (T 270, 710). The 08.02 and 10.02 trains from Sydney Terminal are recommended connections. Phone (063) 53 1795 or, for recorded information, (063) 51 4826.

Queensland

Ballyhooley Express, Mossman Central Mill, North Queensland. A 60 minute ride on narrow gauge (610mm) sugar cane lines between Port Douglas and Mossman. Operates on weekdays July–October, commencing 09.30 from Port Douglas, with another departure from Mossman Central Mill at 13.30 and several "commuter" trips between Marina and St Crispins at Port Douglas. Fares vary from $17 adult round trip. For details phone Cairns (070) 98 1400 or call tourist offices in Cairns. Coral Coaches operates a regular bus service between Cairns, Mossman (1hr 20min) and Port Douglas (1hr 50min). (T 107)

At the time of writing, this service has been discontinued but it is hard to believe this will be other than temporary.

Big Pineapple Railway, Nambour. A miniature rail circuit of pineapple plantations, built on the lines of sugar cane railways. Features a steep climb on a reverse curve. Situated 6.4km (4 miles) south of Nambour on the Bruce Highway, ten minutes by frequent local buses from Nambour railway station (T 160). Nambour is 1hr 40min by electric train from Brisbane, with an average of eight trains a day each way (T 159). The Moreton Central Sugar Mill also operates cane trains which may be seen crossing streets in the town.

Brisbane Tramway Museum, Ferny Grove. 500m (550yards) from the railway station on the Brisbane suburban electric line, 25min from Central. Open Sundays 12.30–16.00. An operating electric tramway.

In the **Brisbane** area there are frequent excursions operated by the ARHS and by Trainaway Tours. These are well advertised locally at stations and tourist agencies and frequently cover routes not served by regular services. Rolling stock includes vintage carriages and motive power is usually steam, including such locomotives as the 10-Class 0-4-2 locomotive No. 6 built by Nelson & Co in 1865 and a magnificent restored Beyer Garratt 4-8-2+2-8-4 built in Manchester in 1949.

Excursions are also operated by Swanbank Railway near

Ipswich and at the Rosewood Railway Museum at Cabanda. Unfortunately, both are accessible only by private transport, despite the existence of rail track to Bundamba and Rosewood respectively, both on the Brisbane Citytrain network.

Brampton Island Railway runs from the jetty to the resort on Brampton Island, reached by launch from Mackay, but the railway station is somewhat distant from the jetty. There is a similar railway at **Hayman Island** resort in the Whitsunday Islands near Proserpine, which is perhaps more accessible, involving a 45-minute bus ride from Proserpine station to Shute Harbour (T 132), followed by a short sea crossing. Proserpine Mill, close to the station, is a major centre for Queensland cane train activity.

Brisbane–Proserpine–Cairns

Times valid September 1996 but changes after January 1997 are likely.
C 9013

	TuThSa	Thu	Sun
Dep Brisbane	09.55ᵃ	15.40ᵇ	09.55ᶜ
	WeFrSu	Fri	Mon
Arr Proserpine	05.20	11.00	05.20
Dep Proserpine	05.25	—	05.25
Arr Cairns	18.00	—	18.00
	MoThSa	Fri	Tue
Dep Cairns	08.00ᵃ	—	08.00ᶜ
Arr Proserpine	19.50	—	19.32
Dep Proserpine	20.05	12.15ᵇ	19.42
	TuFrSu	Sat	Wed
Arr Brisbane	16.10	07.00	14.55

ᵃ *Sunlander*.
ᵇ *Spirit of the Tropics*.
ᵈ *Queenslander* and *Spirit of the Tropics*.

Callemondah Yard, Gladstone. Gladstone is full of railway interest, both in the layout of the tracks through, around and behind the town, in the variety of trains you will encounter, and in the almost constant activity. At Callemondah Yard, 5km (3 miles) north of Gladstone station, is a vast complex of sidings, where electric and diesel locos are assigned their respective tasks. From Callemondah, the catenaries reach north and west to Emerald, via the Bowen Basin coalfields to Hay Point on the coast, and south to Brisbane; while diesel-operated routes strike inland to the mines of the Callide and Dawson Valleys. Gladstone is worth a break of journey for the enthusiast, but much may be observed merely passing through. The *Sunlander* and other long distance trains pass Gladstone but the best viewing is in daylight on the all-electric *Spirit of Capricorn*. (C 9013)

Dreamworld, Coomera. On the Pacific Highway west of Gold Coast city, the Dreamworld complex includes a 3km (2 miles) railway at the sugar line 610mm gauge with ex-Canefield locomotives. Local buses meet QR Cityrail Gold Coast express trains at Coomera Station. The trains take one hour from Brisbane and run hourly on weekdays from early morning till nearly midnight, half hourly on Saturdays and Sundays. (T 194)

Dreamworld is open daily, except Christmas Day. Admission to the park includes other features and shows. Phone (075) 73 1133 or, for current admission charges, toll free on 008 07 3300.

Durandur Railway and Museum, Woodford. This is a 610mm gauge operating railway (Sundays, mostly in winter months), on the trackbed of the former Wamuran–Kilcoy branch at Woodford, 24km (15 miles) west of Caboolture. Phone (07) 3269 1873 or (07) 3269 2468 evenings. Brisbane Bus Lines and Suncoast Pacific operate infrequent buses through Woodford from Caboolture, which is a 50-minute journey on the half-hourly service from Central on the regular Citytrain network. Bus timetables in *Travel Times*. (T 155 & 163)

The Forsayth Mixed – *Train 7A90*. Described as "The Last Great Train Ride" from around 1990 until its withdrawal in 1995, this almost unique train, a goods consist with passenger accommodation, crossed 423km (262 miles) of mountain range and savannah country every week between Cairns and the old gold mining centre of Forsayth. It is included because with the change of government in Queensland in early 1996, a promise of restoration has now to be kept. Failing this, a railcar substitute, the *Savannahlander*, operates over two of the longest of the many scenic sections of the line, between Forsayth and Mount Surprise, a 121km (75 mile) trip accomplished in 5½ hours.

Golden Mount Railway, Mount Morgan. What might have been the slowest passenger train in the world (Thangool–Rockhampton, 178km or 110 miles at an overall mean speed of 11.25 km/h or 7mph) ran on this line in Central Queensland until the mid-1980s. Among the few still operational remnants of the former Callide Valley branch of Queensland Rail from Kabra Junction to

Thangool is the privately operated 3.5km (2.2 miles) Golden Mount Railway between historic Mount Morgan and Cattle Creek siding. Four bridges and a tunnel, plus Mount Morgan's imposing railway station building, are features of the route. Trains depart at 14.00 on Saturdays. For more details phone (079) 38 2312.

Mount Morgan can be reached by bus from Rockhampton, 38km (24 miles) to the northeast. (T 145 & 150)

The Gulflander and **The Kuranda Tourist Train**, are fully described on pages 103 and 64 and 144 respectively. Both are a "must" for every rail enthusiast, not to mention the everyday tourist.

The Mulgrave Rambler, Gordonvale. Currently operated only as a charter train or by excursions advertised locally, this cane line is the most accessible of all, since the station immediately adjoins QR Gordonvale station, which is 22km (14 miles) south of Cairns and a regular stop for the *Sunlander*. Hauled by the *Nelson*, a restored Fowler 0-4-2 oil-fired steam loco, the route circles Mulgrave Mill, then by canefields, river and rainforest to Orchid Valley where tropical plants, entertainment and refreshments are among the attractions.

When the trains run, a connecting coach is provided from Cairns. For details contact Mulgrave Central Mill Company Limited (070) 563 300 or phone Mike Kent on (070) 563 904. At the time of writing, the mill management appear not to favour the *Rambler* activity but, as with so many things, public demand and encouragement from tourist bodies may induce a change of attitude.

RAILCo, Ravenshoe. The Ravenshoe Atherton Insteam Locomotion Company, to give it its full title, operates weekend and holiday services on the Ravenshoe–Atherton section of the former QR branch south of Mareeba in the Atherton Tablelands. The 22km (14 mile) section includes Queensland's highest railway station at Tumoulin, 965m (3,165ft) above sea level, and a 7km (4 miles) climb at 1-in-33 through the ranges. Phone (070) 976 698, or (070) 976 698 for recorded information. Ravenshoe is accessible from Cairns or Kuranda (see above) by Whitecar and Cairns–Karumba Coaches. (T 110, 112 & 115)

Rockhampton Rockhampton, 630km (390 miles) and 9½ hours by train from Brisbane, is the northern limit of the QR electrified main line and terminus of the *Spirit of Capricorn* inter-city service, a place of great interest to rail enthusiasts. (C 9013)

Most long distance trains stop at least 25 minutes in

Rockhampton, when there is time to explore the station environs. Just beyond the station the railway goes along the middle of a public street before swinging north across the river. Near the station is the original roundhouse, built in 1915 with a central turntable serving 52 locomotive bays, and other historic buildings. If changing trains or staying overnight, ask the station master if a visit to the Central Train Control is possible. Other Rockhampton railway attractions include the Archer Park Railway Museum and Rockhampton Steam Tramway.

Seaworld, Gold Coast, reached by bus connection from Helensvale station on the Cityrail Gold Coast branch (T 194). Australia's first monorail in an entertainment complex.

South Johnstone Sugar Mill and **Sugarworld Gardens**, Hambledon Sugar Mill, Edmonton, both operate tourist trains on parts of their 610mm cane railways. Hambledon Mill is at Edmonton, 15km (9 miles) south of Cairns, a station on the *Sunlander* route. South Johnstone is 11km (7 miles) from Innisfail, the nearest station on the QR north coast line. A hire car from Cairns would be the best way to visit both these railways.

Buderim Ginger Factory, Yandina. There is a 1km (0.6 mile) 610mm loop railway at the world's largest ginger factory on Pioneer Road, Yandina, 8km (5 miles) north of Nambour. Open daily 08.30–16.30, except certain public holidays. Shops, a restaurant, gardens and wildlife enclosure are among the other attractions; phone (074) 941 555. Interurban trains of QR serve Yandina, but not frequently as at the time of writing. In fact, a day trip from Brisbane is impractical by rail, but the Tewantin Bus Service connects with Cityrail trains at Nambour. See *Travel Times* T 160a and local timetables. The factory is about ten minutes walk from the station. Round trip fares from Brisbane are $21.

Brisbane–Yandina
T 159 and local
By rail. Times are from Roma Street but all trains call at Central.

	Mon–Fri	Sat	Mon–Fri	Sun
Dep Brisbane	12.23	17.26	17.33	17.56
Arr Yandina	14.27	19.26	19.31	19.52

	Mon–Fri	Sat	Mon–Fri	Sun
Dep Yandina	06.50	07.22	15.06	17.13
Arr Brisbane	08.44	09.13	17.00	19.11

Brisbane–Nambour–Yandina
T 159, 160a + local
Rail/bus connections. Times at Yandina are approximate. Buses not covered by Austrailpass. Changes to these timings are planned for early 1997 but details were not available as this book went to press.

	Sat	Mon–Fri	Sun	Sat	Mon–Fri
Dep Brisbane	06.40	07.51	07.55	09.35	10.58
Arr Nambour	08.33	09.37	09.33	11.40	12.38
		Change to bus			
Dep Nambour	09.30	09.45	09.40	12.20	12.55
Arr Yandina	09.40	10.00	09.55	12.35	13.10

	Sat	Mon–Fri	Sun	Mon–Fri	Sat	Mon–Fri
Dep Yandina	09.10	09.25	09.25	12.33	13.45	17.55
Arr Nambour	09.25	09.40	09.40	12.48	14.00	18.10
			Change to bus			
Dep Nambour	10.05	10.05	10.10	13.07	14.42	18.25
Arr Brisbane	11.50	11.43	11.57	15.00	16.46	20.13

Yaraka branch, Queensland Rail. The Yaraka branch is one of only three in Queensland at the time of writing on which scheduled goods trains still, at least notionally, carry some "passenger accommodation". The others are the Kingaroy branch and the Hughenden–Winton line. Such accommodation is most likely to consist of a grey-painted crew van and not only may the train not run to time; it may not carry any such accommodation or even run at all in some circumstances. Enthusiasts should therefore check not only the timetables (T 140 for Yaraka, T 122 for Hughenden–Winton) but also enquire from the appropriate district headquarters of Queensland Rail a few days before travel.

Trains on such lines, although timetabled, tend to run only according to customer requirements, and you would not want to get off the comfortable *Spirit of the Outback* only to find that week's Yaraka mixed was cancelled. A phone call to the Supervisor's Office, Coal and Minerals Division, at Rockhampton District Control (079) 320 287 would be a good investment.

The Yaraka branch is 271km (168 miles) long, from Jericho on the Rockhampton–Longreach line. Just under half way along is Blackall, where shearer Jackie Howe hand-sheared 321 sheep in one day. At Blackall is the "Black Stump" in the grounds of the state school; the only problem being almost every state in Australia claims its own black stump. But Blackall does have a 225 million year old fossil tree stump in Shamrock Street.

Hughenden, on the Mount Isa line, to Winton is 212km (132 miles), and Kingaroy is 131km (81 miles) from Theebine, itself

34km (21 miles) from Gympie North, the nearest regular passenger station on the North Coast line.

Although these branches all commence at main line junctions, connections in the normal sense of the word are usually non-existent and departure and arrival times tend to be at rather unattractive hours. The following timetables summarise the situation as of January 1997. Times for each are given in 24-hour notation with the first figure representing the day of the week (1 = Monday, 7 = Sunday). C 9011, 9013, 9015, T 140, and local

Brisbane–Kingaroy

Dep Brisbane	1:17.33	3:20.25[r]
Arr Gympie N	1:20.31	3:23.21
railway bus connection Gympie N–Gympie		
Dep Gympie	2:03.45	4:03.45
Arr Kingaroy	2:10.00	4:10.00
Dep Kingaroy	2:11.30	4:11.30
Arr Gympie	2:17.45	4:17.45
railway bus connection Gympie–Gympie N		
Dep Gympie N	3:06.00	5:06.00
Arr Brisbane	3:08.52	5:08.52

Brisbane–Yaraka

Dep Brisbane	2:18.55[r]
Arr Gympie N	2:22.00
Dep Gympie N	2:22.10[r]
Arr Alpha	3:14.25
Arr Jericho	3:15.32
Dep Alpha	5:06.00
Dep Jericho	5:07.15
Arr Yaraka	5:16.25
Dep Yaraka	5:18.45
Arr Jericho	6:02.58
Arr Alpha	6:04.42
Arr Emerald	6:09.48
Dep Jericho	7:09.53[r]
Dep Alpha	7:10.50[r]
Dep Emerald	7:14.40[r]
Arr Gympie N	1:03.40
Dep Gympie N	1:03.50[r]
Arr Brisbane	1:06.50

[r] Reservation required.

Brisbane–Winton via Hughenden

Times are given in 24-hour notation with the first figure representing the day of the week (1 = Monday, 7 = Sunday).

Dep Brisbane	2:09.55ʳ
Arr Townsville	3:10.00
Dep Townsville	3:18.00ʳ
Arr Hughenden	4:01.30
Dep Hughenden	4:03.00
Arr Winton	4:10.30
Dep Winton	4:20.00
Arr Hughenden	5:03.45
Dep Hughenden	6:04.10ʳ
Arr Townsville	6:11.00
Dep Townsville	6:15.40ʳ
Arr Brisbane	7:16.10

ʳ Reservation required.

Victoria

Ballarat Vintage Tramway. This runs for 1.3km (0.8 mile) through Botanic Gardens, part of Ballarat's original tramway system opened 1887 and closed in 1971. Open Saturdays, Sundays and Holidays; phone (053) 34 1580. Reached by bus route no.15 from Post Office Corner near the railway station, which is itself a recognised historic monument. Ballarat is 119km (74 miles) from Melbourne Spencer Street and is reached by a fairly frequent (approximately two-hourly) V/Line train service taking just over 90 minutes. (C 9031)

Puffing Billy Railway, Belgrave. The *Puffing Billy* Preservation Society, part of the statutory body known as the Emerald Tourist Railway Board, operates this narrow gauge (2ft 6in or 762mm) branch of the former Victorian Railways system. The pioneer and best-known of Australia's preserved railways, it is gradually being extended to the original terminus at Gembrook, 24km (15 miles) from Belgrave. Mostly operated by steam, trains run at least twice daily except Christmas Day. The round trip fare Belgrave–Lakeside (about 2 hours) is $15.

A shorter trip, to Menzies Creek, where the society also has a steam museum, costs $9.50.

Access by frequent suburban train from Flinders Street or Spencer Street, Melbourne–Belgrave, 75min (C 9023). Leaflets describing the *Puffing Billy* Society are also available at Spencer

Street station, or phone (03) 9754 6800, or (03) 9870 8411 for recorded information.

Bellarine Peninsula Railway, Queenscliffe–Drysdale. A 16km (10 miles) remnant of the former Geelong–Queenscliffe branch, reached by frequent Melbourne–Geelong trains (60min, C 9023), with connecting bus (T 462) to Queenscliffe. Operates Sundays and on public holidays with additional days during school holiday periods. Adult round trip fare $9. For detailed timings and days of operation, phone (052) 52 2069.

Bendigo trams, travel past historic buildings, old tram depot, and Central Deborah Gold mine. Trams operate from 09.30 daily except Christmas Day, running through the city centre, within walking distance of Bendigo station. Phone (054) 43 8117. Bendigo is 162km (100 miles) from Melbourne, served by V/Line trains approximately every 2 hours. (C 9032)

Castlemaine & Maldon Railway, runs Sundays and holidays, except February, on 8km (5 miles) of a former Victorian Railways branch. Maldon station is a National Trust listed building and the town itself is subject to special preservation policies. Fare $8, phone (054) 75 2966 on operating days, (03) 889 2804 at other times. Castlemaine, 125km (78 miles) from Melbourne on the Bendigo line is the nearest station, 16km (10 miles) from Maldon, from where there is a very limited bus service. (C 9032; T 422, 723)

Central Highlands Tourist Railway, Daylesford. Partly restored 1600mm gauge Daylesford–Karlsruhe branch line. Ex-Victoria Railways vintage railmotors operate on Sundays hourly from 10.00–15.00; phone (053) 48 3503 or (053) 48 3927. Daylesford railway station in Raglan Street is 125km (78 miles) from Melbourne, reached by V/Line train and road coach, changing at Woodend, a two hour journey overall. There is no bus service on Sunday until evening, so prospective travellers on this railway must stay overnight Saturday in Daylesford if relying on public transport. (C 9032, T 427, 721)

South Gippsland Railway, Korumburra. Australia's newest steam railway (also operates ex-South Australian diesel railcars and a diesel-electric railmotor ex-Victoria Railways) has brought passenger services back to the twice-closed South Gippsland line between Nyora and Leongatha, up to 80km (50 miles) of route. Days of running vary. Between December 1995 and April 1996 four return trips between Korumburra and Leongatha were operated on various days of the week, mostly Sundays. All trains have refreshments; evening trips may include a "sausage sizzle" and charter trips may be arranged. Current timetables obtainable from major V/Line stations in the Gippsland area, such as Traralgon, and by phoning (056) 581 111 or (056) 581 511. Round trip fare to Leongatha $12. Korumburra station is a 2–2½ hour journey by V/Line coach from Melbourne or Dandenong. (C 9023, 9096)

The Vintage Train, Steamrail Victoria. Runs various excursions advertised locally. Phone toll free (008) 13 6036. Typical price: Melbourne–Bendigo and return $33.

Yarra Valley Tourist Railway Trains operate half-hourly on the second Sunday of each month and on holidays over 8km (5 miles) of the former Victoria Railways Healesville branch from Yarra Glen, north of Lilydale, the current terminus of the Melbourne Met system. Phone (03) 730 1811 for recorded messages. Frequent suburban electric trains from Melbourne–Lilydale (a 55 minute journey), and thence by private bus to Yarra Glen (15min) and Healesville (32min). (C 9023)

South Australia

St Kilda Tramway Museum The museum has a 2km (1.2 miles) operating tram track to the seafront, by taxi from Salisbury station on suburban system (Gawler line, C 9030). Open 13.00–17.00 Sundays and most public holidays; phone (08) 9110, 339 3671 or (08) 297 4447.

Glenelg Tramway A frequent service daily on the 11km (7 miles) former private railway from central Adelaide (Victoria Square, 1.6km or one mile from City station) to the seaside suburb of Glenelg. To avoid the walk or local bus, take a local TransAdelaide Belair or Noarlunga train from the City station or the Keswick suburban platforms to Goodwood where the tram route intersects the railway. (C 9030, T550, 552)

Pichi Richi Railway, Quorn. Narrow gauge (1067mm), mostly steam, (including a steam motor coach, the *Coffee Pot*), this was part of the original Great Northern Railway intended to link Port Augusta with Darwin. It was at Quorn that the Great Northern Express to Oodnadatta was first nicknamed the *Afghan Express*, later shortened to become the *Ghan*. Trains run on various days, mostly during school holidays, public holidays and some Sundays. The return trip from Quorn–Woolshed Flat ($19) takes almost 3 hours. Refreshments on all trains. Usual departure times from Quorn are at 10.00 and 14.00. Quorn is accessible from Port Augusta, a major stop on the route of the *Indian Pacific* and the new *Ghan*, by Stateliner buses 5 days a week (45 minute journey) but overnight stays in Quorn are needed for those wishing to travel on the railway. Timetables and days of running have been published in *Travel Times Australia* (T 567 and 736); for up-to-date details phone the Society at Quorn station, (08) 276 6232.

Steam Ranger, Goolwa. The *Steam Ranger* depot which formerly adjoined Dry Creek station on the Adelaide suburban network had to be relocated in 1996 following standardisation of the Adelaide–Melbourne line. The new depot is at Mount Barker, about 5km (3 miles) from Mount Barker Junction on the standard gauge line. The *Steam Ranger* (which in this transitional situation may sometimes be diesel-hauled much of the way) is again operating between Mount Barker, Goolwa and Victor Harbour. At Goolwa is the option of a boat trip on the lower reaches of the Murray. The train runs every Sunday May–November, departing Mount Barker at 10.30, arriving back at 18.10. The adult fare is $32. It includes vintage compartment coaches, with tavern car. Details from Steam Ranger, Box 8226 Hindley Street, Adelaide, SA 5000; or phone (08) 8391 1223 during office hours. The only public transport access to Mount Barker is by Hills Transit buses from Adelaide via Aldgate, Bridgewater (both also on the railway but with closed stations) and historic Hahndorf. These run several times daily; phone (08) 8339 1191. (T 547)

Steamtown, Peterborough. Operates excursions, usually on Sundays, over the southern part of the Peterborough–Quorn 1067mm railway, between Peterborough and Eurelia; 57km (35 miles). For timetables, fares and other details phone the Society on (086) 51 2106.

The Tea and Sugar Train

Based on Port Augusta, the "Tea and Sugar" is a supply train, without air-conditioning, sleepers or refreshments except from the shop at scheduled stops. Although a passenger carriage is attached, special permission is needed to travel on this train. Prior arrangement is essential and application would need to be made in writing, explaining why permission is sought. An indemnity may be required. Departure, arrival and crossing times must be checked in advance and on day of travel.

The train may, however, be seen (and, if time permits, entered to make a purchase from the shop) at times when it is parked at one of the stations on its route between Port Augusta (Spencer Junction) and Kalgoorlie (Parkeston). A brief glimpse is possible when it is crossed or passed by the *Indian Pacific* or the *Ghan*. For a longer inspection, a break of journey would be required. This is not recommended except at the few places where accommodation of some sort is available or where private arrangements have been made locally.

Known officially as Train 4205 shunt goods, returning as Train 4280, the "Tea and Sugar" timetable is not publicised and, like all timetables for trains of this type, is prone to alteration. The following may therefore prove to be quite inaccurate.

At 15.34 on a Wednesday the westbound *Indian Pacific* stops at Rawlinna, where the returning "Tea and Sugar" should be waiting to depart at 18.10 for Cook. The westbound "Tea and Sugar" has a scheduled four hour stop on Wednesday afternoon at Tarcoola, while at Cook both the westbound and the eastbound "Sugars" are scheduled to stop for two hours or more late on Thursday morning. None of these times coincides with the arrival or departure of a regular passenger train, so overnight stops would be needed. Tarcoola has a hotel, and at Cook you could always follow the injunction to "go crook" and stay a couple of days in their hospital. They say it needs your support.

The northbound *Ghan* calls at Tarcoola around midnight on Thursday, at which time the returning "Tea and Sugar" should be somewhere in the station area. By staying a night at the hotel near the station, the keen passenger could catch the returning *Ghan* to Adelaide at about the same time the next night, or wait an hour or two more to join the westbound *Indian Pacific*. If the relief Ghan is running on its former timings it should cross the westbound "Tea and Sugar" around 04.40 on a Wednesday at McLeay, an hour after it has departed from its stop at Pimba.

Western Australia

Bassendean Rail Transport Museum, 136 Railway Parade. An ARHS railway museum 400m (0.25 mile) north of Ashfield station, on the Perth suburban system (Midland line). Open Sundays and public holidays 13.00–17.00; phone (09) 279 7189.

Bennett Brook Railway Situated 8km (5 miles) north of Perth, a 5.7km (3.5 miles) long 610 mm gauge loop line through bushland, linking items of railway interest in Whiteman Park. Operating

11.00–17.00 Sundays, and 11.00–16.00 Wednesdays–Saturdays; phone (09) 294 3861. The Whiteman Park Tramway Museum, including a 4km standard gauge electric tramway is part of the park complex. Access is by taxi from Guildford station on the Midland Line of Perth's Fastrak suburban system. (C 9037)

Boyanup Transport Museum Home of the *Leschenault Lady* and *Koombana Queen*. Regular steam train trips operate from Boyanup station, 18km (11 miles) from Bunbury, according to demand. Access by Westrail coach from Bunbury station or Brunswick Junction, both served by the *Australind* service from Perth. Boyanup is half way between Bunbury and Donnybrook on the Western Highway. Phone (097) 31 5250 or (09) 457 3229 for all information and bookings. (C 9036, 9134; T 615, 625)

Golden Mile Railway, Boulder. A 7km (4.4 miles) narrow gauge (1067 mm) loop line, linking Boulder, Golden Gate, and Trafalgar. Trains depart Boulder station 10.00 daily with an extra service on Sundays and public and school holidays. Phone (090) 93 3053 (answering service) or (090) 93 1157 for ticket information; or enquire at Kalgoorlie Tourist Bureau.

Kalgoorlie is on the Sydney–Perth Trans-Australian rail route served both by the *Indian Pacific* and the *Prospector* from Perth (655km/406 miles). The Golden Lines bus service operates between Kalgoorlie and Boulder (5km/8 miles) daily except Sunday. (C 9033, T 611)

Hotham Valley Tourist Railway operates steam trains on the Pinjarra–Dwellingup line, with connections from Perth City. For details and booking phone (09) 451 6734.

Oliver Hill Railway, Rottnest Island. A re-built military railway, 8.5km (5.3 miles) long, links the old jetty to the Oliver Hill gun batteries. Trains operate hourly from Settlement Station, Kingstown. The island is accessible by ferry from Perth and Fremantle. Phone (09) 222 5600. (C 9037, 9059, T 635)

Tasmania

There are no main line passenger railways in Tasmania, so access to any private or preserved railways has to be by other forms of transport. The following, which all include actual train travel, are particularly worth visiting.

Derwent Valley Railway, New Norfolk operates rail tours, usually monthly on Sundays, on the scenic Derwent Valley line from New Norfolk station, 38km (24 miles) northwest of Hobart to Mt Field National Park and Maydena. The adult fare is $26. Bookings and details of operations from Birch Travel; phone (002) 34 6049 or (002) 23 7264 or from the Preservation Society itself at (002) 21 0381 or (002) 49 3250 outside office hours. New Norfolk is 55 minutes by bus from Hobart. (T 525)

Don River Railway   The Van Diemen Light Railway Society Inc. operates a 4km (2.5 miles), 1067mm gauge branch railway, closed in 1963 and restored in 1971. Steam hauled vintage trains run along the Don River to Coles Beach, 3.5km (2.2 miles) west of Devonport. Trains operate from 11.00–15.00 daily, except Christmas and Good Friday. There is also a museum. On selected dates, special trains venture onto the Australian National system. Phone (004) 24 6335 (museum) or ask at the Tasmanian Government Tourist Bureau. (T 502, 507, 731)

Ida Bay Railway (T 730) Tasmania's longest operating 610mm gauge railway, 6.8km (4.2 miles) in length, 113km (70 miles) south of Hobart on the Huon Highway (T 730). Operates thrice daily throughout the year. Adult fare $8. Hobart coaches run on weekdays to Dover (1½ hour journey), from where Ida Bay is a further 20km (12 miles). Phone (002) 983 110 for further details.

Tasmanian Transport Museum, Glenorchy. By northern suburbs bus from Hobart. Open Saturdays, Sundays and public holidays, includes short (0.5km) rides on track of former Hobart–Launceston main line. Phone (002) 34 1632.

Wee Georgie Wood Steam Railway, Tullah. 1.8km (1.1 miles) of the former tramway from Farrell to the silver mining centre of Tullah on Tasmania's west coast has been restored and steam trains operate from September–Easter on alternate Sundays. For details, contact the Tasmanian Government Tourist Bureau, phone (002) 34 6911.

On the 1067mm gauge **Emu Bay Railway**, Burnie–Melba Siding, Rosebery, 130km (80 miles), passengers may be carried in the guard's van. The daily train leaves Burnie about 05.00. Enquiries to Secretary, Emu Bay Railway Co Ltd, PO Box 82, Wilson Street, Burnie, Tas 7320. Phone (004) 30 4211.

Northern Territory

The Old Ghan The Ghan Preservation Society operates a four or
five days a week service over 26km (16 miles) from McDonnell
Siding–Ewaninga Sidings on the original Marree–Alice Springs
narrow gauge line. The adult round trip fare (1½ hour journey) is
$15. Trains carry refreshments and an evening dinner trip is
operated on Friday nights. For further details and times phone (089)
55 5220 or for bookings through the Central Australian Tourist
Industry, (089) 55 5199. The local Asbus service from Alice
Springs town centre calls at the siding regularly during the day.

Chapter Eight

Planning Your Own Australian Itinerary

Many people prefer to plan their own itinerary. But even the most detailed, such as some in this book, can be varied to get the utmost value from Austrail or other passes. This chapter explains firstly the ways in which some long interstate journeys can be varied, and secondly the various day trips and other excursions you can make from the major centres where you might be based. More important, it tells you how to make sure of getting back when you have long distance trains to catch, or when your ticket is about to expire.

For convenience the various options are described in an order which corresponds broadly to the key sections of the 30 day Austrailpass Itinerary, described in Chapter Four on page 57. Where times are given they are for normal weekday trains except where stated. Different times may apply at weekends and on public holidays. All should be checked locally before travel.

From Sydney north to Brisbane

Assuming a daylight start from Sydney refreshed and ready for the "road" just after breakfast (whether this has been taken on an overnight express from Melbourne or Adelaide or in a hotel) you have the opportunity of starting north later than the rather early *Murwillumbah XPT* but much earlier than the 16.24 departure time of the *Brisbane XPT*. The *Tablelands Xplorer* at 11.05 or the morning *Grafton XPT* at 11.35, or one of the numerous fast double-deck air-conditioned electric inter-urban trains north from Sydney will give you time to visit all sorts of places en route.

Newcastle, terminus of the electric inter-urban services from Sydney, is a coal town, but has maritime, local history and shell museums and an art gallery. Nearby **Hamilton**, first stop on the spur line to Newcastle, where you change trains for the locals to Maitland, is an attractive place for a break of journey. It is regarded as Newcastle's Sunset Strip or Bondi, a major night activity spot offering a strong selection of good, mostly ethnic, restaurants as well as cheap accommodation, all within a stone's throw of the station.

Maitland, 31km (19 miles) west of Newcastle, is a historic town with a thriving city centre just north of the station. See the heavy coal trains on their way to the port area of Newcastle. Visit the Grossman House Historical Museum, just past the pubs north of the station forecourt. From Maitland you could take a taxi to the Pokolbin wine district, 31km (19 miles) away. North coast and Tableland trains go direct to Maitland from Sydney and the *Brisbane XPT* leaves there at 18.59 so make sure your taxi is booked for the return in time if you are continuing north.

However, the Hunter Valley wine growing area is also served by the stations at **Singleton** and **Muswellbrook**. The town centre is just north of Muswellbrook station on the New England Highway. This is a good centre for visiting the wineries of the Upper Hunter, of which the nearest, Queldinburg, open seven days a week, is just two kilometres away. **Branxton**, just east of Singleton, is the nearest station for the Pokolbin vineyard district but the local train service is vestigial and there are no reasonable connections. Most big names in Australian wine are in this area, between Rothbury and Bellbird, 10-16km (6-10 miles) south of the railway. Most wineries are open every day of the week. There are cabins, a wine village, and motor lodges where, if in a hired car, you can stay the night to sober up before going back to the train.

Whether visiting the Hunter vineyards by taxi, car, or public transport, an overnight stop is recommended, since rail and bus schedules are not conducive to a quick visit. Connections to and from north coast trains are shown in the following table. (*See also* the table of trains and bus connections at Branxton on page 110).

Maitland–Singleton–Muswellbrook
C 9017, 9018; T 235b, 247

Rail	ExSa	M–F	Sun
Dep Sydney	15.12[a]	05.41[b]	11.05
Dep Maitland	18.12[c]	08.52	13.40
Arr Branxton	18.31[c]	09.11	—
Arr Singleton	18.50[c]	09.30	14.07[d]
Arr Muswellbrook	19.23[c]	10.03	—

Bus	ExSu	M–F	Sun
Dep Muswellbrook	05.35	12.35	13.35
Dep Singleton	06.10	13.10	14.10[d]
Dep Branxton	06.30	13.30	14.30
Arr Rothbury	06.36	13.36	14.36
Arr Pokolbin	06.45	13.45	14.45
Arr Kurri Kurri	07.15	14.15	15.15

Bus		ExSu	M–F	Sun	
Dep	Kurri Kurri	17.10	20.10	20.40	
Dep	Pokolbin	17.40	20.40	21.15	
Dep	Rothbury	17.50	20.50	21.25	
Arr	Branxton	17.53	20.53	21.28	
Arr	Singleton	18.15	21.25	21.50	
Arr	Muswellbrook	18.50	21.50	22.25	

Train		ExSu	M–F	Sat	Sun	Daily
Dep	Muswellbrook	20.39	—	21.01	—	13.16
Dep	Singleton	21.12	—	21.34	—	13.50
Dep	Branxton	—	21.28	21.51	21.51	—
Arr	Maitland	21.48	21.48	22.10	22.10	14.18
Dep	Maitland	—	09.39e	09.39e	09.39e	18.59f
	(for north coast)					

a Five minutes later on Sundays. Change at Hamilton.

b Change at Broadmeadow.

c Five minutes later on Sundays.

d A very doubtful connection (3 minutes) unless advance arrangement made with bus company to wait for train.

e To Grafton and Murwillumbah. Also at 14.03 to Grafton.

f To Grafton and Brisbane.

Another option for the northbound traveller is to take the *Murwillumbah* or *Grafton XPT* during daytime to Dungog, Gloucester or even Taree, from where a seat or berth on the *Brisbane XPT* can be taken overnight. Options are also possible travelling south from Queensland if you have a day in hand. Break your journey at a Northern New South Wales town such as Casino, Grafton or Coffs Harbour, staying the night and continuing south next day.

North from Brisbane
On a journey from New South Wales to north Queensland you need not spend a night on the Gold Coast or in a Brisbane hotel. Budget conscious travellers wishing to make the train their travelling hotel can leave Brisbane the day they arrive from the south, whether the *Sunlander* runs that day or not, by taking the earlier *Spirit of Capricorn* up to **Rockhampton** and spending a day or more there before continuing northward. For anyone interested in the working of a railway system a visit to the Central District Train Control Centre at Rocky (always learn what the locals call a place) is a must.

Alternatively, there is time for sightseeing closer to Brisbane. Take a local Nambour or Cooroy train in the morning or early afternoon up to the remarkable **Glasshouse Mountains** and pick up the Gympie train there in the evening. You can then either stay the night in Gympie, or change there for Rockhampton on the *Spirit of the Outback* at 22.10 on a Tuesday or Friday, or the "Night Spirit" (which local railway people refer to as the "Capricornian", the name of the former Brisbane–Rockhampton overnight service) at 23.23 on a Wednesday or Sunday. On a Thursday, you would need to leave Glasshouse Mountains station at 13.26 to catch the northbound *Spirit of the Tropics* at Nambour or, if you had an appropriate rail pass, you could return south to Caboolture on a local at 15.55 to catch the northbound *Tropics* there at 16.32. A stop at Glasshouse Mountains is worth making, even though you would see the same scenery in passing on the *Sunlander*.

Gladstone, reached after dinnertime on the northbound *Sunlander* (or just before if travelling on the *Spirit of Capricorn*) is a colourful town, with its juxtaposition of magnificent coastal scenery, massive industrial development and a small boat harbour. The coal terminals, modern as any in the world, and the railway marshalling yards set in undulating bushland at Callemondah, present a most unusual picture. Break your journey here and take a cab up to the vantage point on Round Hill.

Alternatively you can break the journey further south at **Bundaberg**, heart of sugarland and home of Queensland's famous rum. You'll have time to see how they make it, and taste it, between the arrival of the *Spirit of Capricorn* northbound and the departure of the *Sunlander*, or between the arrival of the *Sunlander* southbound and the departure of the *Spirit* to Brisbane. Better still, on some days you can continue south by a comfortable sleeper on the *Spirit of the Outback*.

Mackay is a sugar exporting port with the largest bulk sugar terminal in the world. You may see the burning cane fields light up the sky after harvest, although different harvesting methods have largely transcended this feature.

Proserpine, terminus of the mid-week *Tropics*, is only a short bus ride away from Shute Harbour in Conway National Park, gateway to the tropical islands of Hayman, Daydream, Hamilton, Lindeman and South Molle in the Whitsundays.

With an Austrailpass or Flexipass you can break the journey at many other centres north of Brisbane. Inland excursions are also possible, offering a marked contrast to the scenery of the north coast line. A diversion from Rockhampton into central Queensland or from Townsville inland to Mount Isa will easily fill two days or more with experiences of rural and outback Australia many tourists never manage to see at all, and which you are unlikely readily to forget.

At **Townsville**, just to the right near the end of Flinders Mall, you will find Ross Creek. Dotted with myriads of small boats, the quayside is lined by an excellent restaurant and bar complex, which you have ample time to visit if changing at Townsville for the train to Mount Isa.

Half day city bus tours are operated by Ansett Pioneer in Hanran Street just east of Townsville station. There are day cruises to the Outer Barrier Reef but for around $10 you can enjoy an hour or two among the marine wonders of Reefworld just off the Strand, or take a ferry from Hayles Wharf on Ross Creek over to nearby Magnetic Island.

The attractions of **Cairns** and its surroundings have already been described in Chapter Four and elsewhere.

Canberra and southern New South Wales

If your itinerary includes Canberra, or you have time for a 2-day trip there from Sydney, then there are plenty of interesting features to see in this national capital city, such as Parliament House (the new and the old), the Prime Minister's Lodge, the National Library with its modern art display, the Academy of Science and the War Memorial and Museum. An inexpensive tour is offered by ACT Tourist Bureau, located in the Civic Centre. There are marvellous views from Mt Ainslie, Mt Pleasant, or Red Hill Lookout. See the 6,000 native Australian plants in the Botanic Gardens, the old locomotive bell in All Saints Anglican Church, and if you have time, the Tidbinbilla Nature Reserve 39km (24 miles) away or the rather delightful model English village at Cockington Green.

The former *Canberra Monaro Express* continued south from Canberra past Tuggeranong New Town to **Cooma** on the edge of the Snowy Mountains, where buses (State Rail operated) connect south to Bombola and have now replaced the train. Cooma is the gateway to Mt Kosciusko, highest peak in Australia, where the Perisher SkiTube (*see* page 113) takes skiers and tourists by a funicular railway to the slopes of the Snowy Mountains National Park.

Between Sydney, Albury and Melbourne the overnight sleeper is supplemented by the daylight train. Any itinerary which includes a day or more in either capital city therefore allows the option of a break of journey in southern New South Wales or northeast Victoria. If leaving Sydney on the daylight train you could break your journey at Cootamundra, Junee, or Wagga Wagga. Or, if you prefer, carry on to Albury and stay there beside the River Murray for the night.

Albury-Wodonga, largest town on the Murray and a planned growth centre, partly in Victoria and partly in New South Wales, is a centre for tours of the historical gold towns, river centres, wineries, and snowfields of northeastern Victoria. Attractions include the fine railway station itself, Hume Weir (for trout fishing), historic Beechworth and Yackandandah, and the many wineries around Rutherglen. There is a free bus tour of Albury-Wodonga and coach tours operate to the surrounding places of interest.

A V/Line bus (Austrailpass valid) from Albury or Benalla also brings the traveller to **Echuca**, an important historic centre of early river transport.

In the morning you can, if a compulsive early riser, board the *Southern Cross XPT* from Albury at 03.54 to go on to Melbourne, or you can wait for a V/Line InterCity at 06.20 or 12.25. You can break the journey again at Chiltern, Wangaratta or Benalla, but watch your times if you intend catching the *Overland* to Adelaide the same night. The last connection from Chiltern is at 16.29 on Saturday only; from Wangaratta and Benalla respectively 16.13 and 16.37 daily, plus 16.56 and 17.22 on Saturdays. (C 9028)

If it is fruit harvest time you might prefer a diversion to **Shepparton** in Victoria's fertile Goulburn Valley to try some of their luscious pears. Change trains at Benalla if on the XPT from interstate and change again, or otherwise, at Seymour where you will have time to spare before going on to Shepparton. Travelling north, a trip to the Goulburn Valley will still bring you back to Melbourne in time for the Sydney XPT, the *Southern Cross*, but you can change instead at Seymour and take the InterCity north to Benalla, Wangaratta, or Albury. Stop for dinner, then join the train for Sydney afterward.

Sydney westwards

The *Indian Pacific* interstate train on the western route from Sydney starts in the early afternoon and returns in the morning. This allows an optional morning start or evening finish to an interstate journey by using one of the frequent inter-urban trains to break the journey at Lithgow in the Blue Mountains. Going west there is also the option of taking the XPT to break the journey for several hours further west, at Bathurst, Blayney or Orange.

Bathurst is Australia's oldest inland settlement, proud of its old buildings which can mostly be seen on a walking tour. See the humble cottage where former Australian Prime minister Ben

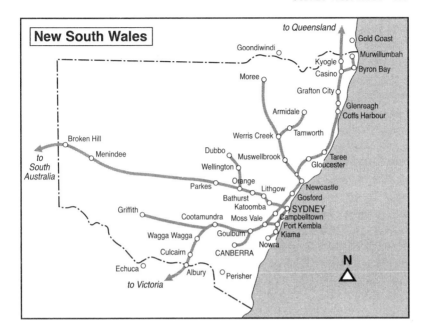

Chifley lived, and the steam engine he drove as a railway employee.

Orange is an excellent centre for exploring the Conobolas country (not a Greek name as it may sound but formed from two aboriginal words). The mountain of that name, some 14km (9miles) southwest of the city, is the highest point between the Blue Mountains and the Indian Ocean. The Hotel Conobolas is round the corner from the station, as is the restful civic park and the new library and regional gallery, well worth a visit. Call at the Visitor Centre for information on a walking tour of the historic buildings. Coach tours of the surroundings are operated to co-ordinate with the arrival and departure of the XPT train; phone (063) 62 4822 for information.

Note that to join the *Indian Pacific* to continue west it is necessary to go to Orange East Fork, 1.8km (1.1 miles) from Orange main station, from where it leaves at 21.05.

Travelling further west from Sydney you should wake up in time to see the Menindee Lakes, which contain more water than Sydney Harbour. You reach Broken Hill around breakfast time. You have half an hour before the train continues westwards, but if travelling east on the *Indian Pacific* you have less – and are advised not to leave the station precincts. (There is a 30 minute time zone adjustment to be made here, so beware!)

Broken Hill merits a longer visit and it is worth breaking your journey to stay the night there. Unfortunately this involves waiting between two successive calls of the *Indian Pacific* (not less than three days for trains going in the same direction, two days if on a there and back trip from Adelaide, or at least one day if going there and back from Sydney). The only other option (apart from aircraft or bus) is the new Countrylink Outback service to and from Orange or Sydney which widens the possibilities. These are summarised in Chapter Seven under the heading "Broken Hill Transport Museum", *see* page 107.

Being built over rich deposits of silver, lead and zinc, Broken Hill is rich in mining (and railway) history and boasts some of the finest vernacular architecture of the period. Do not fail to look at the magnificent iron-verandahed Palace Hotel and ask proprietor Mario about the painting on the ceiling. For tours of the mine area contact the City Council's Tourism Development and Marketing Department, corner of Blende and Sulphide Streets; phone (080) 88 9266. See the collection of coins, minerals, shells and aboriginal artifacts at Carlton Gardens and Art Gallery, and the restored Afghan mosque, once used by camel drivers imported to carry supplies through the region.

Scenic air tours operate from "the Hill" to nearby places of interest such as the diggings of the world's only source of black opals at White Cliffs. Trips are also possible to Kinchega National Park and several outback stations. The restored Silverton ghost town is nearby, and further afield at Mootwingee, 132km (82 miles) northeast, are aboriginal rock carvings. You will learn just as much perhaps, but not see it all, by simply spending some time in the bar of one of this industrial town's many fine old hotels and talking to its warm and friendly people.

Day trips from Sydney

From Sydney there are frequent electric trains down the coast to **Wollongong**, of Australia's "Aunty Jack" TV fame, with its "What's wrong with Wollongong" quip. You'll find out, but be prepared for a surprise. Wollongong, like all hard-earning industrial towns, has a warmth about it many other places lack. You will feel this even more if you go down the branch to **Port Kembla** where the steelworks are. Port Kembla is not everyone's cup of tea, but have a quick beer and say hello to the friendly locals. The pub is five minutes from the station and there should usually be about half an hour before the local train returns to Wollongong.

There are tempting places to break a journey most of the way between Unanderra and Nowra (Bomaderry), the end of the line.

At Bombo the beach is just over the track from the station platform. There is a little restaurant just down the road from **Kiama** station, a good place to linger that extra few minutes over lunch or stay the night and see the nearby blowhole and Cathedral Rocks.

Sydney to the south coast C 9014; T 295

One class only trains leave Sydney for **Nowra** at more or less at hourly intervals (two hourly on mornings and at weekends) from 04.52 on weekdays, 05.44 weekends, and arrive at Kiama on average in about 2 hours 20 minutes and Nowra 2 hours 50 minutes. Return services depart from Nowra just as frequently but at more erratic intervals (varying from 32-121 minutes). All trains involve a change between local electric and diesel *Endeavour* units at Dapto. Last return times from Nowra if catching the Melbourne XPT from Sydney are 16.51 on weekdays, 17.32 Saturdays, Sundays and on holidays, Kiama departures being 17.30 and 18.10 respectively. There are much later trains to Sydney itself.

On Mondays, Tuesdays, Saturdays, Sundays and public holidays (except Christmas Day) a delightful circular trip is possible, down the coast to Wollongong, then up through the rainforest to Moss Vale and back into Sydney via Campbelltown. There is a 15 minute stop at Summit Tank to view the scenery. This trip can be made in either direction and a break of journey is possible using the timetable below.

Sydney–Wollongong–Moss Vale–Sydney
C 9014, 9021; T 295, 308, 712

Trains between Unanderra and Moss Vale are mostly steam hauled and operated by 3801 Limited. Round trip fare (not covered by Austrailpass) is $20. Phone toll free 1800 64 3801 for further information and booking.

	Mon Tue	Sat Sun
Dep Sydney[a]	07.58[b]	07.44[b]
Dep Wollongong[a]	09.32[b]	09.15[b]
Dep Port Kembla[a]	09.30	09.30
Dep Unanderra	10.00	10.00
Arr Moss Vale	12.40	12.40
	Change trains	
Dep Moss Vale	13.42	14.35[e]
Arr Campbelltown[c]	15.00	15.41[e]
Arr Sydney[c]	15.54[d]	16.26[e]
Dep Sydney[c]	11.15	10.59[d]
Dep Campbelltown[c]	11.54	11.54
Arr Moss Vale	13.14	13.14
	Change trains	

		Mon Tue	Sat Sun
Dep	Moss Vale	13.50	13.50
Arr	Unanderra	16.05	16.05
Arr	Port Kembla[a]	16.30	16.30
Arr	Wollongong[a]	16.43[b]	16.54[b]
Arr	Sydney[a]	18.16[b]	18.16[b]

[a] Frequent additional trains Sydney to Wollongong and Port Kembla from 04.52, and from Wollongong to Sydney up to 22.10 (Port Kembla 21.57), weekdays, varied at weekends.

[b] Change at Unanderra

[c] Frequent local trains between Campbelltown and Sydney.

[d] Change at Campbelltown. Other trains Moss Vale–Campbelltown–Sydney at various times. Check before travel or at Moss Vale.

[e] XPT. Reservation required. Carries buffet. For connection to Brisbane same day change at Strathfield.

State Rail Day-a-Way Tours

Some all-in Day-a-Way tours operated by Cityrail include coach and ferry with lunch or other refreshments en route. Rail fare is deducted from the inclusive price if you have a rail pass. The tours start and finish at Sydney Central. Itineraries include parts of the south coast, the Blue Mountains, the Hunter valley, "The Riverboat Postman" covering the Hawkesbury River and one to "Old Sydney Town", a recreated historic settlement near Gosford. Local enquiry is necessary.

Sydney to the Southern Highlands

Frequent suburban electric trains serve Campbelltown, while diesel *Endeavour* sets of Cityrail, plus *Xplorer* or XPT trains together offer a somewhat erratic but roughly hourly service to and from Moss Vale, Goulburn and intermediate stations, with three trains daily continuing to Canberra. Day trips can easily be made to all destinations from early morning. Last trains for return the same day are at 17.20 from Canberra, 19.45 from Goulburn (21.18 on Fridays and Saturdays, 18.47 Sundays and holidays), and 20.42 from Moss Vale (plus 22.15 on Fridays and Saturdays). (C 9014, 9021)

Sydney to the Blue Mountains

Possibly the most scenic part of the continent, at least of readily accessible places, the Blue Mountains west of Sydney feature towering escarpments, waterfalls, deep bush, and scenic lookouts, accessible by coach tours from the principal centre, **Katoomba**, or by bush walking tracks, a steam railway, cable car, and the world's steepest funicular railway. Katoomba is reached by fast and frequent trains from Sydney. **Springwood**, with its Norman Lindsay gallery and museum, **Wentworth Falls**, **Leura**, **Blackheath**, and **Mount Victoria** are other convenient stations for access to this National Park.

Just short of the inter-urban terminus at Lithgow is a tiny platform called **Zigzag**, a request stop and station for the Zigzag Railway, which operates at weekends. Here you can take a steam train up a private line on the old switchback route which crossed the mountains before they built the present line which pierced the ranges with its ten tunnels. At Top Points you turn around and return to the bottom, where you must hail the train for the return to Sydney. Frequent trains serve the Blue Mountains area (C 9014, T 270). From Katoomba and Leura are tours such as the Freedom of the Blue Mountains Explorer bus.

To the Central West C 9020, T 255

A day trip from Sydney is possible to the Central West using the XPT from Sydney at 07.10 returning from Dubbo at 14.10, Wellington 14.49, Orange 15.55 and Bathurst 17.14. This service reaches Sydney at 20.48, just missing the overnight *Southern Cross* XPT to Melbourne, but passengers can change from the returning train at Strathfield at 20.34. Prior booking for this is essential.

Wellington has nearby Mount Arthur and the Wellington caves are within 9km (6 miles) of the town. See the historical museum and the phonograph parlour and try the Bite-Te-Eat BYO for fast foods with a difference. Nearby **Stuart Town**, scene of a former gold rush and immortalised by Banjo Patterson's poem *The Man from Ironbark* (its former name) is a place where the casual prospector can still readily find a little "colour" in a pan. The XPT calls at this station.

In **Dubbo**, see Victoria Park Zoo and the old Dubbo Gaol with its self guided tour and souvenir shop.

To the Central Coast and Newcastle
C 9014, T 232, and local

There are frequent trains to Mt Ku-ring-gai and Hawkesbury River (55 minutes), Gosford (72-82min) and Wyong (85-100min); also to Newcastle at intervals up to 16.12 which arrives in Newcastle at 18.40 (Broadmeadow 18.31). You don't have to go back to Sydney if you are going north overnight because the *Brisbane XPT* calls at Hornsby at 16.57, Gosford 17.41 and Broadmeadow 18.36. There are later trains to the Central Coast and Newcastle if you intend a longer break of journey by staying overnight.

If travelling south from Sydney that day you will have less time to spare. Deadline times to return for the *Southern Cross* XPT to Melbourne on weekdays are 18.02 from Newcastle, 18.12 from Broadmeadow, 19.02 from Wyong, 19.17 from Gosford and 19.42 from Hawkesbury River. Weekend and holiday times are around 40 minutes earlier. These connections all involve changing at Strathfield to the Melbourne train. If you have left your luggage at Sydney and not booked it on the XPT you will have to leave earlier but times vary at weekends so local enquiry is recommended.

Day trips further north are summarised below.

Sydney–Dungog–Gloucester
C 9016, 9017; T 235b & local

Daily XPT trains with buffet. A more frequent service to and from Dungog only, changing at Hamilton, is available.

Dep Sydney	07.05	11.35	16.24
Arr Dungog	10.22	14.44	19.41
Arr Gloucester	11.15	15.37	—
Dep Gloucester	—	12.28	17.16
Dep Dungog	07.10	13.22	18.11
Arr Sydney	10.30	16.34	21.35

If continuing north to Brisbane the same day, the overnight train must be picked up at Maitland at 18.57 or Dungog at 19.41. From Gloucester it is necessary to leave at 17.16, returning south to pick up the northbound XPT at Dungog, or take a Countrylink bus at 20.03 connecting with the XPT at Taree.

For the overnight Melbourne XPT departure deadline you must return to Sydney by the local connecting trains from Dungog at 15.23 Mondays–Fridays, or 14.08 Saturdays. On Sundays the XPT from Dungog at 13.22, or Gloucester 12.28, is the only return connection.

Two-day trips from Sydney
A two day trip from Sydney can take you into the Northern Tablelands of New South Wales or to Moree. Daylight travel is by *Xplorer* air-conditioned diesel train with buffet facilities; all trains normally require reservations. For times and other details see Cooks C 9018.

Tamworth is famous for its country music festival held over 11 days in January. Historic buildings, galleries, friendly family pubs, and surrounding bush walks are other features. **Armidale** holds a people's market in the mall on the last Sunday of each month. Worth visiting too is the folk museum in Faulkner Street. Follow

Barney Street east from the station to reach the town centre. At
Moree there are hotels close to the station. Take your swimwear
(or cozzie as this is known in Australian English); no visitor to
Moree should miss an early morning bathe in the spa pool just a
block or two away from the station.

The limitations on other possibilities for rail travel in New
South Wales depend only on how long you have before going on
interstate (or home) from Sydney. It is a good idea to make a
provincial town your base for part of the time. Places such as
Maitland, Orange, or Goulburn, all rail junctions, will shorten
many of your trips. Longer inclusive Country Link Holiday tours
are also offered by the State Rail Authority.

Deadline departures from Sydney

If you have to get back to Sydney for an interstate journey, make
sure you take account of the following deadlines:

14.40	*Indian Pacific*	to Adelaide and Perth
16.24	*Brisbane XPT*	
20.43	*Southern Cross*	to Melbourne

Useful bus/rail connections in New South Wales

Road coaches owned or contracted by State Rail can extend the
range of places you can visit in New South Wales (and some go
into Victoria). Maps and timetables can be be obtained at railway
stations. The following places are served by bus from the stations
named.

Barraba and Inverell	from Tamworth
Cooma, Bega and Eden	from Goulburn and Canberra
Cooma, Bombola and Eden	from Canberra
Cowra and Grenfell	from Bathurst and Blayney
Deniliquin and Echuca (Vic)	from Wagga Wagga
Forbes and Eugowra	from Orange and Parkes
Glen Innes and Tenterfield	from Armidale
Griffith, Hay and Mildura (Vic)	from Cootamundra
Gundagai and Tumberumba	from Cootamundra
Mudgee and Coonabarabran	from Lithgow
Narrandera and Griffith	from Wagga Wagga
Nyngan, Brewarrina, Cobar and Bourke	from Dubbo
Oberon	from Mt Victoria
Tocumwal and Echuca (Vic)	from Albury
Walgett and Lightning Ridge	from Dubbo
Young	from Harden and Cootamundra

In addition, railway buses provide potentially useful cross-country links between some of the railway routes, as follows:–

Cootamundra Main south line	to Condobolin Western main line
Cootamundra Main south line	to Orange and Bathurst Western main line
Cootamundra Main south line	to Dubbo Central west line
Dubbo Central west line	to Parkes and Broken Hill Western main line
Grafton City North coast main line	to Moree Northwest line
Wagga Wagga Main south line	to Griffith
Yass Main south line	to Canberra

Day trips west from Brisbane

Helidon is worth a visit for its mineral springs but, apart from the *Westlander* on two evenings a week, it is now only accessible by private coach from Ipswich, although passengers with a rail ticket are allowed a discount. If you don't like natural mineral water there is a pub just opposite the station and a coffee shop 100m down a street of colourful Jacaranda trees. Otherwise **Rosewood** is as far west as you can go in a day by rail at the present time.

Day trips north from Brisbane

Gympie, at the end of the climb through the Eumundi ranges, is an old gold mining centre. A friendly town, full of historic relics; they hold an Annual Show in late May and a Gold Rush Week in mid-October. Local fruit – oranges and pineapples – is plentiful and cheap. Worth a day trip or break of journey between Brisbane and north Queensland. The train service is limited, and better suited to an overnight stay in Gympie. Services will alter in early 1997 and up-to-date details should definitely be checked locally before you travel. (C 9013, 9015)

Nambour, further south, is another good place to break your journey or for a day trip, being the gateway to the Sunshine and Sun Coast resorts. A short cab ride or bus service (approximately hourly) will bring you to the "Big Pineapple" complex where you can buy local products and ride a cane train through the pineapple plantation.

If your itinerary includes time for a whole day in this area, you do not need to hire a car or take a cab as buses operate between

Nambour and Maroochydore, and from **Eumundi** and **Cooroy** to the Sun Coast at Noosa, worth visiting for a look at the coloured sands of Cooloola National Park, and with many excellent beaches within easy striking distance. A reasonable service of local inter-urban electric trains links Brisbane with Nambour (approximately 2 hours journey). (C 9015)

Day trips from Brisbane to the coast C 9015
Frequent local trains serve Sandgate on Bramble Bay and Shorncliffe on Moreton Bay, also Lota on Waterloo Bay, and Ormiston and Cleveland on Raby Bay. Journey times vary from 30 to 50 minutes. These bayside suburbs are all in fact on part of the greater Moreton Bay and are more in the nature of commuter suburbs than coastal resorts. From Cleveland, Stradbroke Ferries operates a water taxi service to **Stradbroke Island**, with courtesy bus from the railway station to the ferry terminal (T 175), and from Caboolture, 60 minutes by City train, buses connect to **Bribie Island** (40min, T 166).

The Citytrain network is being extended to the **Gold Coast**. Currently, hourly express trains serve Coomera and Helensvale, from where connecting buses link with the Dreamworld complex and various Gold Coast destinations. *Travel Times* T 194 and local timetables give the full details, but check locally for the latest information. Reduced fares are available at weekends.

Longer Queensland trips
If you have time for more than one nightstop in Brisbane area, you can take a rail trip up the ranges to **Toowoomba**, the garden city of the Darling Downs on the edge of the escarpment. The Early Settlers' Museum and other old buildings are a few kilometres southwest at Drayton, and other old buildings are at Oakey and Jondaryan, both on the railway west of Toowoomba – but Oakey unfortunately is served by train in either direction only in the middle of the night, and Jondaryan is no longer even a stopping place.

Longer trips from Brisbane, Gympie, Rockhampton and Townsville are described in Chapters Six and Seven.

Day and two day trips from Cairns
Cairns is a useful base for local trips, by train, by coach, by launch, or by hired car. A day trip to one of the islands on the Great Barrier Reef is easily undertaken from Cairns if you have a whole day there. Full day coach tours are available to Atherton Tableland, with crater lakes, orchid gardens and waterfalls; or to Cape Tribulation and Mossman gorge. At **Mossman** the *Ballyhooley*

Express (not covered by Austrailpass) runs through canefields to historic Port Douglas and at Gordonvale the *Mulgrave Rambler* offers a similar yet more accessible adventure, although neither train runs regularly at the time of writing *(see* Chapter Seven, pages 114 and 117 respectively).

Kuranda, the "village in the rainforest" is famous for its station, Barron Falls, markets (held on Sunday and Wednesday mornings), noctarium, butterfly farm, and the Bottom Pub for a cold beer.

Although there are daily trains (two or three most days) between Cairns and Kuranda (C 9007) there are also many private coach tours which allow the outward or return trip to be taken by train. There is also the option of taking the newly opened Skyrail rainforest aerial cableway from Caronica Lakes station 2 minutes from Smithfield Shopping Centre and 11km (7 miles) from Cairns city centre. The Skyrail fare is $23 one way, $39 round trip, or $49 round trip including transfers to and from hotels. The local Marlin Coast Beach Bus service Route 208 has a half hourly service past Smithfield; phone (070) 577 411.

An alternative, covered by your rail pass, is to go up to the Atherton Tableland. Take the Kuranda Tourist Train to have a quick look around Kuranda (the station itself is like a botanical garden), then catch the railway bus to Mareeba, Atherton, Herberton or even Ravenshoe, stay the night and be back in Cairns next day.

Another alternative is to take the *Sunlander* south from Cairns on Monday, Thursday or Saturday and stop a night or three in Gordonvale, Babinda, Innisfail, or Tully. You can then carry on south another day, but if that is a Tuesday, make sure your night-stop is either at Innisfail or Tully as Tuesday's train is the *Queenslander* which does not stop at any of the other places in this area. If you want to return to Cairns instead there are trains back on Sunday, Monday (from Tully or Innisfail only), Wednesday or Friday.

Babinda is among the many places where a stopover can be recommended. It features a nature reserve, the Boulders, where a small river plunges among rocks, scene of both legend and recent tragedy when a foolhardy swimmer ignored the warnings. Keep to the excellent deep pool where it is safe.

Innisfail, in sugar cane country, is set between the ranges and the sea and is noted for its Chinese Temple and Pioneers' Monument. Nerada tea plantation, several kilometres inland, is

Australia's first venture into this crop. Palmerston National Park is further inland on the road to Millaa Millaa and Ravenshoe on the Atherton Tableland.

Closer to Cairns, at **Gordonvale** (32 minutes by train), set among canefields and backed by rainforest, the Mulgrave Mill is open for inspection tours even if the *Mulgrave Rambler* steam train is not taking its scenic 15km (9miles) narrow gauge rail trip to Orchid Valley.

Mareeba, an aboriginal name for "meeting of the waters", at the junction of the Barron and Granite rivers, is a former stopping place of Cobb's coaches and a centre for timber and tobacco. The sawmill yard to the right of the station is worth a look. The town centre adjoins the station. Dunlop's Hotel, just over the road, has the local reputation of offering the best tucker in town. At the time of writing Mareeba is not served by rail (not counting the Queensland Rail bus to the Atherton Tableland) but this is most likely to change in the near future. Mareeba is a useful base for a coach (or, hopefully, rail) excursion through tobacco country to Dimbulah and the old mining centre of **Chillagoe** or for coach trips south into the Atherton tableland. Mareeba rodeo is held every July in nearby Kerribee Park. A granite gorge, west of the town, has boulders the size of 8-storey buildings.

Close to **Ravenshoe**, former end of the Atherton railway (and where a private railway now operates – *see* page 117), are the Millstream Falls, the widest in Australia, and dense eucalypt forests. Atherton Tableland is one of the oldest land masses in the world. Its has many attractions including a giant curtain fig tree and the tranquil crater lakes of Eacham and Barrine, all about 15km (9 miles) east from Atherton. While in the area, do your best to urge restoration of full rail services to this scenic paradise!

Longer trips in Queensland, of which there are many (it would take weeks of non-stop travelling to cover all possible Queensland rail routes where passenger trains or mixed freight and passenger trains are run), are described in Chapters Six and Seven. The former Forsayth train, described as the world's "Last Great Train Ride" should appeal not only to rail buffs, since (assuming that it is soon resurrected in one form or another) you can, even without taking it all the way, experience the ranges at night, visit Mareeba or break your journey at **Mount Surprise** to visit the unique system of volcanic lava tubes at Undara. (Stay at Undara Lodge).

One other option in Queensland deserves to be mentioned. Between April and October, during most weeks, there is a six day rail tour between Brisbane and Cairns, covering the whole route by daylight and including meals and nightstops at hotels. Pre-booking is essential and the fare is not covered by the Austrailpass or Sunshine Rail Pass, since the train is contracted out to the Queensland Tourist and Travel Corporation. The train, the "Sunshine Daylight Rail Experience", usually runs fortnightly. The itinerary varies, but tours normally start on a Monday in each direction and include photostops and visits to offshore islands.

Sometimes this train operates to other Queensland destinations such as the "Granite Belt" in the ranges south of Toowoomba. Details of running, costs, and booking, from railway stations or Queensland Rail Travel Centre, *see* Chapter 2 page 12.

Bus/rail connections in Queensland

By and large, Queensland Rail does not operate bus services to anything like the extent seen in New South Wales or Victoria. The few rail-contracted bus services that exist simply replace trains on some of the remote branch lines (Cunnamulla and Quilpie from Charleville, Winton from Longreach and Toogoolawah from Ipswich) or link new stations on the outskirts of some towns with the older stations in the central area (as at Gympie and Maryborough).

There are no railway bus services linking railheads, but private buses do offer some useful cross-country connections. To list all these would be beyond the scope of this book. Many of them make very poor connections or connections at unreasonable times of day. The following are those that might just prove useful to a traveller with an Austrail Flexipass who is willing to endure some hours in a bus to go from one remote destination to somewhere equally obscure. The buses are private, many but not all operated by McCafferty's, a Toowoomba based company with an office in the Roma Street Transit Centre, Brisbane. Phone 13 14 99 toll free from anywhere in Australia. For further details see *Travel Times Australia*.

Barcaldine–Blackall–Charleville Buses run daily between Barcaldine (Midland line) and Charleville (Western line) via Blackall (Yaraka branch) at 17.10 and 17.35, returning from Charleville at 03.50. An alternative northbound service returns from Morven (Western line) at 17.10, reaching Barcaldine at 22.35.

Kuranda–Mount Surprise–Croydon A bus links Kuranda with Mount Surprise (Forsayth line) and Croydon (Normanton

Railway), on Mondays, Wednesdays and Thursdays, departing 07.15, returning from Croydon at 10.00 on Tuesdays, Thursdays and Fridays.

Croydon–Georgetown–Forsayth On Thursday, the bus from Croydon at 10.00 connects with a bus leaving Georgetown for Forsayth at 13.30 (with time for a lunch break in between).

Cloncurry–Normanton On Thursdays a bus links Cloncurry (Mount Isa line) with Normanton, leaving at 12.30 and arriving at 17.10, returning at 08.45 on Wednesday.

Cloncurry–Winton–Longreach Buses leave Cloncurry daily for Winton and Longreach (Midland line) at 09.20 and 09.55. Return services from Longreach are at 10.15 and 23.45.

Mount Isa–Alice Springs McCafferty's service 131 leaves Mount Isa daily at 19.15 for Alice Springs via Tennant Creek, arriving 08.35 next day. The return leaves Alice Springs at 20.30 to reach Mount Isa at 11.05. There is also a Greyhound service on this route (C 9075, 9125), but not fitting in so well with train times. Neither can really be recommended to the train traveller unless in emergency.

Day trips east from Melbourne

The rail system east of Melbourne serves the industrial towns of Moe, Morwell and Traralgon in the Latrobe Valley, then goes on through Rosedale to Sale in East Gippsland (C 9029). Another branch used to serve South Gippsland (see page 122 for details of the private service replacing part of this route) and there is a local line to **Stony Point** for the ferry trip across to Philip Island (in summer only) with its penguins. Take the suburban train to Frankston and change to the railcar there. The ferry crossing takes only a few minutes. (T 365, 367)

All stations in Gippsland are within day return reach of Melbourne but to see the sights of the region two or three days are needed. **Bairnsdale**, reached by connecting V/Line bus from Sale (approximately one hour, C 9029) is the gateway to the coastal lakes of eastern Victoria. Paynesville on Lake Victoria (10km from Bairnsdale) and Lakes Entrance (35km) are specially popular resorts, the latter adjoining Victoria's Ninety Mile Beach. At **Nowa Nowa**, north of Lakes Entrance, is the largest timber trestle bridge in the Southern Hemisphere, on the former freight-only Orbost branch of the railway, now closed to traffic altogether. Between Nowa Nowa and Orbost the bushland off to the right is full of kangaroos and wallabies, a wonderful ride when trains ran. This

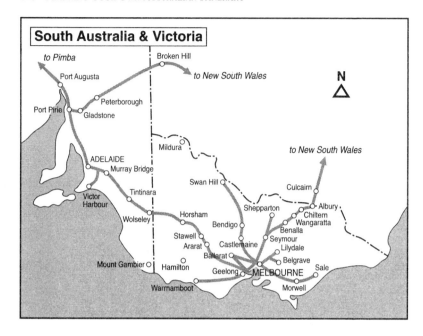

part of East Gippsland remains accessible by V/Line bus. (T 350)

Day trips north from Melbourne

Wodonga, Wangaratta and Benalla are on the main line from
Sydney, and also served by V-line InterCity trains. For local
InterCity services see Cooks C 9028. All Melbourne–Albury local
trains stop at Seymour (70min from Melbourne), Benalla (another
hour), Wangaratta (an hour from Albury) and Wodonga, Albury's
Victoria twin city.

A day trip into the Goulburn Valley is another option. Trains go
only as far as Shepparton, from where V/Line buses connect to
Cobram on the New South Wales border (T 402). From Cobram it is
only 5km (3 miles) to Barooga in New South Wales, where a visitor
from Victoria can sample the club life and facilities of New South
Wales with its "pokies" (slot machines) and the excellent catering
they help to subsidise.

Another northern Victoria line is that to Bendigo and Swan Hill.
Bendigo, scene of a gold rush in 1851, has a wealth of Australian
history, perhaps typified by its magnificently opulent Shamrock
Hotel. See the original Chinese Joss House, still open. Take a ride
on the tram, visit the pottery and climb to the top of the Central
Deborah Mine.

En route to Bendigo, you pass **Castlemaine**, another historic centre, from where the old railway to Maldon is being restored. In contrast to the several "re-created" historic townships, Maldon is a living example of a small mining town of the last century, where an enlightened local council maintains strict control of all new building. Bendigo has a reasonably good service from Melbourne, on which Victoria's new Sprinter railcars have recently begun operating. When these come fully into service, schedules should improve. Current times average about 2 hours and there are 4 to 8 services a day. (C 9032)

Day trips west from Melbourne

The western line of Victoria was historically the main interstate line to Adelaide, but since standardisation of another route between Melbourne and Ararat via Geelong, few trains are left serving the former route and all passenger trains have been withdrawn from former branches to Maryborough, Mildura and Hamilton. The *Wimmera Limited* linking Melbourne and Ballarat through Horsham to Dimboola has been replaced by a bus; the Warrnambool trains to the southwest coast have gone over to private enterprise, and the only V/Line services west of Melbourne, are now to Ballarat.

Ballarat, a historic mining centre, is a convenient day trip from Melbourne and also worth an overnight stay. Attractions include the vintage tramway and museum, many historic buildings and interiors, Sovereign Hill (a recreated mining settlement where you can pan for gold), and the railway station itself, a particularly fine building with arched roof, old fashioned level crossing gates, signal cabin and gantry, classics of industrial archeology. The Begonia Festival is held during the first two weeks in March, and there is also the Yellowglen Winery, specialising in *méthode champenoise* sparkling dry wine of fine quality.

Ballarat trains take on average around 90 minutes, running approximately every two hours (C 9023, T 445). Some follow a different route, via Geelong North Shore. If taking this route, look out on the left for the wharves and industry of Port Philip Bay after leaving Footscray (10 minutes from Spencer Street), and the massive industrial areas towards Geelong. Also on the left on this route, watch for the delightful old stone rail station building at Lal Lal, about 40 minutes after North Shore. The normal, more direct route to Ballarat west from Melbourne features a steep climb towards Ballan half an hour to an hour after leaving Melbourne Spencer Street station, with views back over the lights of the city.

Further west, **Ararat** is a centre from which to explore

Victoria's Grampians, Pyrenees and Central Highlands. The only options for travel are via the *Overland* at 01.17, returning to Melbourne at the even less appealing departure time of 03.35. Those wishing to see this part of Victoria, with its many attractions, might consider the V/Line bus as an alternative, there being three services a day (two on Saturdays and Sundays), all connecting with V/Line trains at Ballarat, and continuing west to Great Western, Stawell, Murtoa, Horsham and Dimboola (C 9090a). Ararat station adjoins the town centre. From here until 1981, Australia's then fastest train served **Hamilton**, wool capital of the world and a good centre for a western Victoria stay, now served by bus from Ballarat (2¼ hours), or from Terang or Warrnambool on the West Coast Railway (1hr 40min). (C 9027, 9117; T 452)

Stawell attractions include a unique chiming clock on the town hall tower, a "world in miniature" and the winding Gold Reef mall. This is a good centre from which to explore the Grampians National Park since the former railway to Fyans Creek and the heart of this scenic area was abandoned. **Horsham**, regional capital of the Wimmera, hosts conventions and sporting meetings. Wimmera wool factory is open from 10.00–16.00 all year round.

To the southwest coast

Warrnambool, end of the passenger line now operated by West Coast Railway, features safe wide surf beaches and a lookout from which, from around June to October, the rare southern right whales can be seen coming in to calve in the sheltered waters. The Maritime Village recreates the days of sail. Nearby Port Fairy, Hopkins Falls and Tower Hill Reserve – a tour through an extinct volcano – are among the other attractions which the Tourist Information Centre in Raglan Parade will tell you all about; phone (03) 5564 9837; open 7 days a week).

There is a frequent V/Line service between Melbourne and **Geelong**, Victoria's second city, centre for touring the Bellarine Peninsula and parts of the southwest coast, and a good out-of-town base for Melbourne sightseeing. Trains run approximately every hour from Melbourne to Geelong returning mostly around half past the hour until 21.05 Mondays to Fridays, 20.25 Saturdays and Sundays (C 9023). The last departure to connect with the *Southern Cross* for Sydney or with the *Overland* for Adelaide (until the proposed new station is opened at North Shore) is at 18.25 (Mon–Fri), 18.30 (Sat) and 17.30 (Sun). The *West Coaster* from Warrnambool on Sunday, calling at Geelong at 19.20, reaches Melbourne only 3 minutes before the *Overland* departure – not a recommended connection – but hopefully a stop at North Shore may remedy this problem in future.

Two and three day trips from Melbourne

There are evening trains to most of the places already described, so that stopovers of two or more nights can be made. **Swan Hill**, north of Bendigo and on the River Murray, is interesting and cannot be reached by train on a day trip. Attractions include the re-created pioneer settlement, featuring the largest paddle steamer to operate on the Murray, numerous restaurants, a military museum, and historic homesteads. River cruises operate daily 10.30–14.30. Other historic river centres such as **Echuca** are now accessible only by bus (but still covered by a rail pass). This makes places like Bendigo and Ballarat good centres from which to explore the Victorian hinterland.

Echuca was the scene for filming the TV series *All The Rivers Run*. The first port on the Murray to be reached by rail, it is full of history. See the old wharves of massive red gum logs, the historic buildings, and the art and craft shop. Take a trip on a riverboat or visit Tisdall's winery. The railway shares right of way with the road across the bridge to Moama and Deniliquin, where passenger trains used to go. Bus services (usable by Australpass holders) can still cross to the New South Wales network by this route. The bus connection to Echuca from Bendigo takes 1½ hours. An alternative route, of equal time, is from Murchison East on the rail line to Cobram.

If you have time to spare in Victoria it would be a pity to miss a trip to **Mildura**, a city of flowers and vines on the banks of the Murray near historic Wentworth where the Murray and the Darling meet. Mildura is capital of "Sunraysia" district, noted for its wineries and dried fruits, Hattah Lakes National Park, and the Mildura Workingmen's Club with the longest bar in the world.

An interesting variation on any itinerary is to take a V/Line bus from here to Broken Hill, a useful shortcut if five hours on a bus does not appal you, especially after having to reach Mildura by bus in the first place. A unique geological feature, the Walls of China, at the ancient bed of Lake Mungo, is accessible by day coach tour from Mildura.

For several years the only regular train to Mildura was the *Vinelander*, a pleasant sleeping and sitting car train with buffet, which left Melbourne's Spencer Street nightly, Saturdays excepted, to arrive in "Sunraysia's" capital at breakfast next day. Now there is only a daily bus connection from the train at Swan Hill, but you

can still have a night and most of a day in Mildura if you leave
Melbourne on a Thursday at 17.42 or Saturday at 18.10; returning
to Swan Hill by bus, leaving at 13.15 on Friday or 14.20 on
Sunday. Otherwise, a Mildura trip, with any useful time there at
all, means three full days from Melbourne. Fortunately Mildura is
the kind of place you will happily linger at. (C 9032, 9105)

Bus/rail connections in Victoria

Although V/Line has abandoned many of its former passenger rail
routes, the Austrailpass holder (and to a limited extent the Victoria
Pass holder) may use the following bus services, some of which
augment the rail service on major routes:

Bairnsdale and Orbost	from Sale.
Balranald (NSW), Robinvale and Euston (NSW)	from Swan Hill.
Beechworth, Bright and Corowa	from Wangaratta.
Benalla and Albury	from Seymour.
Daylesford	from Woodend (Bendigo line).
Echuca and Moama	from Shepparton.
Eildon	from Lilydale (on Melbourne Met)
Hopetoun	from Stawell.
Maldon and Maryborough	from Castlemaine.
Portland and Mount Gambier (SA)	from Warrnambool.
Tocumwal and Barooga (NSW)	from Cobram.
Yarrawonga and Mulwala	from Benalla.

Rail operated coaches also provide useful links between some rail
routes:-

Albury	to Cobram
Ballarat	to Camperdown and Warrnambool.
Ballarat	to Bendigo.
Benalla	to Shepparton.
Shepparton	to Pyramid (on the Swan Hill line) via Echuca.

Deadline departures from Melbourne

To make sure you get back in time from wherever you have been
in Victoria, here again are the deadline departures from Melbourne
interstate:

20.05	*Southern Cross*	to Sydney
20.20	*Overland*	to Adelaide

The *Southern Cross* also picks up at Benalla at 21.58 and
Wangaratta at 22.23. The *Overland* may pick up at Geelong North
Shore, time as yet undetermined; or, if you really like catching trains

in the middle of the night (it's the only one there is), at Ararat 01.17, Stawell 01.43, Horsham 02.39 and Dimboola 03.08.

Day and two day trips from Adelaide

Adelaide is not well situated for day trips much beyond the suburban area, but you can go up into the Mount Lofty ranges by local train as far as Belair where there is a natural recreation park. Although the railway continues much further into the ranges, only buses now serve places east of Belair such as Aldgate, Bridgewater and Mt Barker. (T 547, 550 & 552)

The **Coorong National Park** near Meningie, about 60km (37 miles) from Tailem Bend, can be reached by bus from Tailem Bend station on the Adelaide–Melbourne interstate rail route, although bus and train times are such that an overnight stop in Tailem Bend would be needed both on the way there and the way back. For train and bus times see Cooks C 9035, 9123.

TransAdelaide tickets are valid for buses as well as trains but do not cover any travel on the various privately-run bus services which also operate in the metropolitan area.

Two days or more depending on the day, are needed for trips to Port Pirie, Port Augusta or Gladstone, or to the southeast of the state, there being now no regional train services whatever. Highlights of the southeast include the famous vineyards of Coonawarra, left of the Mount Gambier line near Penola, Australia's largest pine forests, and the remarkable Blue Lake of Mount Gambier itself.

Mount Gambier remains linked to the Victorian rail network with regular freight trains, but passengers must now take either the V/Line bus connection from Warrnambool in Victoria, or a private bus from Bordertown – reached around midnight by train from Adelaide, or in the middle of the night by train from Melbourne, or in late morning by V/Line bus from Adelaide (3 hours), or mid-afternoon by V/Line bus connection from Bendigo (5 hours). Whichever way, it is a very long way round, and although an independent arbitrator determined that rail services to Mount Gambier should be restored, there seems little hope of governments honouring former commitments. For full timetables see Cooks C 9035, 9112.

Although South Australia has numerous bus connections to places no longer served by rail, these are not owned or managed by, or contracted to the railway systems and are therefore outside the scope of this book.

Excursions from Perth

From Perth City to **Fremantle**, described on pages 87-89, there are frequent suburban trains from 05.50–23.20 Monday–Saturday, 07.10–20.10 Sunday. Journey time is 20 minutes (C 9037) and this is an easy half day trip with plenty to see.

Rail excursions beyond the suburban system can be taken either on the southwest line to Bunbury or the main trans-continental route to **Kalgoorlie**. Between Perth and Kalgoorlie the *Prospector* trains enable long distance trips to be broken at several places. More gold has been won at Kalgoorlie than at anywhere else on earth, and if your itinerary has not included a Kalgoorlie stopover on the way to Perth it should now be a prime choice for a two or three day excursion to appreciate its real atmosphere. There are comfortable historic hotels where you can stay the night, some just opposite the station. There's another kind of accommodation in Hay Street, just to your right. Coach tour guides will be sure to point it out but be warned – a night there will not appeal to all and it is very expensive.

If in Kalgoorlie during daytime follow Paddy Hannon's golden footsteps to his monument. He was the chap who discovered gold in this area. You can also see the old brewery bearing his name, a historic building but, alas, no longer producing the pale amber fluid. Visit the museum (open 10.30–12.30, 14.30–16.30), Boulder and the "Rattler" train on the Golden Mile, Hainault gold mine and the lookout. The tourist bureau is in Hannan Street, four blocks from the station. Some 40km (25 miles) from Kalgoorlie and 14km (9 miles) south of **Bonnie Vale** railway station is historic Coolgardie, well worth a visit if you are staying in the Goldfields region for a day or two.

For those tourists with a week or more to spend in Western Australia, Westrail's famous wildflower tours are a good way to see the amazing colours of the desert flora. Usually held from August to October, they last a week, but rail passes are not valid. Details from Westrail Travel Centre or Perth Terminal station.

Chapter Nine

New Zealand's Railways

Unlike Australia, New Zealand has long had just one national rail system. This has greatly facilitated reforms and improvements in recent years and has avoided (though not completely) features like the non-connections between trains so noticeable on many other railways. Information is readily available too.

Originally New Zealand Government Railways, the system was corporatised in 1982 and in 1990 was privatised. Together with the Cook Strait inter island ferry operations, the railways were acquired by a new company, New Zealand Rail Ltd. This in turn, in 1993, was purchased by a consortium headed by the US regional railway Wisconsin Central.

Tranz Rail became the official overall name late in 1995 when the company was divided into distinct operating units, all bearing the Tranz logo; Tranz Link is the freight arm of the business, Tranz Scenic the main passenger service name, and Tranz Metro the name of the commuter services in Wellington and Auckland. Headquarters are in the national capital, Wellington, at the railway station close to the town centre.

The whole of New Zealand's main railway system is of 3ft 6in (1067mm) gauge. Part of the North Island Main Trunk Line, between Hamilton and Palmerston North, is electrified, so is the Wellington suburban system and a short stretch through Otira tunnel on the Midland Line of the South Island.

Elsewhere diesel is the motive power, either suburban multiple units, railcar sets, or locomotive-hauled trains. Steam haulage appears on special occasions and on preserved railways like the short Kingston–Fairlight section of the former 140km (87 miles) branch from Invercargill to Kingston on Lake Wakatipu.

Being of less than standard gauge, the New Zealand rail system is not noted for high speeds. In 1985 the maximum permissible running speed on any line was only 90km/h (56mph) but since then track improvements and new bogies on carriages have allowed line speed limits to be raised on some sections.

In 1996 the overall mean speed of all services other than the purely suburban trains of Wellington and Auckland was just under 63km/h (39mph), the fastest complete run being by the Friday night Dunedin to Christchurch *Southerner* in South Island at a fraction under 70km/h (43mph). Slowest, not surprisingly, was the steam-hauled heritage train, the *Kingston Flyer*, at 27km/h (17mph) for its 30-minute run over 13.6km (8.5 miles) of preserved track. Average speeds varied little between the two islands, the fastest North Island service being the *Kaimai Express* from Auckland to Tauranga at 69km/h (43mph).

INFORMATION AND RESERVATIONS

Since Tranz Rail owns very few of the actual railway stations, they are not, except for those in the major cities and at the termini of regular rail services, such as Rotorua, the places at which to make reservations or to obtain tickets. The telephone number of the Central Reservation office of Tranz Rail Limited is (04) 498 3000, extension 43302/3, fax (04) 498 3090, or toll free within New Zealand 0800 802 802. For calls made from outside New Zealand the international dialling country code "64" replaces the initial "0" of the "04" (Wellington) area code. Information on the Interislander ferry is available on 0800 658 999.

Most cities and even small towns in New Zealand have an information and ticketing office; many have more than one (*see* Appendix, page 206).

Outside New Zealand, bookings can be made through offices of Thomas Cook and most other travel agents. Tranz Rail also has agents in various countries around the world (*see* Appendix, page 206, for a list).

If there is an office of the New Zealand Tourism Board in your city or region, that will also be able to help. Details of various New Zealand Tourism Board offices are also given in the Appendix, *see* page 207.

RAIL FARES

Tranz Scenic publishes a comprehensive Fares and Timetables booklet, free of charge, which contains almost all the information a traveller might require except details of suburban trains and InterCity coaches, for which separate timetables are available at main stations and from city coach terminals.

Tranz Scenic fares are unlike those of most other railways,

being more genuinely "market oriented". They do not necessarily alter in proportion to the distance travelled. Also, although the standard of accommodation varies between trains, gone is the traditional distinction between "first class" and "economy" or whatever else second class may be called. Instead, Tranz Scenic sets the fares according to what is offered and what the passenger may seek.

A good example is the fare between Wellington and Auckland. On the daylight *Overlander* the standard adult fare is $129. On the "sit up all night" *Northerner*, with the same seating and taking the same time on the journey, the fare is $109.

On both trains there are also economy, saver and super saver fares, which can have the effect of reducing fares by from 20% to 50%. There are limited numbers of such tickets available and various conditions apply to these reduced fares, such as a requirement to purchase and pay for them a specified period in advance of travel, no refund being payable on cancellation in some circumstances, and free on board snacks not necessarily being offered to those using them, though this appears to depend largely on passenger loading.

Children's fares are approximately 50% of adult fares. Students, war pensioners and senior citizens (called Golden Age – meaning 60 and over – in New Zealand) also enjoy discounts. Discount and concession fares may be purchased only in New Zealand.

For visitors who like to be partly organised, Tranz Scenic offers a wide range of packages which include train and coach travel, accommodation and other activities such as wine tasting, bush walking, rafting and jet boat riding. Examples range from day-return trips to the Waitomo caves from Auckland ($99) to the Wild West two-day round-trip package from Christchurch at $349 including accommodation.

The "Queenstown Connection" is a special package allowing travel from Christchurch to Queenstown or vice versa in from one to six days, at a one-way cost of $134. This covers the *Southerner* train between Christchurch and Dunedin, the *Taieri Gorge* train to Pukerangi, and the Pacific Coachway tour from there to Queenstown. Accommodation costs are not included if stops are made at Queenstown or en route.

The following specimen fares should enable the traveller to determine whether a New Zealand Travel Pass, described below, is a better bargain than having separate tickets.

Standard adult single (one-way) fares

Valid in 1996. All fares in New Zealand dollars, subject to checking prior to travel.

Auckland	to Hamilton	$33.00	$28.00 on *Northerner*
	National Park	$66.00	$56.00 on *Northerner*
	Palmerston North	$103.00	$87.00 on *Northerner*
	Wellington	$129.00	$109.00 on *Northerner*
	Tauranga	$49.00	
	Rotorua	$59.00	
Wellington	to Palmerston North	$28.00	$24.00 on *Northerner*
	Napier	$63.00	
	Picton	$44.00	*via* Interislander ferry
Christchurch	to Picton	$59.00	
	Greymouth	$74.00	
	Dunedin	$61.00	
	Invercargill	$97.00	
Dunedin	to Invercargill	$41.00	

Tranz Scenic also offers combination fares covering rail and ferry journeys between places in North Island and South Island and numerous day excursions at special rates.

Special through fares

Auckland	to Christchurch	$138.00
Wellington	to Christchurch	$69.00

These fares do not apply to travel on the *Lynx* fast ferry service.

Some day excursion return (round-trip) fares

Tauranga	to Auckland	$69.00
Auckland	to Rotorua	$83.00
	Otorohanga	$55.00
Christchurch	to Greymouth	$99.00
	Timaru	$42.00
	Oamaru	$59.00
Wellington	to Napier	$88.00
	Palmerston North	$39.00
Invercargill	to Dunedin	$57.00

The New Zealand Travelpass

The New Zealand Travelpass is of two types; the 3-in-1 Travelpass and the 4-in-1 Travelpass. The 4-in-1 type includes a domestic flight on Ansett New Zealand Airlines, useful if you plan, for example, a north to south tour ending up in Dunedin or Invercargill and having to return to Auckland. The 4-in-1 Travelpass costs $205 more than the 3-in-1 version.

The Travelpass is of the flexible variety, covering from 5 days travel over a period of validity of 10 days, up to 22 days travel over

8 weeks, the prices (valid to September 1996) ranging from $350 to $690. Children's fares are two thirds of the adult fare. The Travelpass includes a book of discount vouchers (called a Sightpass) for various sightseeing attractions such as glacier walks, cruises, meals and Maori concerts. More to the point, and especially valuable to the traveller, the pass covers not only rail journeys on Tranz Scenic, but the Interislander ferries and InterCity coaches.

There are two main bus companies in New Zealand; Newmans Coachlines and InterCity Coachlines. References to coach connections in this book are confined to InterCity Coachlines unless otherwise stated – not that this suggests any superiority of one over the other – but that it is prudent for the visitor with a Travelpass to take advantage of buses on which an additional fare does not have to be paid. InterCity Coachlines covers most of New Zealand; for information phone toll free within New Zealand 0800 731 711.

The Travelpass does *not* cover the suburban or inter-urban rail services operated by Tranz Metro in Auckland and Wellington.

The New Zealand Travelpass may be purchased from any Tranz Scenic ticketing agent or the Tranz Rail travel shops in Wellington or Christchurch. For reservations and enquiries within New Zealand call toll free 0800 802 802.

NEW ZEALAND TRAINS

Tranz Scenic trains are air conditioned and all journeys require reservation. As is common with airlines, there is a check-in time for trains, usually 15 minutes before scheduled departure, although it is difficult to see how this can be applied at the many unstaffed stations at which Tranz Scenic trains call. On all Tranz Scenic trains luggage is restricted to two items per passenger, which should be checked into the baggage compartment at the station of origin. Additional hand luggage may be taken into the carriages. Bicycles may be taken on trains for a charge of $10 subject to space being available: pre-booking is advised. Animals other than seeing-eye dogs are not permitted and radios and cassette players must be used only with earphones. Smoking is not permitted on trains, except in the special circumstances of the *TranzAlpine*, as noted in its entry on page 164 below.

Some places are "restricted" stops (either for picking up only or setting down only) or "conditional" stops (where the train only stops on prior request for confirmed bookings). Where the letter (c) follows a place name given in this book, it means there are some such restrictions, about which intending passengers should always enquire before attempting to travel to or from those places.

The Overlander
Auckland–Wellington

Not to be confused with Australia's *Overland* (Melbourne–Adelaide) which is sometimes wrongly called the "Overlander", New Zealand's *Overlander* is a new day train introduced in 1992 to replace the ageing and rather inadequate *Silver Fern* railcar set as a day train between Auckland and Wellington.

Departs Auckland 08.50, Wellington 08.40 daily; 681km (423 miles) in 10 hours 40 minutes, calling at Middlemore (c), Papakura (c), Pukekohe (c), Huntly, Hamilton, Te Awamutu, Otorohanga, Te Kuiti, Taumaranui, National Park, Ohakune, Waiouru, Taihape, Marton, Fielding, Palmerston North, Levin, Otaki, Paraparaumu (c), and Porirua (c).

Pride of the North Island Tranz Scenic fleet, the *Overlander* is loco-hauled (sometimes electrically between Hamilton and Palmerston North) and consists of comfortable carriages, with reclining seating on a 2+2 layout with centre aisle, most seats facing the direction of travel. Although the carriages seem almost new they date, like most of TranzRail's rolling stock, from the 1930s/40s era but have been extensively refurbished with new bogies, new sides, windows, roof, seating, furnishing, lighting, and amenities such as drop down tables, ceiling lights, overhead reading lights and luggage racks. The windows are curtained but not double glazed. The luggage racks are not very commodious but there is also a luggage van into which bulky items can be placed at the beginning of the journey and reclaimed later at the station of disembarkation. There is also space at the ends of the carriages for some additional items, such as travelling wardrobes,

Old style toilets, open to the track, have been replaced by the retention style, although the toilet paper dispensers tend to defy all but the most determined attempts to persuade them to give up any of their contents! Probably only the carriage ends, couplings, under-frame, and entrance doors remain of the former carriages. Similar refurbishment is being carried out to all the Tranz Scenic passenger rolling stock; differences can still be observed between different trains. The exceptionally large windows particularly facilitate scenic viewing. In this the *Overlander* is somewhat reminiscent of Switzerland's *Panoramic Express*, but has far better catering.

Complimentary snacks and lunch are included except sometimes to passengers travelling on super saver fares. The free lunch
is small but adequate and well presented – a bit like the better
economy airline meals. Other refreshments, including substantial
fork meals, and drinks can be obtained at the licensed bar or served
at seat. Typical menu items are hot roll, curried chicken and rice,
savoury potato and meals of the day. Beer costs $3, wine $5 for a
quarter bottle and the meals range from $3 to $7.50. Lion Red beer
is typical New Zealand, somewhat akin to Britain's Newcastle
Brown Ale, unlike Australian beer which is more like German or
Dutch lager.

A commentary is given on points of scenic and other interest,
and a mobile phone is available for hire at a modest charge. There
is usually an observation lounge in the rear carriage. The seats in
this lounge are not bookable, and some passengers will sometimes
seek to monopolise the space available.

The Northerner
Auckland–Wellington

Daily; 681km (423 miles) in 10 hours 40 minutes, calling at the
same stations as the *Overlander*. An overnight train without sleeping
accommodation which Tranz Scenic wisely and honestly advertises
as providing "a comfortable journey for the budget-conscious
traveller". The seating is described as "reclining airline-style"
which it is, but like all such seating, whether on airlines, trains or
coaches, is designed essentially for daylight travel, not sleeping.
Complimentary snacks are offered and there is a buffet, though
without any bar service. In all other respects, the *Northerner* in
1996 is the *Overlander* on a night run, the only New Zealand rail
service in which the standard of comfort and amenities has fallen
over the last ten years.

The Bay Express
Wellington–Napier

Daily; 317km (197 miles) in just under 5½ hours, calling at
Porirua (c), Paraparaumu (c), Otaki, Levin, Palmerston North,
Woodville, Dannevirke, Ormondville, Waipukurau, and Hastings.

A train of refurbished rolling stock replacing the former
Wellington–Gisborne *Endeavour* service. Loco-hauled, with carpeted
carriages, table and at seat service, buffet and bar, informative
commentary, mobile phone, and some complimentary refreshments. The seating may differ from that on the *Overlander*, such as
having seats facing across tables instead of all facing the same

way. The same exceptionally wide windows are fast becoming characteristic of Trans Scenic rolling stock. In 1992 the *Bay Express* became the first New Zealand reconditioned train to include a rear observation lounge.

The Geyserland
Auckland–Rotorua

A journey of 275km (171 miles) taking just over 4 hours. One of two new trains introduced in 1992 (the other was the *Kaimai Express*), the *Geyserland* restored passenger rail service to North Island's thermal wonderland, obviously in an attempt to attract tourist traffic to an area which had not seen regular passenger trains for over two decades.

The former *Silver Fern* railcars, made redundant by the introduction of the *Overlander* between Auckland and Wellington, were redeployed to the Rotorua and Tauranga routes after refurbishment. The fleece-covered seats give a distinctive New Zealand flavour to this train, echoing the fleece-covered creatures seen thronging the track-side grassy slopes. The seats recline; they are in a 2+2 formation with a pitch of 99cm (39in), comfortable enough for medium distance travel as on the routes on which they are now used, but with rather hard armrests. The seats face the direction of travel, the windows are large and well spaced in relation to the seats, and the train is air conditioned. A mobile phone is available for passenger use. It is brought to your seat and costs $2 for the service, plus $1 per minute on connection.

Departs Auckland 08.20 and Rotorua 13.05 daily, with an additional Friday and Sunday service at 12.55 returning at 17.50, the *Geyserland* calls at Middlemore (c), Papakura (c), Pukekohe (c), Huntly, Hamilton, Morrinsville, Matamata, Putaruru, and Rainbow Springs (c). Complimentary morning and afternoon teas are served at seats. Light meals and bar service (beer, wine, spirits and soft drinks) are also available. There is a commentary on points of interest.

The Kaimai Express
Auckland–Tauranga

Daily; 236km (147 miles) in $3\frac{1}{2}$ hours, calling at Middlemore (c), Papakura (c), Pukekohe (c), Huntly, Hamilton and Morrinsville. This train consists of refurbished *Silver Fern* railcar stock and apart from its destination and the final part of its route is otherwise indistinguishable from the *Geyserland* – in fact one train becomes the other on arrival at Auckland daily. The *Kaimai Express* offers "supper" (on the evening run) as well as afternoon tea. The supper on one occasion when I travelled consisted of a piece of cake plus tea or coffee or fruit juice, the same as morning or afternoon tea.

The Capital Connection
Palmerston North–Wellington

A commuter express running Mondays to Fridays only, operated by Tranz Metro. Departs Palmerston North 06.20, returning from Wellington at 17.17; 136km (84 miles) in 2 hours southbound, 2hr 10min northbound. Locomotive-hauled with mixed rolling stock. Seats in different coaches may vary, some refurbished, others not; some similar to main line Tranz Scenic stock but others more typical of ordinary suburban carriages. A small buffet bar operates rather sporadically, since the buffet attendant doubles as ticket collector which takes a considerable part of his or her time.

Calls at Shannon, Levin, Otaki, Waikanae, and Paraparaumu, where it connects with a Tranz Metro Paraparaumu express serving some other suburban stations.

The Wairarapa Connection
Masterton–Wellington

Another commuter express, diesel-hauled, with five return services on Fridays, two on Saturdays and Sundays, and four daily on other days. These trains mostly run express between Waterloo (Hutt Central) and Upper Hutt on the electrified section of the Tranz Metro system. Calls at other stations vary with some conditional stops on some trains at certain times. The 91km (57 miles) is covered in 88-96 minutes with 9-12 intermediate stops.

The Coastal Pacific
Picton–Christchurch

A journey of 347km (216 miles), taking 5 hours 20 minutes. Departs Picton 13.40 and Christchurch 07.30, calling at Blenheim, Seddon, Kaikoura, Mina, Waipara and Rangiora. Connects with the Interislander ferries leaving Wellington at 09.30 and Picton at 13.30. The train is similar in consist to the *Overlander,* but without the observation lounge (though this may soon be added). A "backpacker" car is sometimes a feature of this train, which carries many people to and from the Cook Strait ferries. This is a car set aside for people on super saver fares. While they may not obtain free refreshment packages, they have equal access to the buffet, in which excellent value "meals of the day" such as chicken chasseur can be obtained, with wine at startlingly reasonable prices in spite of impositions like New Zealand's Goods and Services Tax.

The refreshment package even includes a little refresher towel. Such thoughtful touches help make New Zealand trains pleasantly surprising and a welcome change from the worst traditions of railway catering.

The Southerner
Christchurch–Invercargill

Departs Christchurch and Invercargill at 0830, a 589km (366 miles) journey in 8 hours 50 minutes, calling at Ashburton, Timaru, Oamaru, Palmerston, Dunedin, Mosgiel, Milton, Balclutha, Gore, Mataura and Edendale. The schedule varies on Fridays, with the 08.30 from Christchurch terminating at Dunedin (from where a coach connection runs to almost the same timetable as the train) and a later service leaving at 17.15, arriving Invercargill 02.30 next day. In the return direction the Friday train leaves at 06.20 and is supplemented by a train from Dunedin at 17.00, reaching Christchurch at 22.35 (no bus connection from Invercargill). The *Southerner* is the oldest remaining part of the former New Zealand Railways fleet and appears to be the last to be refurbished. In other respects it matches the other Tranz Scenic services in comfort and amenities.

The TranzAlpine
Christchurch–Greymouth

Departs Christchurch 09.00, Greymouth 14.25, calling at Rolleston, Darfield, Sheffield (c), Springfield, Mt White Bridge (c), Bealey Bridge (c), Arthur's Pass, Otira, Jacksons, Inchbonnie, Moana, Kokiri (c), and Stillwater; 231km (143 miles) in 4 hours 25 minutes outbound, 4 hours 10 minutes return.

Once threatened with extinction, this train in the late 1980s had only two or three coaches and very little about it to attract custom. Through the imagination and determination of a local rail-worker its potential was recognised and the name *TranzAlpine Express* was adopted in 1987. Since then, as its rolling stock and its amenities have been improved, patronage has steadily increased. In 1996 eight or nine carriages, including an open observation car and two buffet cars, has been a typical consist, and there are few vacant seats. All round, the current *TranzAlpine* is recognised as the premier passenger rail service not only of the South Island but of the whole Tranz Scenic fleet, and in my view fully merits ranking as one of the top ten train journeys of the world.

The *TranzAlpine* has wide picture windows, seating in 2+2 formation mostly facing between tables, and in the middle of the train (or at one end depending on the number of carriages used) there is an open observation car. This is formed from the power car, the ends of which are open to the elements like a cattle truck. Passengers stand in the breeze to enjoy not only the sight but the sounds and smell of the scenery – and smokers can here enjoy a crafty "drag" which is prohibited everywhere else on New Zealand's trains.

An informed and helpful, sometimes amusing or quirky commentary by the train manager enhances the trip, while the buffet serves the standard Tranz Scenic fare but with extras. The variety in the "blackboard" meals of the day seems greater than on other trains. There is a variety of beers, and wines are offered in quarter, half and full bottles at prices that are quite remarkable in light of normal off-licence (bottle shop) prices, and even by comparison with the prices on trains in Australia, where wines in general are substantially cheaper than in New Zealand.

The Kingston Flyer
Kingston–Fairlight

A tourist steam train operated by Tranz Rail between Kingston and Fairlight, 14km (8.7 miles) in 30 minutes. Runs twice daily between October and April. Includes heritage buffet car and 1898 "birdcage" compartment carriage with leather seats. Kingston is not served by InterCity Coachlines, but is a 45 minute bus journey by several operators from Queenstown at a fare of $13 (C 9803). The nearest station on Tranz Scenic is Invercargill, from where there are also private buses taking 1¾ hours at a fare of $28.

Taieri Gorge Limited
Dunedin–Middlemarch

A journey of 76km (47 miles), taking 2-2½ hours including sight-seeing stops. Runs daily to Pukerangi (57km/35 miles) in summer (September–April inclusive) with less frequent services the rest of the year, and to Middlemarch only on Sundays from October to mid-March plus some extra runs in December and January. Diesel-hauled train with buffet and carriage-end observation platforms. Carries bicycles. Connects with buses to and from Queenstown.

Current fares: Dunedin–Pukerangi $28.50 one way, $45 round trip; Dunedin–Middlemarch $31.50 one way, $49.00 round trip; with reductions for YHA members and students. Each adult may take one child free of charge. Additional children $9.00. Bookings can be made at Dunedin Railway Station, P O Box 140, Dunedin; phone (03) 477 4449, fax (03) 477 4953.

Suburban trains

The **Auckland** suburban system of Tranz Metro consists of three routes, Auckland to Waitakeri (30.4km/18.9 miles), Auckland to Papakura (33.7km/20.9 miles) and Newmarket to Westfield (9km/5.6 miles), a total of 73.1km (45.4 miles), served by one-class diesel multiple units from Auckland station on Mondays to Saturdays at better than hourly frequency from around 06.00 to 19.00 hours. Almost all trains stop at every station.

Wellington has a much more developed suburban system, including the two outer urban commuter services described earlier. The principal route is part of the main North Trunk Line to Paraparaumu (48km/30 miles). Other routes are along the Hutt Valley to Upper Hutt (32km/20 miles) with a 3km (1.8 miles) branch to Melling. Finally, there is the 10.5km (6.5 miles) Johnsonville line, originally part of the main trunk, which climbs into the ranges above the city almost like a Swiss mountain railway. There is also a genuine funicular railway, the Kelburn Cablecar, which links the heart of downtown Wellington with the University area and the botanical gardens above.

Trains for the enthusiast

For the rail enthusiast, apart from the *Kingston Flyer* and *Taieri Gorge Limited*, there are tours operated by Steam Incorporated, based at Paekakariki near Wellington (*see* next chapter, page 176), while at Burkes Pass in the foothills of Mount Cook National Park there is a half kilometre (550 yards) 7¼ in (184mm) gauge "sit on top of the carriages" miniature railway with a 2-6-2 steam locomotive based on one that ran in the northeast USA in the 1920s.

New Zealand has the only preserved and restored Fell engine in the world at Featherston on the North island. This locomotive formerly operated on the nearby Rimatuka Incline, closed in 1955 when it was replaced by the 8.8km (5.5 mile) Rimatuka Tunnel. The Museum is located in the town, open 10.00–16.00 Saturdays and Sundays (13.00–16.00 Sundays May–September) or phone (646) 308 9777/9780 at other times. Featherston is 57km (35 miles) from Wellington on the Wairarapa line.

Chapter Ten

A Comprehensive Tour of Kiwi Rail

This chapter begins with an itinerary describing a comprehensive tour of almost all of New Zealand's passenger lines and many of the major locations in both the North and South Islands. This is followed by a description of the highlights of such a journey, including the Christchurch–Greymouth *TranzAlpine Express*, one of the greatest rail journeys in the world.

Itinerary 14

Fifteen days travel which can be spread over anything up to five weeks with a 3-in-1 New Zealand Travelpass. Commencing and ending in Auckland, with stopovers in Rotorua, Tauranga, Otaki, Napier, Wellington (three), Christchurch (three), Invercargill, Dunedin, and Greymouth, covering all passenger rail routes in New Zealand except the *Kingston Flyer* and private society lines. The travel days are not necessarily consecutive. The term "nightstop" may cover more than one night as desired. The itinerary is confined to rail trips, apart from the Interislander ferry. All journeys are subject to advance reservation.

Day		Programme		
Day 1	Dep Auckland	08.20	*Geyserland*	
	Arr Rotorua	12.25	nightstop	
Day 2	Dep Rotorua	13.05	*Geyserland*	
	Arr Huntly	15.44	3 hours free[a]	
	Dep Huntly	19.09	Kaimai Express	
	Arr Tauranga	21.05	nightstop	
Day 3	Dep Tauranga	08.05	*Kaimai Express*	
	Arr Hamilton	09.28	change trains	
	Dep Hamilton	10.50	Overlander	
	Arr Otaki	18.15	nightstop	
Day 4	Dep Otaki	09.12	*Bay Express*	
	Arr Napier	13.20	nightstop	
Day 5	Dep Napier	14.20	*Bay Express*	
	Arr Wellington	19.45	nightstop	
Day 6	Wellington	suburban rail & sightseeing[b]		
Day 7	Dep Wellington		Interislander ferry	
	Arr Picton		change to train	
	Dep Picton	13.40	*Coastal Pacific*	
	Arr Christchurch	19.00	nightstop	

Day		Programme		
Day 8	Dep	Christchurch	08.30	*Southerner*
	Arr	Invercargill	17.20	nightstop
Day 9	Dep	Invercargill	08.30[c]	*Southerner*
	Arr	Dunedin	11.45	2½ hours free
	Dep	Dunedin	14.30	*Taieri Gorge Railway*[d]
	Arr	Pukerangi[e]	16.35	
	Dep	Pukerangi[e]	16.45	*Taieri Gorge Railway*[d]
	Arr	Dunedin	18.30	nightstop
Day 10	Dep	Dunedin	11.45[f]	*Southerner*
	Arr	Christchurch	17.15	nightstop
Day 11	Dep	Christchurch	09.00	*TranzAlpine*
	Arr	Greymouth	13.25	nightstop
Day 12	Dep	Greymouth	14.25	*TranzAlpine*
	Arr	Christchurch	18.35	nightstop
Day 13	Dep	Christchurch	07.30	*Coastal Pacific*
	Arr	Picton	12.50	change to ferry
	Dep	Picton	13.30	Interislander ferry
	Arr	Wellington	17.05[g]	nightstop[h]
Day 14	Dep	Wellington	08.40[h]	*Overlander*[h]
	Arr	Auckland	19.20[h]	
Day 15		Auckland	suburban rail & sightseeing[b]	

[a] Option of changing at Hamilton or continuing on to Auckland or one of its outer suburban stops, subject to advance booking.

[b] The cost of any Wellington and Auckland suburban trips is not covered by the New Zealand Travelpass.

[c] Except Fridays.

[d] Not covered by Travel Pass. Check days of running (C 9802a).

[e] Middlemarch is a possible alternative, depending on day & season.

[f] On Fridays depart 09.35, arrive Christchurch 15.05.

[g] Ferry arrives at terminal 35 minutes earlier; bus from ferry is 20 minutes later on Mondays.

[h] Option of taking overnight train from Wellington at 19.45 on Day 13, arriving Auckland 06.45 next day. No sleeping berths.

WHAT TO SEE FROM THE TRAIN
North Island

Auckland, the "City of Sails" (it has more sailing boats and yachts per head than any other city on earth) is probably the first place the visitor to New Zealand sees – unless they have travelled by Kiwi Air or some other charter airline using Hamilton as base port, or unless they have come into Wellington or Christchurch on a flight from Australia or one of New Zealand's Pacific near neighbours.

This brief travelogue will assume Auckland as your starting point. On the way into the city from the airport, watch out for the famous One Tree Hill, a dormant volcano like most other hills around the city. Some bright larrikin tried to chop the tree down a few years ago, making headlines around the world.

Auckland station is one of those sad reminders of the former glories of rail. It is too much on the edge of the central area, and although airport and other buses serve it well, it has a depressing emptiness and isolation about it. A new station closer to the town centre is proposed. In the meantime, Auckland station is a place to get away from, whether by Tranz Scenic or Tranz Metro. Not that there are many suburban services left – basically two destinations, Waitakere on the north and Papakura on the south, although there are two routes to the latter. The local train service consists of diesel multiple units which somehow look older than they probably are. They tend to rattle, and the furnishing is somewhat spartan.

Nevertheless, the service has improved immeasurably over the past decade. In 1985 there were 20 daily trains on weekdays on the main suburban line to Papakura, with 10 more going half way, to Otahuhu via the longer route of the main trunk line through Tamaki. None ran express and there was no weekend service at all. Ten years later the total had increased to 40, with most going all the way, alternately following the two different routes, and including morning and evening commuter expresses.

On the north of the city the improvement has been still more dramatic. Little more than a peak hour service of only eight trains a day has increased to 21. On both routes Saturday services have been introduced. A consequent increase in patronage has been noted. (C 9752)

Scenes from the train in Auckland are mostly disappointing. The main trunk route south passes through some residential suburbs rather lacking in character, interspersed with industrial buildings and yards. The shorter alternative route runs mostly parallel to a freeway. The suburban line to the north is more interesting. First stop is Newmarket, an inner city commercial area where the train reverses out of the station before turning onto the North Auckland line. It then winds through the attractive semi-rural environment of West Auckland suburbs, past busy suburban shopping areas at New Lynn and Henderson, to the terminus at Waitakere, 30km (19 miles) from Auckland.

The suburban railway network certainly serves commuters but it is possibly not the best way for the visitor to see the many and

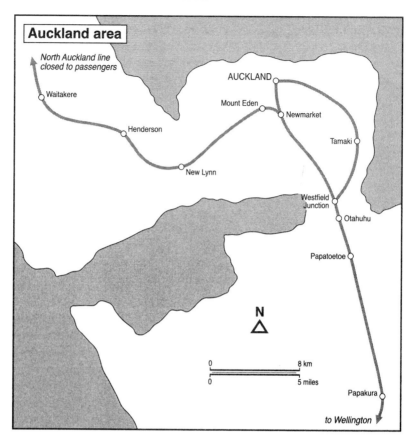

varied attractions of this colourful and thriving city, New Zealand's largest, in which one can actually walk across New Zealand from the Pacific Ocean to the Tasman Sea in three hours. Walking is popular and encouraged in Auckland, provided you don't mind climbing hills; the only level parts are reclaimed land near the water! Waitemata harbour, which includes a ferry terminal, is half a kilometre (550yd) north of the railway station, while Onehunga Wharf on Manukau harbour is 12km (7.5 miles) to the south.

Great views of the city, its harbours and beaches can be obtained from the Centennial Memorial Park or from the top of Mount Eden, By contrast, the railway station at Mount Eden bears the ravages of graffiti artists to an extreme degree, perhaps in an effort to hide its otherwise near derelict appearance.

Nearer at hand (1½km or about one mile from Auckland station) is the Domain, an extensive park area containing winter gardens, natural bushland and the Auckland War Memorial Museum, which holds some of the finest Maori and Polynesian anthropological and ethnological exhibits in the world.

Going south on the main trunk line the suburbs are soon left behind, but main line Tranz Scenic services can be joined at Middlemore (18.5km/11.5 miles) or Papakura (33.7km/20.9 miles), the limit of the suburban rail system.

After Pukekohe, the main line swings east to follow the Waikato river upstream, the countryside faintly reminiscent of Ireland in the upper reaches of the Shannon. This area is known as the Whangaramino wetlands. Look out for the Meremere power station, New Zealand's biggest, 20km (12 miles) south of Pukekohe near Mercer, and then Lake Waikare on the left just south of Te Kauwhata, 37km (23 miles) and about half an hour after the stop at Pukekohe. Here the river, New Zealand's longest, is on the right (assuming you are facing the way the train is going).

Hamilton is the major stop on this route, being the junction for the lines to Rotorua and Tauranga. The new station lies within the angle of the junction and is called Hamilton Frankton, being just south of Frankton yard where the motive power changes over to electricity. The original Hamilton station was on the branch at Hamilton Travel Centre 1.7km (one mile) from Frankton Junction and was in a tunnel. It was closed because it had become a haunt of undesirables at night, when it was presumably unmanned. East of the old station the line to Tauranga, known as the East Coast Main Trunk, crosses the Waikato River on a 144m (157yd), 21m (69ft) high bridge.

Morrinsville is the next station, the junction for the freight only Thames Branch, and is in the heart of lush farming country, said to be the most fertile in the world. Between Morrinsville and the first stop on the Rotorua branch, Matamata, the train speeds over fairly flat farmland. Allowed 24 minutes for an easy 30km (19 miles), the train has ample recovery time built into its schedule. This allows it to make up any time lost by waiting to cross freight or timber trains from Rotorua or the Kinleith branch at passing loops on the single track.

Waharoa, a depot for New Zealand Co-operative Dairy, is the junction where the Rotorua line branches from the East Coast Main Trunk and, after more dairying country, comes to the small station of Putaruru where it leaves the Kinleith branch with its timber traffic and starts its climb over the Mamaku volcanic plateau. Here the gradient is 1-in-35 and from about 15km (9 miles) before Rotorua, as the train winds down the range, an excellent view of Lake Rotorua may be seen to the right ahead.

The current station at **Rotorua** is about a kilometre short of its former terminus in town. A shuttle bus operates, at a fare of $2, to meet arriving trains and to collect railway passengers from town. The station here is not staffed by Tranz Rail but is run (unpaid) by a local society, the Second Chance Trust, dedicated to bringing back steam trains to the scenic route between Rotorua and Mamaku. Jill at Rotorua station asserted: "It's the smallest, cleanest and friendliest station in New Zealand – at least we reckon so".

To spend only the hour or so between arrival and departure of the *Geyserland* daily train is unthinkable – although it is surprising how many people you can meet who are doing just that. However, the additional Friday and Sunday services allow five hours in the area, time to see some of its main attractions such as the thermal wonderland of Whakarewarewa, but a whole day or more is really needed – Rotorua has so much. The Tourism Centre is at 67 Fenton Street; phone (07) 348 5179.

Beyond Waharoa junction the East Coast Main Trunk line turns sharply left to enter the Kaimai tunnel through the mountain range of that name. New Zealand's and the Southern Hemisphere's longest tunnel at 8.85km (5.5 miles), this was opened in 1978, shortening the distance between Hamilton and the East Coast by over 50km (30 miles). New Zealand's railways are noted for tunnels; there are 180 altogether, totalling approximately 100km (62 miles) in length.

Immediately west of the tunnel the track crosses the 230m (250yd) Wainui viaduct, 34m (112ft) high, then skirts the wonderful coastal sedgeland country of Tauranga harbour. Most unusual, to British or Australian visitors, are the hedges or narrow windbreaks of pines or similar tall evergreen trees, very narrow, in single rows, but close together and 10-15m (30-50ft) high. New Zealand farmers seem to be more aware of the dangers of wind erosion than those in most of Australia. Gorse, pampas grass, and daisies beside the track are other features of plant life in this part of the world.

At **Tauranga**, motels, pubs, cafés, shops etc. all adjoin the railway opposite the station, while on the other side is the seafront of the Bay of Plenty. Flannagan's, the "Irish" pub, is good for an impromptu evening of amateur musical entertainment. Tauranga station is unmanned except when the train is in. This makes it difficult to "check in" 15 minutes before it is scheduled to leave if it does not arrive from the sidings somewhere east of the station much before departure time. However, this train staff are friendly and helpful, baggage is taken care of, seat allocations checked, and orange juice is served immediately on departure. Newspapers are available for sale – a feature of most New Zealand trains.

On the main trunk line south from Hamilton the next brief stop is **Te Awamutu**, now unmanned but formerly allegedly the busiest station in New Zealand, with extensive cattle sidings and continual rail activity. The only sign of animal life on a recent visit (not counting a local character repairing a motor truck in the yard) was a litter of puppies in a makeshift enclosure, yelping for attention and apparently in constant danger of jumping out onto the platform or track.

The next stop south is **Otorohanga**, a good place for a break of journey or a day excursion from Auckland, arriving at 11.30 and leaving again at 16.35. From the railway station there is a connecting shuttle bus to the famous Waitomo limestone caves ($14 round trip, not including caves entry fee). For information, phone Waitomo (07) 878 7640 or Otorohanga (07) 873 8951.

Te Kuiti, the next stop, at 205km (127 miles) from Auckland, marks the start of the railway's climb into the central mountain ranges of North Island. In this area the scenery is very rugged, somewhat reminiscent of the mountain ranges of northern Spain but greener, with little gullies and broken ridges and hillocks, an ever undulating skyline. Some parts are rather like the fells of Lakeland in Britain but much more broken. It is altogether a unique landscape. Little terraces of grass on the mountain slopes show evidence of soil creep, and everywhere there are sheep, sheep, sheep, in their millions.

At **Okahukura** the New Plymouth branch turns away to the west. Closed to passengers since 1983, this 191km (119 miles) line follows a tortuous route along mountain ridges to Stratford, on the slopes of Mount Egmont, before descending to the coast. En route, it passes through 24 tunnels, four of which are over a kilometre (0.6 mile) long. If any excursions on this line are advertised, they would be well worth taking.

Taumarunui, in the heart of the central highlands, reached after successive crossings of the Ongarue river, is another place suitable for a break of journey, being within day round trip distance (283km/176 miles) of Auckland. The railway station adjoins the main street, among hotels, shops and cafes.

Still climbing, 39km (24 miles) further south and 421m (1,380ft) higher in the mountains, the train reaches the famous Raurimu spiral, where it first negotiates a horseshoe bend to the left, before climbing through the spiral itself with its two tunnels. The scenery near Raurimu spiral provides a wide panorama of very broken, mostly green, undulating sheep farm country with a backdrop of mountains of ever changing shapes. Palmetto type ferns, brambles, gorse, broom, bracken, foxgloves and yellow lupins are the most noticeable among plant life.

National Park, where the north and southbound *Overlanders* cross, is the next station. The train is now nearing the summit. Seen off to the left is Mt Ruapehu, North Island's highest at 2,897m (9,508ft), often snow-covered even in summer.

After crossing the 262m (287yd) Makatote viaduct, the disused station of Pokaka, and the smaller Mangaturuturu viaduct, the train attains the highest point on New Zealand railways, at 814m (2,672ft). Shortly after this, the line crosses the new reinforced concrete Hauawhenua Viaduct, opened in 1987 as part of the Main Trunk electrification project of the 1980s, 414m (453 yd) long and 51m (167ft) high. The old viaduct, which may be seen from the train, is kept as a historic structure and used as a platform for bungy jumping.

The descent from the mountains is more gradual, averaging about 1-in-212 down to the River Rangitikei north of Marton as against 1-in-190 up from Te Kuiti to the summit, although much steeper gradients occur in parts, including a 1-in-58 average for the last 20km (12 miles) towards National Park from the north.

Just south of Mt Ruapehu and 17km (10 miles) after the next station, Ohakune, is the former station of Tangiwai, where in 1953 a crater lake overflowed and breached both the railway and the adjoining highway at the Wangaehu River Bridge. The next stop is Waiouru, following which the track twists and turns like a snake to **Taihape**, where a brief stop now replaces the 25 minute lunch break of the old *Silver Fern*.

Between Taihape and Marton the line crosses the deep gorge of the Rangitikei River by a series of high viaducts and bridges; the Toi Toi Viaduct, only 59m (194ft) long but just as high; North Rangitikei Bridge 181m by 77m high (198yd by 252ft); Kawhatau Bridge 181m by 72m high (198yd by 236ft); South Rangitikei Viaduct 315m by 75m high (345yd by 246ft); Makohine Viaduct 229m by 73m high (250yd by 240ft); and the inevitable crop of tunnels. From Marton to Palmerston North is comparatively easy going, 44km (27 miles) taking exactly 44 minutes including an intermediate stop at Fielding.

Palmerston North is one of New Zealand's major cities. It is also an important station on the railway, marking the southern end of the Main Trunk electrification, the junction for the Gisborne line and the outer urban terminus of the Tranz Metro system of Wellington. There is therefore a choice of trains between Palmerston North and the capital, as summarised in the following table.

Palmerston North and Wellington

C 9750 and local

All trains have refreshment service and most require reservation.

Dep Palmerston North	05.18	06.20[b]	17.20	17.35
Dep Levin	05.56	06.56[b]	17.54	18.09
Dep Otaki	06.17	07.16[b]	18.15	18.30
Arr Paraparaumu[a]	06.38[c]	07.37[b]	18.40[c]	18.52[c]
Arr Wellington	07.35	08.21[b]	19.30	19.45
Dep Wellington	08.00	08.40	17.17[b]	19.45
Dep Paraparaumu	08.52[d]	09.33[d]	18.10[b]	20.36[d]
Arr Otaki	09.12	09.54	18.34[b]	20.57
Arr Levin	09.32	10.14	18.53[b]	21.17
Arr Palmerston North	10.14	10.55	19.27[b]	22.00

[a] Interchange for Tranz Metro suburban services.

[b] Mondays to Fridays only.

[c] Calls to set down only.

[d] Calls to take up only.

In Itinerary 14, **Otaki** is suggested as one possible nightstop, if travelling to Napier the following day. Palmerston North, Levin or Paraparaumu could equally serve this purpose. Otaki is suggested partly because the times of arrival and departure are convenient for dinner and breakfast, partly because there is sensibly priced accommodation adjoining the station (the Railway Hotel – what else?) and many travellers prefer a small town to a large city. For those deciding on a longer stay, Otaki beach is just 3km (1.8 miles) from the railway. Main line trains may not stop at Otaki unless booked in advance – or unless the train staff are warned at one of the previous stations.

If continuing by train into Wellington (though this is best covered in either direction on a morning run), note Kapiti Island off the coast opposite Waikanae, just before Paraparaumu. There is another good view of the island between Paekakariki and Muri.

Paraparaumu marks the start of the suburban electric system, and from here on into Wellington the coastal scenery is superb, the railway line on some stretches being as close as you can get. They call it the Golden Coast, starting just south of Paekakariki, the first stop on the Tranz Metro after Paraparaumu. A railway preservation group, Steam Incorporated, is based at Paekakariki, where there is a railway museum and vintage rolling stock may be seen in the sidings. Between Paekakariki and Muri the railway goes along the side of a steeply sloping cliff behind the foreshore. Below it the road follows the cliff base. There are many tunnels on this section.

South from **Paremata** the line skirts the picturesque harbour of Porirua. Paremata was an American naval base during World War II.

After Porirua (a conditional stop for main line trains) the railway leaves the Tasman coast, cutting inland to plunge into the Tawa tunnels, the first of which in this direction (known as No.2 tunnel since the numbering starts from Wellington) is New Zealand's fourth longest at 4.32km (2.69 miles). The tunnels were opened in 1937, replacing the original mountainous route via Johnsonville opened in 1885.

Bursting out of the No.1 tunnel there is a great view of the harbour, but it is on a different side. The train has crossed the North Island from the Tasman to the Pacific and the view is of Lambton Harbour and Port Nicholson, Wellington.

The original trunk line is still in use as far as Johnsonville, a winding, climbing route through seven tunnels to a terminus only 10.5km (6.5 miles) from Wellington (only 6.5km/4miles as the crow flies) but 140m (460ft) above. As a suburban line this is most unusual and scenic. The lineside is festooned with wild flowers. The catenaries are supported on timber stanchions, the seven intermediate stations are all close together and houses in the suburbs near them are perched high up above the track, with access by steep paths. Johnsonville is a 50 minute return trip from Wellington and the service is half hourly or better. (C 9751)

The other Wellington suburban service is to the Hutt Valley, the main stations being Hutt Central or Waterloo, and Upper Hutt. At peak periods express services augment the normal half hourly frequency and there are a few longer distance services out to Masterton, 91km (57 miles) from the capital (the *Wairarapa Connection* referred to in Chapter Nine). Upper Hutt is 32km (20 miles) from Wellington. Stopping trains take 50min and expresses 41min on the trip. A three kilometre (1.8 miles) branch from Petone to Melling has a peak hour service only. (C 9751)

No visit to Wellington's rail system would be complete without a trip on the Kelburn Cable Car, a one metre gauge railway which runs for 628m (687yd) from its base on Lambton Quay (the name of one of the town centre's principal streets, not an actual wharf, although only three blocks from the harbourside) up the hill to the Botanic Gardens, passing Victoria University, which has its own intermediate station, on the way. There is a restaurant at the top station, and fine views over the city and across to Mount Victoria. Even finer views are obtained from Mount Victoria's summit at 167m (506ft), but this is unfortunately not linked by cable car or other railway.

Wellington, as New Zealand's capital, has many other attractions. The Wellington Visitor Information Centre is at 101 Wakefield Street (Civic Square), just over a kilometre (0.6 mile) from the railway station – there are frequent local buses. The phone number is (04) 801 4000, and fax (04) 801 3030.

Day trips by train from Wellington can cover all the Tranz Metro network, north up the main line as far as Ohakune, also by the *Bay Express* to Woodville, Hastings or Napier.

The Napier line branches from the North Island Main Trunk just beyond Palmerston North, from where it swings east through a pass between the Tararua Range on the south and the Ruahine Range on the north. Through this pass flows the Manawatu River, giving its name to the resultant steep sided gorge in which the railway generally hugs the left bank (travelling east or upstream) with the road on the right. The gorge is not unlike some valleys in the Italian Alps or Dolomites, although the mountains are much lower. Landslides are a frequent hazard affecting the highway where loose scree slopes abut the road edge. In the middle of the river there is a rock with a red top – said to be the blood of a Maori Chief. The *Bay Express* observation lounge is a good place to be for viewing this part of the route.

Beyond Woodville, where the line is joined by a former passenger route from Wellington to Palmerston North via Masterton, the valley opens out and the railway runs between the Ruahine and the Puketoi Ranges to **Dannevirke**, a useful turning point for a day or two-day excursion, with the convenient Merrylees Hotel just opposite the station.

Numerous viaducts are a feature of the line north from here to Takapau, 87km (54 miles) from the junction with the Main Trunk line. Most dramatic of all of these is the Ormondville Viaduct, immediately north of Ormondville station where the train calls at 11.35 northbound and 16.07 on the return trip. Ormondville Viaduct is 281m (307yd) long with the rails 39m (128ft) above the valley floor.

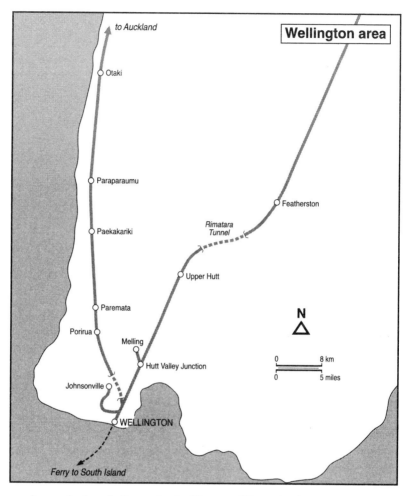

An early lunch from the buffet car (if stocks have not run out, as they sometimes can, and did on the writer's last trip when a party of Japanese unexpectedly consumed the lot) will take you to Hastings, the last stop before the turnaround at Napier. Hastings is very much industrial; the railway here becomes double track and serves the Hawkes Bay Fruitgrowers, Nelsons (New Zealand) Ltd, and the Hawkes Bay Farmers Meat Co. Ltd at nearby Whakatu. The Whakatu industrial park is something of a blemish on the scenery of Hawkes Bay – but short-lived when passing on the train. The industrial landscape north of Hastings soon gives way to extensive apple and pear orchards and vineyards. Hawkes Bay is the most prolific wine-producing region of New Zealand, noted especially for its dry whites, and also produces excellent dry cider.

The railway station at **Napier** has been moved by some half a kilometre south from its original position in the days when it was a refreshment stop on the *Endeavour Express* to Gisborne. Trains still go to Gisborne on special occasions – this is a highly scenic and dramatic route which finishes up with a run across the airport runway. The new Napier station is nevertheless handy for local amenities and if you are unsuccessful in obtaining a meal on the train there is just time for a quick one (a counter lunch that is!) at a hotel within a stone's throw of the station.

Napier is worth far more than an out-and-back rail trip, however. Imported deciduous trees from Britain line some of the main streets. Adjoining the seafront on Marine Parade is a statue which is dedicated to a legendary but true character famed in Napier's history, Pania of the Reef. The model for the bronze figure, a local schoolgirl, could certainly have had a career in modelling or films, had she lived these days!

South Island

While freight is taken aboard the Cook Strait train ferries in railway wagons, this is not the case with passenger cars. There is no need, at least with the train schedules as now and as they have existed for many years. With trains arriving and departing at Wellington in the North Island in the morning and evening, and arriving and departing around midday at Picton in the South Island, an immediate connection or an overnight stop in Wellington is indicated.

The crossing of the Cook Strait on one of the Interislander ferries or on the *Lynx* is in fact one of the highlights of travel by Tranz Rail. Scenically, it is a ferry journey with few equals anywhere and in terms of amenities, the Cook Strait ferries offer everything that would be expected on an ocean liner; restaurant, cafeterias, bars, shops, cinema, video games, play areas and, of course, comfortable seats in saloons and on deck where the ever changing scenery of the crossing can be enjoyed.

The *Lynx* is a 74m (240ft) catamaran, operating as a high speed summer ferry service. Crossing time is 1¾ hours instead of the normal 3 hours or 3 hours 20 minutes depending on which of the two "regular" ships is used, the facilities are a little more limited, and there is a surcharge of $8 for Travelpass holders.

The crossing of Cook Strait follows a winding course, first sailing east into Port Nicholson from the Interislander ferry terminal (reached by complimentary bus from Wellington railway station), then turning south between the heads, Sinclair Head on the west and Baring Head on the east, west across the strait, passing Cape Terawhiti to starboard and heading roughly west by north for the narrow entrance to Tory Channel between the mainland of South Island and Arapawa Island. Turning northwards again, the ship enters Queen Charlotte Sound, where a south westerly course is set for Picton Harbour. So that whether you are on deck breathing the salt air, or in the cinema (a bit of a waste, surely), relaxing in the saloon or chatting to fellow travellers in the bar, there need never be a dull moment on this sea crossing.

At Picton a courtesy bus again awaits passengers for the short ride to the station, where the train is ready waiting.

Between Picton and Blenheim are mountains both sides of the railway, with forests of conifers, rushing streams, rocks, colourful broom, gorse, and daisies with eagles or hawks floating lazily overhead.

Blenheim, the first stop, reached in half an hour, is the centre of the South Island's vineyard district, home of Marlborough wines. Sauvignon Blanc from this district is particularly fine but Marlborough Riesling is also great and Marlborough Cabernet Franc is a promising red – obtainable on the train.

South of Blenheim, at **Seddon**, the train crosses a double deck bridge where the railway is on the top deck with the highway below, so that in case of flood the highway is closed and the railway keeps going, evidence of sound thinking on the part of the early engineers!

The railway then crosses Lake Grassmere where salt is produced – and its presence is very evident. The lake adjoins Clifford Bay and Tranz Rail is understood to be making some investigation into a possible shortened sea crossing by constructing a new ferry port in this area. This would by-pass much attractive scenery, both on the crossing and on the rail route, not to mention the town of Blenheim. No doubt economic aspects will have to be considered against social, environmental, tourist and other factors.

South of Lake Grassmere the railway runs along a narrow strip of land between the Kaikoura Ranges and the coast, kilometre after kilometre of blackish pebble beaches, reminiscent of the black sands of Papeete on Tahiti – but a little colder! Rocks and kelp break the surface, yet hardy characters in wetsuits can be observed struggling against the surf.

Although the railway hugs the coast in this area some parts of the coast on this stretch may seem dull – but if the scene looks flat and uninteresting on the seaward side one has only to look to the mountain hinterland on the west, where snow capped peaks will likely be towering in the distance.

Kaikoura, once a dismal "refreshment stop", marks a change in scenery. Here the coast is broken by promontories and islands. The Kaikoura Peninsula dominates the scene, and the views are memorable both to the seaward and landward. Whale watching is a year-round attraction at Kaikoura. Dolphins may also be seen in summer, along with hundreds of fur seals sunbathing or grooming their fur.

The view of Kaikoura Peninsula and bay is outstanding when viewed from the railway just north of the 975m (1,067yd) Amuri Bluff tunnel, for which it is best either to be facing the rear of the train, or travelling north. Scenic appreciation is not an exact science, despite many attempts by landscape architects to classify and evaluate scenery of different kinds. However objective one tries to be there remains the subjective element, personal to the viewer, and while there are undoubtedly scenes over which most normal people would gasp with wonder and pleasure, there are always those like the alleged English Lakeland farmer, mystified by a visitor effusing over the scenery, who said "There's nowt but hills and trees and watter!"

John Price, in various issues of the *Thomas Cook European Timetable*, has listed rail journeys he considers the finest scenically. But much depends on where one is looking at what time, and which way the train is going. This may explain why I personally have formed the opinion that the scenery of the *Coastal Pacific* route is better seen travelling north than south.

At Ferniehurst, 143km (89 miles) north of Addington (Christchurch) the bridge crossing over the Conway River marks the boundary between Canterbury Province to the south and Marlborough to the north. There is no town named Marlborough, which visitors can find confusing. The railway between the Conway River and Kaikoura is especially scenic. About 6km (4 miles) north of the Conway River mouth, the train crosses the 21m (69ft) high Okarahia Viaduct, then plunges immediately into the Amori Bluff tunnel, exiting to hug the foot of the limestone cliffs almost on the water's edge past the little township of Oaro on Goose Bay.

On this section of line, the most difficult encountered during the construction period in the 1920s, the road had to be pushed out over the beach by landfill to make room for the railway. The line hugs the coast rather like Britain's Great Western coast line near Dawlish in Devon. But Goose Bay is unlike the Devon sands. Dark masses of seaweed, with shags dotted around on the rocks, mark the scene seawards, while on the landward side, where the cliffs do not obscure the view, the Seaward Kaikoura Range dominates the horizon.

Just south of Kaikoura, between Goose Bay and Kowhai, are nine short tunnels in succession. At one point there are three together through the base of a cliff, but not all are railway tunnels; the railway has one, and there are twin tunnels for the adjoining road. To seaward you may catch a glimpse of a tiny rock island known as Riley's Lookout. Riley was a noted whaler. Ask the train attendant to tell you the story.

When starting north from Christchurch on the *Coastal Pacific* route, the countryside is comparatively uninteresting before **Waipara**, the second stop, reached in just under an hour. Waipara will be noticed by rail enthusiasts; there is a collection of old locomotives and rolling stock to the east of the station. North of Waipara, the track moves further inland, climbing between hills which are rather bare of vegetation, the countryside very much reminiscent of the Cheviots of Northumberland in England. Indeed, the line from Addington to Parnassus was originally called the Cheviot Branch and place names are suggestive of England's north: Scargill, Greta, and Cheviot itself. Even the sheep could be on the Northumberland Fells. Approaching Mina, 120km (75 miles) north from Addington there are views of distant Tapuaenuku Mountain, 2,885m (9,469ft), in the Inland Kaikoura Range, ahead left, which would never be noticed on a southbound journey.

Christchurch, regarded as the most English city outside England, has been laid out on more of a grid street pattern (quite un-English!) than Wellington or Auckland, where the topography tends rather to get in the way. It is a clean city, well endowed with parks and with the Avon River (named after that in Christchurch's namesake city in Hampshire) winding through its centre. Until 1976 there was a suburban rail service on the 10km (6 miles) branch to Lyttleton Harbour. This, and the Main South Line from Christchurch was originally built to the 1600mm broad or "Irish" gauge (in fact Christchurch to Lyttleton was combined 1600mm and 1067mm until 1877).

Christchurch is New Zealand's second largest city and until recently, when limited charter flights have begun using Dunedin, had South Island's only international airport.

The Coastal Pacific crosses the Okarahia Viaduct immediately before the Amuri Bluff tunnel, Marlborough Province, South Island. (TR)

Above left: *The* Overlander *climbs the Raurimu spiral section of its route across the North Island.* (TR)

Above: *Railway motifs on a stained- glass window at Dunedin's elaborate station* (RS)

Left: *The decorative exterior of Dunedin station, completed in 1907 to a design by the future Sir George Troup.* (RS)

Far left: *Travellers on the* Taieri Gorge Limited *enjoy a break in their journey at The Notches viewpoint.* (RS)

*Dramatic volcanic scenery is one of New Zealand's many attractions. This is
Mount Tarawera, a short distance east of Rotorua.* (RH)

The railway station moved recently from its location south of the central area to Addington, 3km (1.8 miles) from Christchurch, at the junction between north and south lines and on a former workshop site. Day trips can be made by train to Ashburton, Timaru, Oamaru and Palmerston on the south line, to Greymouth in the west and anywhere up to Picton in the north.

The country around and particularly south of Christchurch is known world wide as the Canterbury Plain, characterised by large sheep stations, the field boundaries often marked by healthy dark green shelter belts, and famous for succulent Canterbury lamb which, oddly enough, seems hard to find in New Zealand itself.

When compared with the north line, with its views of dramatic coastline, cliffs, and high mountains, the south line, by general consent, is "relatively unspectacular" as Geoffrey Churchman and Tony Hurst put it in their book *South Island Main Trunk* (IPL Books, 1992). There are nevertheless many points of interest, both to the rail fan and to the general sightseer. The coast from just north of Palmerston to Dunedin is varied and attractive, alternating between bays and headlands, with some excellent beaches. However, these are unfortunately inaccessible to the rail traveller, since the stations adjoining them are closed.

Approaching and beyond Waikouaiti, 14km (9 miles) south of Palmerston the coast is varied, very rugged and hilly from Merton to Seacliffe where the line climbs from almost sea level up to the Puketeraki tunnel at 63m (207ft), then descending past Seacliff and Warrington to Evansdale, where it follows the shore of Blueskin Bay to Waitati. The beaches near Warrington and at Waitati are most tempting. From almost sea level at Waitati the track skirts the shore of Blueskin Bay, then climbs past Michie's Crossing to Cliffs Tunnel, where it rounds the headland before turning south again, still ascending, to the 1,408m (1540yd) Mihiwaka Tunnel. Emerging above Otago Harbour it slopes down into Port Chalmers, where the Otago Harbour Board wharves are joined by a 2km (1.25 miles) branch to the Main South Line at Sawyers Bay.

From Port Chalmers to Dunedin the railway follows the north side of Otago Harbour. Until 1979, a suburban service operated on this part of the line.

Dunedin, the Edinburgh of the south, is a historic city, and the influence of early Scottish settlers is still felt in this region. It is certainly a place to break the journey, if only to travel on the Taieri Gorge line, owned and operated by Dunedin City Council.

I am indebted to writer Roy Sinclair of Christchurch for the following description of the **Taieri Gorge Railway**.

"Anyone who has ridden above the Animas Canyon on the narrow gauge Durango and Silverton Railroad in North American Colorado, is likely to feel at home on the Taieri Gorge Railway in Central Otago. This railway is often called "the Colorado of New Zealand". A 63km [39 miles] section is used to run the Taieri Gorge Limited, a tourist train making regular departures from Dunedin. Features of the railway include deep river gorges, several tunnels, and iron and steel viaducts. Many structures, including bridge piers, are made from the distinctive Central Otago schist stone.

"The full length of the Otago Central Railway, 236km [147 miles] from Wingatui Junction (12km [7.5 miles] west of Dunedin) to Cromwell, was built over a 42 year period starting from 1879. It was intended as transport to the goldfields, but as with most of the world's railways built for this purpose, the gold rush was over long before the railway got there.

"In its last years the railway served to supply construction materials to the huge Clyde Dam hydro project which was destined to flood the last section of the railway through the Cromwell Gorge. These days just the 63km [39 miles] of the line, between Wingatui and Middlemarch, remain. Luckily, this is the best part and it survives because, in 1990, it was purchased from the government by the Dunedin City Council. Trains on the Taieri Gorge Railway are operated by the Otago Excursion Train Trust which owns several restored turn-of-the-century vintage carriages, three new carriages built by the Trust, and a small fleet of Japanese-built Dj class diesel-electric locomotives of 1960s vintage.

"Regular trips to Pukerangi or Middlemarch depart from Dunedin's magnificent Edwardian station throughout the year. When the TGR summer timetable is in use (September to April), afternoon trips connect with the Tranz Scenic *Southerner* service from Christchurch. A return [round] trip from Dunedin to Pukerangi (the name is Maori and translates as "Hill of Heaven") lasts about four and a half hours.

"That such wild spectacular country exists so close to a large city never ceases to amaze visitors. An informed commentary, photo stops, a chance to walk across a high viaduct or visit the remnants of an isolated railway construction camp, and a well-stocked licensed buffet, are among the delights of taking the *Taieri Gorge Limited* which is an excellent train in every respect. Photographers, especially, can enjoy the trip by getting great shots from the open platforms at each end of the carriages.

"If you have seen the spectacular alpine scenery from the *TranzAlpine Express* further north, you will also enjoy an equally spectacular, but quite different ride, on the Taieri Gorge Railway. But allow time to look over Dunedin's splendid railway station, also owned by the Dunedin City Council.

"The granite and bluestone station, built to a Baroque design between 1904 and 1907, is meticulously decorated. Heraldic lions crouch at the uppermost corners of the 39m [128ft] southern tower, mosaic tiles adorn the entrance hall, and stained glass windows with railway themes are well worth seeing. The design was by a Scot, 21-year-old George Troup – later Sir George Troup – who went on to become a respected New Zealand Railways' designing engineer. Troup also supervised the construction of the station, but despite his efforts to save considerable sums of money, his work was criticised by Dunedin's strong Scottish element. Even the lavatories were said to be far too lavish!"

The main south line continues past Wingatui Junction a further 211km (131 miles) to **Invercargill**, the present terminus of the passenger line, though only just over a decade ago, trains ran on a further 24km (15 miles) south from there to Bluff. Some of the landscape of the Invercargill region is suggestive of Scottish upland scenery. Enterprising locals have even produced a whisky, "45 South", which is closer to the real thing than most other imitations of the famous *usgiebeatha*.

The approach to Invercargill station is not the usual expected assortment of warehouses, scrapyards, sidings etc. but through an attractive park.

Invercargill lies at 46 degrees south – claimed to be the farthest south of any railway station in the world, though Bluff would hold the true honours if still operative. Railways in the Northern Hemisphere, however, extend much closer to the Pole. Latitude 46 north is only the level of Lausanne in Switzerland, and most of Canada lies north of this line!

Christchurch to Greymouth – The Midland Line
Keeping the good wine to the last, no visit to New Zealand, whether touring by rail or any other mode, would be complete without a journey on the *TranzAlpine* route across South Island from Christchurch on the Pacific coast, westward to Greymouth on the Tasman Sea. This is unquestionably New Zealand's finest rail journey, and is attracting visitors from all over the world. It is much like a trans-continental trip, although it takes only four and a half hours. The round trip can easily be achieved in a day.

So much has been written recently extolling the merits of this route that a detailed description of the journey in this guide would be superfluous. Geoffrey Churchman's book *The Midland Line – New Zealand's Trans-Alpine Railway* (IPL Books, first published 1988) has run to four editions and the journey is one of the 30 "most exciting rail routes" of the world described in the British Automobile Association's publication *Train Journeys of the World* (1993, revised 1995).

The journey has to be experienced. It is far different in 1996 from what it was ten years previously. The scenery is the same, but the train, its amenities – and the presentation – have improved out of recognition.

The train was inaugurated under the name *TranzAlpine Express* in 1987. Before that, the passenger service between Christchurch and Greymouth was pathetic. Following the process of attrition so widely practised when managements lack imagination or incentive, the train was not widely advertised, and had no amenities whatever, not even drinking water. Seats and toilets, yes, but no catering on board. The journey of over five hours included two refreshment stops, both of uncertain, unspecified, and certainly inadequate length.

November 1987 changed all that. With refurbished, comfortable, well furnished carriages, an improved schedule, quality food and drink service – and the scenery still as dramatic as ever – the *Tranz Alpine* certainly merits ranking, in my view, as one of the top ten rail journeys in the world today.

Leaving Christchurch at the comfortable hour of 09.00, the train follows the south line to Rolleston Junction (20km/12.5 miles), where it turns northwest to cross the Canterbury Plain up to Springfield on the Waimakariri River. This is crossed on the 205m (224yd) Big Kowai Viaduct.

Springfield was one of the original refreshment stops, and when the train started carrying its own buffet, it was not only the passengers that enjoyed the refreshments available. Rosie, a border collie dog, began meeting the train and was rewarded with a day-old railway meat pie. This intelligent and enterprising animal was able to distinguish passenger from other trains (the line carries heavy coal traffic, its original *raison d'être* and – perhaps until recently – economic mainstay). Keith Williams, the dog's owner and a former railwayman, calculates that the dog must have eaten at least 7000 pies since 1987. The dog coming for his pie became one of the unusual highlights of the trip, but the animal was old,

130 years in human equivalent, and died in April 1996, an event recorded in many newspapers outside New Zealand. You can still see the place where Rosie was fed and can still buy meat pies to eat on the train. Perhaps soon another dog will take her place.

After Springfield the mountain country really begins; tunnels, viaducts, gorges, in seemingly endless succession. Snow capped mountains loom ahead. Beside the track bloom wild flowers, blue and pink lupins, flashes of yellow broom. By the banks of the streams are willow trees. The mountain pastures have an alpine look, but it is different from the Alps of central Europe. The rivers, the Waimakariri which the line follows upstream from Springfield to Staircase Viaduct and again from Cass to Arthur's Pass, and the Taramakau, which the line follows after the Otira tunnel as far as Inchbonnie, feature wide areas of silt and in places where the railway crosses it has the appearance almost of arctic tundra. But equally often, the rivers are crossed in deep gorges by high viaducts. Some of these have high fences on one side. These are windbreaks, and unfortunately briefly spoil some of the views for photographers.

Between the Kowai Viaduct and Avoca, 25km from Springfield, there are 16 tunnels and four viaducts; Patterson's Creek, the longest, at 37m (121ft) high; Staircase Creek, 72m (236ft) high; Broken River, 55m (181ft) high, and Slovens Creek, 39m (128ft) high. From Avoca past Craigieburn to Cass, about 20km (12.5 miles), the train crosses bleak country somewhat reminiscent of Glencoe or Rannoch Moor in Scotland. One can almost imagine highland warriors with their claymores descending to do battle with rival clans.

After Craigieburn the ascent of the Southern Alps steepens, the elevation rising from 461m (1,512ft) above sea level to 579m (1,900ft) at Cora Lynn after again crossing the river, then to the summit of 737m (2,419ft) at Arthur's Pass. With surrounding peaks towering over 2,200m (7,200ft) the most dramatic section of the line, engineering-wise, begins as it plunges into the Otira tunnel at a descending gradient of 1-in-33. This was New Zealand's first electrified railway in 1923.

Emerging from the tunnel, the railway follows the Taramakau River past Mount Alexander down to Jacksons, renowned for a pub that allegedly sold possum pies. The train is now in Westland, or the West Coast, where the rivers flow down to the Tasman Sea and the weather may be totally unlike what it was at the start of the journey on the other side.

At Inchbonnie the line turns north past Lake Poerua to Lake Brunner, a popular fishing spot occupying a large hollow carved out by former glaciers. A track-side sign at Moana on the shore of Lake Brunner warns that "Trespassers may be prosecuted" – not "will" as it always seems to be in Britain even though legally they can never be prosecuted merely for trespass, only sued.

Much of this route is accessible only by rail. After Moana the line descends past extensive forests of southern beech (*nothofagus*) trees to Stillwater on the Grey River, and so down to Greymouth itself.

Greymouth is worth more than an hour's pause between trains. Apart from its own attractions, the old harbour, the flood wall, the rusting railway bridge, still used by trains from the mines north of the river, and the old pubs, perhaps of most interest to visitors is the chance of a coach trip (if staying at least one night) down the west coast to the Fox and Franz Josef Glaciers.

Useful bus connections

InterCity buses, covered by the New Zealand Travelpass, serve the following major destinations not on the railway:

Fox & Franz Josef Glaciers	from Greymouth (C 9803)
Gisborne	from Napier (C 9759)
Mount Cook	from Christchurch (C 9803)
Nelson	from Picton & Blenheim C 9806)
New Plymouth	from Hamilton & Palmerston North (C 9759)
Queenstown	from Dunedin (C 9803)
Taupo	from Rotorua & Napier (C 9759)
Te Anau	from Invercargill (C 9803)
Thames and Coromandel	from Hamilton (local)
Wanganui	from Palmerston North (C 9759)
Westport	from Greymouth (C 9803)
Whakatane and Opotiki (Bay of Plenty)	from Rotorua (C 9759)
Whangarei, Kawakawa & Kaitala (Northland)	from Auckland (C 9754)

InterCity coaches also link Rotorua with Taihape (North Island Main Trunk) via Taupo three times daily, a 4½ hour journey (C 9759), as well as Rotorua with Napier via Taupo as noted above.

Chapter Eleven

Preparing for the Unexpected

The first edition of this book left the would-be traveller out somewhere in Western Australia among the wild flowers. It is easy in a vast continent to lose track of time and of where you are, and more importantly, of how long it will take you to get back. This chapter, among other things, tells you how much time you will need to allow (barring emergencies like floods, strikes, breakdowns, and so-called "Acts of God" – why blame Him? – which we hope you would have insured yourself against before travelling) – to reach your port of departure to be sure of catching your plane or ship home the next day.

Remember Murphy's Law: "If anything can possibly go wrong, then it will."

After all, you can easily forget. You might become so enchanted with the beauty or romance of some place, or so engrossed in talking to the friendly locals and listening to their yarns, or so enjoying the culinary delights or the cold beer or the wine, or you may have met a congenial companion, possibly of the opposite sex, and be living in such a dream world that time ceases to have meaning – at least to the extent that you miss the train you meant to return on.

You could well mistakenly assume there is another train an hour or two later (as there could have been in the country you came from) but this would be rash indeed in Australia and even in New Zealand, so deceptively small that you might think a train would be waiting just round the corner. Instead, the next train might not be for a whole day, or in Australia even a week, and even then it could be late, or fully booked.

That alone, however, may not be the problem it first seems.

Overcoming booking difficulties

Advance reservations are required on all principal Australian and New Zealand trains and are essential at some seasons of the year (school holidays especially) if you wish to avoid disappointment. Many long distance trains can be booked up to 12 months in advance and most others at least one month in advance. A traveller from overseas with limited time in which to use an Austrailpass or New Zealand Travel Pass would be wise to seek bookings at least two months in advance for key journeys. Shorter distance travel can usually be booked a week or two in advance but some trains, particularly on weekends, may be fully booked. Key journeys on such trains as the *Indian Pacific* (Sydney–Adelaide–Perth), *The Ghan* (Adelaide–Alice Springs), the *Brisbane XPT* and the *Murwillumbah XPT*, the *Sunlander* (Brisbane–Cairns) and New Zealand's *Overlander* and *Northerner* (Auckland–Wellington), *Coastal Pacific Express* (Picton–Christchurch) and the *TranzAlpine* (Christchurch–Greymouth), must also be planned well ahead but, as in other countries, you can sometimes obtain a seat or berth without prior booking. It depends on the time of year and the route.

Australian holidays vary from state to state. January is the worst month when many firms regularly close down and schools are on holiday everywhere. This is of course the height of the southern summer. New Zealand also has holidays (like Waitangi Day, 6th February) you may not know about until you suddenly find places closed you expected to be open.

Extra coaches are added to some trains when booking is heavy, and occasionally relief trains may be advertised locally. These may not have the usual catering and in New South Wales when booking is heavy any relief service is more likely to be by bus (some are even regularly scheduled).

Passengers wishing to avoid this sort of experience should make their requirements clear at the time they make reservations. Advance booking is possible on those relief trains which run fairly consistently at certain periods. These and others are listed in the table below, and it is worth asking about them if you are facing booking problems.

Relief trains operating in holiday periods
Australian interstate

| Relief *Ghan* | Adelaide | 14.00 | Mondays | to Alice Springs |
| | Alice Springs | 14.00 | Tuesdays | to Adelaide |

A Saturday departure from Adelaide, returning on Sunday is also possible at periods of peak demand, though departure times may vary.

Queensland

| *Reeflander* | Rockhampton | 18.10 | Mondays | to Cairns |
| | Cairns | 10.00 | Wednesdays | to Rockhampton |

This has not been advertised recently. Enquiry necessary.

New South Wales
An overnight version of the *Tablelands Xplorer* may operate on Fridays and/
or Sundays but recent experience suggests this is more likely to be a bus.

New Zealand
The *Lynx*, a Christchurch–Picton express train connecting with the fast
catamaran Picton–Wellington ferry (also named *Lynx*), operates in the
summer only.

Alternative routes and trains

The holder of an Austrailpass, or other valid pass, always has the
option of changing destination or route – even though the change
may necessitate re-booking. A fully booked train, whether relief or
regular, is not therefore an insuperable obstacle. Go somewhere
else, change your itinerary. The chances are the train you wanted
may have seats or berths a day or a week or two later. If not, your
options are more restricted but, with a few exceptions, you may
still be able to go where you want although it will doubtless take a
little longer. Alternative routes are unfortunately very few, and
have become fewer still in recent years.

In Australia, extensive closures of secondary routes in the early
1970s, again in the early 1980s and between 1989 and 1994 have
left a basic network which is little more than one long curving
spine with a series of dead end branches.

New Zealand has lost the former North Island links between
Masterton and Woodville and east coast link through Stratford during
the same period, but services have been restored on North Island
branches from Hamilton to Tauranga and Rotorua.

Even where there is only one train on a particular section it is
often possible to find one seat for part of the journey and another
for the rest of the way. If you are anxious to be on the move the
minor inconvenience of changing seats half way through the journey
should not deter you. So press your case and do not be put off just
because they say the train is fully booked!

Except when a scheduled train is diverted because of flooding,
major engineering work or some other similar emergency, the few
alternative routes which remain open are used only by freight
trains or special excursions. North of Townsville or west of Port
Pirie there are no alternative routes at all, so if the line is blocked
you may just have to wait. But the lack of an alternative route does
not necessarily mean that if the principal through express, the
obvious first choice the travel agents told you about, is fully booked,
there is no other train. On some parts of some long distance routes

there may be other services you can use – services the average tourist would not know about and that the railway booking offices might not think of telling you about.

Dealing first with the most restricted routes, the options are these.

Australia

Perth–Kalgoorlie Between Perth and Kalgoorlie (the western-most part of the transcontinental Perth–Sydney route served by the *Indian Pacific*) there is the *Prospector* six days a week in each direction between Perth and Kalgoorlie. Operating in daytime, this service enables the traveller to avoid one night on the long distance trains in each direction and it is in the sleepers that the most critical shortages of accommodation occur.

Kalgoorlie–Tarcoola Between Kalgoorlie and Tarcoola, over the Nullarbor, there is no real choice since passenger accommodation was withdrawn from the "Tea and Sugar". However, some of the fast freight trains have accommodation for truck drivers. A trip on one of these lacks the comfort of air-conditioning, dining car, and bar, but tourists who experience it would probably look back on it as a highlight of their trip. Whatever head office says, Australian railwaymen will not willingly abandon tourists in the middle of the Nullarbor and, if you find yourself stranded at somewhere like Cook (by being crook or jailed, for example), then by all means go and see the railway people before you phone for a charter plane!

Tarcoola–Adelaide Between Tarcoola and Adelaide, the *Ghan* is an alternative to the *Indian Pacific*, giving a choice of trains, sometimes two within a few hours of each other. While this may be just as heavily booked as the *Indian Pacific,* remember that if you have a first class Austrailpass you have the option of travelling holiday or economy class if all the first class berths are booked.

Shorter Australian National trips For shorter daytime journeys on Australian National, such as between Adelaide and Port Pirie or Broken Hill, you may even be allowed to occupy space in the lounge car. On some sections of the trans-Australian route it was formerly possible to book such accommodation but this would not now be permitted except in an emergency. If you don't need a sleeper they can almost always find room for you in the buffet or lounge car. See the chief conductor (or train manager as they are nowadays mostly called) and explain your predicament. They are a friendly crowd on Australian National.

Broken Hill–Sydney Between Broken Hill and Sydney there is the added choice of the *Central West XPT* (Dubbo–Sydney with bus connection to and from Dubbo), which operates daily in each direction and the new, once weekly, *Outback,* a Broken Hill–Sydney loco-hauled Countrylink train, though this operates overnight and has no sleeping accommodation.

Adelaide–Sydney Passengers wishing to travel between Adelaide and Sydney who are unable to book on the *Indian Pacific* can instead travel via Melbourne, using the daily *Overland* and *Olympic Spirit* services which connect.

Melbourne–Sydney Between Melbourne and Sydney the traveller has two main options: the daytime *Olympic Spirit* or the overnight *Southern Cross*, both XPT, the latter with a limited amount of sleeping accommodation.

However, there are other alternatives covering parts of this route. V/Line operates day services between Melbourne and Albury and State Rail of NSW has several trains between Goulburn and Sydney. Breaking the journey in two places is therefore a viable option, and very convenient if a side trip to Canberra is also considered. There are coach services also linking Albury (Wodonga) with Canberra which increase the options if you don't mind several hours on a bus.

Since March 1995 Countrylink has also run an extra service once a week between Goulburn and Junee in each direction, which leaves only the Albury–Junee section with no alternative to the interstate trains other than the bus.

Sydney–Brisbane Between Sydney and Brisbane there are quite a number of options except for the most northern part of the route across the state border. Here the only alternatives for the rail ticket holder to the Sydney–Brisbane XPT are the Countrylink bus connection between the *Murwillumbah XPT* and Brisbane, involving an unattractive two hour trip, or between Murwillumbah and Helensvale, a 70-minute trip, there to catch the QR Gold Coast train which takes only another hour to reach Brisbane, running express from Beenleigh.

There is absolutely no need to endure the tedium of a bus journey between Queensland and northern New South Wales in one go unless you are in a desperate hurry. It can be made less traumatic by breaking it at Surfers Paradise. After all, to visit Australia and not see the famous Gold Coast surfing centre would hardly be right. There are lots of things to do at Surfers besides surfing. Take the launch over to Anglers Paradise on South Stradbroke Island or hire a small boat and cruise around the warm passages of the Broadwater, then perhaps have a meal at one of the many excellent restaurants specialising in the unique Queensland seafood like mud crabs or Moreton Bay bugs.

South of Grafton City, which is 293km (182 miles) south from Brisbane there is the daily *Grafton XPT* which augments the service to and from Sydney. Cityrail and Countrylink services also cover the north coast line as far as Dungog, 245km (152 miles) north of Sydney.

There are long term prospects of extending the *Indian Pacific* to Brisbane, and this is certainly something about which you should enquire as a more attractive option than the XPT.

It is strongly recommended, however, that any Sydney–Brisbane sections of your itinerary be booked well in advance. Although the XPT has limited sleeping accommodation and some semi-reclining seats, it is possible you will have to face the discomfort of a 14 hour sit-up journey. If so, you can plan ways to make it less tedious. Breaking the journey will be found to make even an overnight sit-up endurable and some of the ready made itineraries in this book provide for this. Joining a train around or even after midnight to leave it again just after six in the morning is tolerable once in a while, much more so than sitting in the same upright seat for the whole 14 hours.

When breaking a journey in such a way it is important to note that luggage cannot be checked through from train to bus or vice versa but has to be transferred by hand – one of many inconveniences imposed on rail passengers in New South Wales.

North of Brisbane North of Brisbane there are daily "ICE" trains (as railway people call the *Spirit of Capricorn* inter-city express) to supplement the *Sunlander, Queenslander* and *Spirit of the Tropics* services to Rockhampton, with extra shorter distance services as far north as Gympie, 173km (107 miles) from Brisbane. The twice weekly *Spirit of the Outback* also serves this route and is especially attractive for an overnight Brisbane–Rockhampton trip.

On the rest of the "Sunshine route" there are no alternative services except the weekly Brisbane–Proserpine *Spirit of the Tropics* and the occasional *Reeflander* already referred to. Devious links through inland centres involving limited bus travel and uncertainly scheduled goods trains with some sort of passenger van attached offer different ways for the adventurous to travel between central and north Queensland.

North of Townsville there should never be any real difficulty about accommodation. Even if they tell you the train is fully booked, my advice is to get on and ask for the train manager or a conductor. The chances are it could be half empty for the part of its route you wish to travel. There is now computerised booking and it should be foolproof but there are still traces of the horse and buggy methods used previously. I have known whole blocks of seating to be allocated seemingly irretrievably to different stations of origin, and the operators may not always ask their colleagues the right questions.

Attempting once to book a sleeper from Cairns south on a relief *Sunlander* I was told it was fully booked. There had been a whole car empty when they checked it the night before, but they had "given this away" to Townsville booking office where there was presumably heavy demand. Could they get one berth back, I asked? They did. At Townsville I braced myself for the invading hordes, but they did not materialise. Nor did they further south at Bowen or Mackay. Even after Rockhampton, on the final stretch to Brisbane (which in those days was overnight) the sleeping coach was only half full. So much for computers, if they are not properly used.

Be bold, but polite, and don't take no for an answer!

New Zealand
North Island In New Zealand's North Island the only routes outside the suburban areas of Auckland and Wellington where there are options of different trains are between Auckland and Hamilton, where in addition to the day and night Auckland–Wellington main line loco-hauled services, there are the Rotorua and Tauranga railcar sets, and between Palmerston North and Wellington, where the Wellington–Napier *Bay Express* and the inter-urban commuter train, the *Capital Connection* supplement the main line trains.

South Island There are even fewer alternatives to the main services in the South Island. The *Lynx* (Picton–Christchurch) supplements the *Coastal Pacific* express service in the summer, while in each direction between Christchurch and Dunedin an extra train was introduced in 1996 to supplement the *Southerner* on Fridays.

If in doubt, ask
The railways in all Australian states and New Zealand do tend to look after passengers when things go wrong or when a passenger has no reservation and needs to get somewhere in a hurry, or when

a train is over-booked (though this is a fault much more common on airlines than railways). Buses or even taxis can be laid on in case of emergency or breakdown.

The railways will often go to great lengths to make sure that passengers are not stranded or someone does not miss a vital connection, even in the metropolitan areas. I remember the former *Southern Aurora*, which used to be non-stop from Sydney to Melbourne, once stopping at the suburban station of Strathfield (so close into Sydney that it inspired Keith Garvey's poem: "Never been west of Strathfield, never been very far!"). It stopped, they said, to take on a passenger connecting from Newcastle – yet there was no sign of a recognised connection from Newcastle in the timetable!

On another occasion they stopped the *Ghan* at a forlorn crossing loop, Bolivar, between Port Pirie and Adelaide, to allow a German passenger to cross over to the *Indian Pacific* bound for Perth by clambering down onto the track and across to the next line. The train was not scheduled to connect but he had booked in Germany on the basis of the train's previously advertised times and they did not want to upset his itinerary (which he had planned on the basis of the first edition of this book!). The moral of the story is always to check for the latest information when booking.

Departure deadlines

Apart, then, from when some unavoidable delay occurs, how can you make sure of being back in your departure port in time? Clearly, a knowledge of the timetable is required, or you must ask at the station. This, however (depending on where you are), may not always be manned.

It may be useful for you to have a ready-made check list of deadline departures from the kinds of places you might find yourself lingering in for whatever reason.

In case you had been beginning to think Australia or New Zealand were places you could whip round in a few days (by going on a few fast trains and following some of the more intensive itineraries in this book) you will soon learn differently. Only one bad experience is enough to bring you back to reality. Always remember that if your Austrailpass or other ticket expires, while it may be possible to extend it, you may be at some remote station and find you have a lot of complicated telephone calls to make or have to give your name and address to the train conductor or ticket collector!

The table on the following pages is set out in alphabetical order of places; these being most of those which are headlined, highlighted, or otherwise featured in tables in this book as destinations, nightstops, or break-of-journey points of interest. After each is given the last time for a train to be caught (according to the 1996 timetables current as this book goes to press) in order that you can reach the nearest major port of exit from Australia or New Zealand by the evening of any given day (presumably, if you are returning home, the evening before your departure overseas). For this purpose evening arrival is taken as being before 19.00 hours. If the port given is not the port you had booked to leave from and you cannot change your flight plan, then you will need to add more time depending how you go from there to your chosen port (rail or air).

If it will take longer than what is left of the evening to sort out your luggage, buy last minute souvenirs and put your affairs in order, then of course you will need to allow as many extra days as it takes. That is your choice.

Where trains run only once or twice a week you will need to allow extra days. For example, if trains are only once a week, the "last train" you would need to catch to be sure of arrival the day before your departure could be up to six days earlier than if trains ran daily, depending on the day of your actual flight. In the following list, the minimum and maximum number of extra days that need to be added is given. The following example illustrates how this may work.

Assume your return flight is booked from Melbourne and you happen to be in Alice Springs. The trains run once a week. The train leaves Alice Springs on Friday and arrives in Melbourne on the Sunday morning after a change in Adelaide. Two days is therefore the minimum time you must allow if your plane departs on the Monday. But if your flight is on a Tuesday you must allow three days because you still have to catch the Friday train. Likewise, if your flight from Melbourne is on Wednesday you need to allow four days and, to take the worst case, if your flight is on the Sunday, a Sunday morning arrival in Melbourne is probably no good and you must therefore leave Alice Springs by train on the Friday eight days before.

The extra days you need to allow therefore range from 2 to 8, depending on the intended day of departure from Australia. This is indicated by the notation +2 to +8 in the list which follows.

AUSTRALIA: The last chances to return home

Places shown in *italics* are not on the railway or not currently served by any regular train. The times given for these are the departure times by bus or other mode of transport to the nearest railhead which is indicated, the times from which should then also be checked.

The time given for all trains is the departure time of the last train to arrive at the port city named on the evening before departure overseas. Where the services are not daily, or the necessary departure is more than 19 hours before the deadline time of 19.00, the number of additional days required is indicated by +1, +2 etc. The best and worst cases are shown. Where the last suitable train is at a different time on different days, the earliest departure time is given in every case, with the day or days on which it applies stated in the Comments column.

More than one possible departure port is given where the nearest one is not necessarily the most convenient or accessible.

From	To Ï	Time	Extra Days	Comments
Adelaide	Melbourne	19.00	+1	daily
Albury	Melbourne	15.30		daily
Alice Springs	Adelaide	14.00	+1 to +7	
Alice Springs	Melbourne	14.00	+2 to +8	*via* Adelaide
Ararat	Melbourne	03.35		daily
Armidale	Sydney	09.10		daily
Ayers Rock	Alice Springs	—		by air to Alice
Babinda	Brisbane	09.23	+1 to +3	
Ballarat	Melbourne	16.00		weekday times
Barcaldine	Brisbane	05.90	+1 to +4	
Barooga	Shepparton	—		bus connection
Bathurst	Sydney	17.14	+1	daily
Belair	Adelaide	17.35		weekend times
Benalla	Melbourne	16.33		daily
Bendigo	Melbourne	07.35		Sunday time
Birdsville	Try the way you came!			
Blayney	Sydney	16.21	+1	daily
Bonnie Vale	Perth	—		Enquire locally
Bowen	Brisbane	18.30	+1 to +2	
Broken Hill	Sydney	15.20	+1 to +5	
Brisbane	Melbourne	07.30	+3	*via* Sydney
	Perth	07.30	+4 to +8	*via* Sydney
	Sydney	07.30	+1	
Bunbury	Perth	14.40		95min later on Sun
Byron Bay	Brisbane	22.02	+1	*via* Casino
	Sydney	22.02	+1	
Cairns	Brisbane	08.00	+1 to +2	
Canberra	Sydney	12.20		daily
Castlemaine	Melbourne	07.57		Sunday time

From	To	Time	Extra Days	Comments
Charleville	Brisbane	17.45	+1 to +5	
Charters Towers	Brisbane	08.23	+1 to +5	*via* Townsville
Cloncurry	Brisbane	20.15	+2 to +6	*via* Townsville
Coffs Harbour	Sydney	07.56		daily
Cook	Perth	09.10	+1 to +5	WA time
	Melbourne	12.30	+2 to +6	SA time
	Sydney	12.30	+2 to +6	SA time
Cooma	Canberra	10.29		bus to Canberra
Coonamia	Adelaide	03.15	0 to +3	
	Melbourne	03.15	+1 to +4	*via* Adelaide
	Perth	21.05	+2 to +5	
	Sydney	03.15	+1 to +4	*via* Melbourne
Coorong Nat Pk	Tailem Bend	10.50		bus connection
Cooroy	Brisbane	16.04		
Cootamundra	Sydney	01.25		
Croydon, Qld	Brisbane	—	many!	check locally
Cunnamulla	Charleville	14.35		bus connection
Dalby	Brisbane	04.05	0 to +4	
Dubbo	Sydney	14.10	+1	
Dungog	Sydney	13.22		
Echuca	Murchison East	13.45		bus connection
Einasleigh	Brisbane	—	many!	check locally
Forsayth	Brisbane	—	many!	check locally
Fremantle	Perth	frequent		
Geelong	Melbourne	17.25		Saturday time
Gladstone, Qld	Brisbane	09.50		daily
Glasshouse Mts	Brisbane	15.13		Sunday time
Glenreagh	Sydney	07.18		daily
Gloucester	Sydney	17.17		
Gordonvale	Brisbane	08.40	+1 to +3	
Goulburn	Sydney	14.45		weekday times
Grafton City	Sydney	06.45		daily
Hamilton	Sydney	15.29		weekend times
Hawkesbury R.	Sydney	17.34		weekday times
Helensvale	Brisbane	17.32		weekend times
Horsham	Melbourne	02.04		daily
Hughenden	Brisbane	04.10	+1 to +5	*via* Townsville
Ingham	Brisbane	12.35	+1 to +2	
Innisfail	Brisbane	09.49	+1 to +2	
Ipswich	Brisbane	frequent		
Junee	Sydney	00.43		daily
Kalgoorlie	Perth	08.20	0 to +1	

From	To	Time	Extra Days	Comments
Katoomba	Sydney	16.25		daily
Kempsey	Sydney	09.32		daily
Kiama	Sydney	15.50		weekday times
Kuranda	Brisbane	15.30	+2 to +3	daily
Leura	Sydney	16.29		weekend times
Lismore	Brisbane	22.50	+1	*via* Casino
	Sydney	22.50	+1	daily
Lithgow	Sydney	15.05		weekday times
Longreach	Brisbane	07.00	+1 to +4	
Mackay	Brisbane	21.45	+1 to +2	
Maitland	Sydney	14.48		weekend times
Maldon	Castlemaine	09.00		bus connection
Mareeba	Kuranda	09.45		bus connection
Melbourne	Brisbane	20.05	+2	*via* Sydney
	Perth	20.20	+3 to +7	*via* Adelaide
	Sydney	20.05	+1	daily
Merredin	Perth	12.23	0 to +1	
Mildura	Swan Hill	04.29	0 to +1	bus to Swan Hill
Moree	Sydney	08.20		daily
Mossman	Cairns	04.30		bus to Cairns
Moss Vale	Sydney	15.42		weekday times
Mount Barker	Adelaide	16.30		bus throughout
Mount Gambier	Warrnambool	08.20	0 to +1	bus connection
Mount Isa	Brisbane	17.00	+2 to +6	*via* Townsville
Mount Surprise	Brisbane	—	many!	check locally
Mount Victoria	Sydney	15.33		weekday times
Murchison East	Melbourne	15.22	0 to +1	weekday times
Murray Bridge	Adelaide	06.37		daily
	Melbourne	21.41	+1	daily
Murwillumbah	Brisbane	21.15	+1	*via* Casino
	Sydney	21.15	+1	daily
Muswellbrook	Sydney	13.16		daily
Nambour	Brisbane	16.27		daily
Newcastle	Sydney	15.23		weekend times
Normanton	Brisbane	—	many!	check locally
Nowra	Sydney	15.20		weekday times
Orange	Sydney	15.55	+1	daily
Parkes	Sydney	00.05	0 to +4	
Parramatta	Sydney	frequent		
Perth	Brisbane	13.35	+4 to +7	
	Melbourne	13.35	+3 to +6	
	Sydney	13.35	+3 to +6	

From	To	Time	Extra Days	Comments
Port Augusta	Adelaide	02.05	0 to +3	
	Perth	22.50	+2 to +5	
	Melbourne	02.05	+1 to +4	*via* Adelaide
	Sydney	02.05	+1 to +4	
Port Kembla	Sydney	16.09		weekday times
Port Pirie	*see* Coonamia			
Proserpine	Brisbane	19.30	+1 to +2	
Quilpie	Charleville	14.35		bus connection
Ravenshoe	Cairns	08.00	0 to +1	bus connection
Rockhampton	Brisbane	08.25		daily
Roma	Brisbane	23.07	+1 to +5	
Sale	Melbourne	13.40		weekday times
Shepparton	Melbourne	17.45	+1	Sunday time
Singleton	Sydney	13.50		daily
Spring Bluff	Brisbane	06.20	0 to +4	
Springwood	Sydney	17.03		weekend times
Stawell	Melbourne	03.04		daily
Stuart Town	Sydney	15.17	+1	daily
Swan Hill	Melbourne	17.05	+1	Sunday time
Sydney	Brisbane	16.24	+1	daily
	Melbourne	20.43	+1	daily
	Perth	14.40	+3 to +6	
Tailem Bend	Adelaide	06.13		daily
	Melbourne	21.41	+1	daily
Tamworth	Sydney	11.08		daily
Tarcoola	Perth	05.29	+1 to +4	
	Melbourne	18.00	+2 to +5	*via* Adelaide
	Sydney	18.00	+2 to +5	
Toowoomba	Brisbane	05.45	0 to +4	
Townsville	Brisbane	15.30	+1 to +2	
Tully	Brisbane	10.51	+1 to +2	
Urunga	Sydney	08.22		daily
Wagga Wagga	Sydney	00.20		daily
Wangaratta	Melbourne	16.09		daily
Warrnambool	Melbourne	12.20	0 to +1	Saturday time
Wellington, NSW	Sydney	14.49	+1	daily
Wentworth Falls	Sydney	16.35		weekend times
Whitsunday Is	Proserpine	—		by air or sea
Winton	Longreach	04.00		bus connection
Wodonga	Melbourne	12.08		*via* Albury
Wollongong	Sydney	16.39		weekend times
Woodend	Melbourne	08.26		Sunday time
Yulara	Alice Springs	—		by air

NEW ZEALAND

There is basically not the same problem in New Zealand in getting back to a port of departure – the country is so much smaller and almost all trains, certainly the principal ones, run daily. Also, apart from travel to Australia and some nearby Pacific countries and some charter flights, Auckland is the main international port of departure. The following examples bear out these comments.

From	To	Time	Extra Days	Comments
Auckland	Christchurch	20.40	+1	train + ferry
	Wellington	20.40	+1	daily
Christchurch	Auckland	07.30	+1	train + ferry
	Wellington	07.30		train + ferry
Dunedin	Christchurch	09.35		Friday time
Gisborne	Napier	09.15	+1	C 9759
Greymouth	Christchurch	14.25		daily
Hamilton	Auckland	15.20		daily
	Wellington	22.43	+1	daily
Invercargill	Christchurch	06.20		Friday time
Johnsonville	Wellington	frequent		
Masterton	Wellington	09.27		weekend time
Napier	Wellington	14.20	+1	daily
National Park	Auckland	01.17		daily
	Hamilton	14.07		daily
	Wellington	01.57		daily
Otaki	Wellington	06.17		weekend time
Otorohanga	Auckland	03.52		daily
Paraparaumu	Wellington	frequent		
Rotorua	Auckland	13.05		daily
	Hamilton	13.05		daily
Tauranga	Auckland	08.05		daily
	Hamilton	08.05		daily
Wellington	Auckland	19.45	+1	daily
	Christchurch	09.00		ferry + train

WHY GO HOME AT ALL?

Perhaps you lose yourself somewhere in the heart of Australia or New Zealand. In the bush, in the vast emptiness of the Nullarbor, the lush greenery of the tropical rainforest, the sun and surf of Australia's miles of golden beaches, the bustling brashness of the major cities or you are lost in awe at the Geyserland wonders of Rotorua, or are following some obscure track through the glaciers and fiords of New Zealand's Southland. Maybe you are just caught up with the excitement of a party, the "footy", the fever of the Melbourne Cup, when all Australia stands still, or a New Zealand *haka*. Or you succumb to the rich variety of food, from witchetty grub soup to mud crab, from king prawns to barbecued western beef steak, from Canterbury lamb to the variety of tasty morsels offered at a *hangi*. Or you are busy with the fine Australian and New Zealand wines – the golden yellow of Coonawarra Chardonnay, the rich dryness of Marlborough Riesling or the intense ruby purple of the Hunter Valley reds with, so they say, the flavour of a well-worn saddle (it may not sound very appealing until you taste it). Or you are enchanted by the wild life, the myriads of brightly coloured birds, the big black emus and the little kiwis, the possums and the wallabies, not to mention the crocodiles and snakes which are best seen from a protected position.

You may even just be taken by the people, the open friendliness and mateship and the trusting attitude you meet in so many places, especially in small towns and in the bush, or when travelling, or in a pub. Do you know that even in major cities a person can buy a drink at the bar and leave the change on the counter while attending to a call of nature or some other matter? That pile of change, reserved for the next drink, will remain untouched. To violate it would provoke outrage. And in a pub, especially in the outback and in provincial towns, you will hear stories in abundance, tall tales and true ones – the latter often the strangest. Too true, mate, don't you worry about that!

For whatever reason, or for none you can put a finger on, some places will make you want to linger, will draw you back, and if you went there by rail in the first place you can probably go there again. You can see much of both countries and taste their essence without ever going far from a railway or even spending more time out of a train than it takes to wait for the next one – but remember that this may not be until the following day, or even later.

So have a good trip, stay a while, and come again.

Appendix

Useful Addresses

Rail Australia Sales Agents

Canada

Goway Travel (Head Office)
3284 Yonge Street, Suite 300
Toronto
Ontario M4N 3M7
Phone 416 322 1034
Fax 416 322 1109

Goway Travel
Suite 456
409 Granville Street
Vancouver
British Columbia V6C 1T2
Phone 604 687 4004
Fax 604 687 6845

Denmark

Benns Rejser (Head Office)
Norregade 51
DK–7500 Holstebro
Phone 97 425 000
Fax 97 412 827

Benns Rejser
Frederiksberg Alle 18-20
1820 Frederiksberg C
Copenhagen
Phone 33 557 511
Fax 33 557 500

France

Australie Tours
129 rue Lauriston
Paris 75116
Phone 1 4553 5839
Fax 1 4755 9593

Germany

Brits:Australia
Plinganserstrasse 12
81369 Munich
Phone 89 747 0429
Fax 89 725 4516

Hong Kong

Westminster Travel Ltd
16th Floor
Oriental Centre
67 Chatham Road
Tsimshatsui
Kowloon
Phone 2369 5051
Fax 2723 3746

Japan

Japan Travel Bureau
Overseas Travel Department
JTB Building, 3rd Floor
1-6-4 Maraunouchi, Chiyouda-ku
Tokyo 100
Phone 3 3284 7303
Fax 3 3284 7390

Travel Plaza International
NV Tomioka Building, 7th Floor
2-1-9 Tomioka Koto-Ku
Tokyo 135
Phone 3 3820 8011
Fax 3 3820 8014

Travel Plaza International
Jutakukinyukoko – Sumitmoseimei
Building
4-5-20 Minamihommachi
Chuo-Ku
Osaka 541
Phone 6 251 4044
Fax 6 251 4049

Travel Plaza International
Kyoto Tokai Building, 4th Floor
Shijo-Agaru, Karasuma-Dori
Chukyo-Ku Kyoto-Shi
Kyoto-Fu 604
Phone 75 241 9065
Fax 75 241 9073

Toyo World Co Ltd
Adyama Ten-X Bldg, 7th Floor
5-50-60 Jingu-Mae Shibuya-Ku
Tokyo 150
Phone 3 3498 7636
Fax 3 3498 5403

Korea

Seoul Travel Service Ltd
7th Floor, Keumjung Building
1-KA, Ulchl-Ro, Chung-Ku
Seoul
Phone 2 755 9696
Fax 2 753 9076

Netherlands

Incento BV
Stationsweg 40
1404 AP Bussum
(PO Box 1067, 1400 BB Bussum)
Phone 35 69 55 111
Fax 35 69 55 155

New Zealand

Intercity Management Ltd
PO Box 3625
Beach Road
Parnell
Auckland
Phone 9 357 8457
Fax 9 357 8406

Christchurch Rail Station
Clarence Street
Addington
C/–N.Z. Rail Ltd (Private Bag)
Christchurch
Phone 33 728209
Fax 33 728477

Singapore

Linbert Travel Exchange Pte Ltd
1-31 Parkland Shopping Mall
35 Selegie Road
Singapore 0718
Phone 336 7288
Fax 334 4502 or 338 7588

South Africa

Go Australia (Travel Directions)
(Head Office)
Holiday House
158-160 Hendrik Vervoerd Drive
(PO Box 4942)
Randburg 2125
Phone 11 886 7270/6121
Fax 11 886 4460

Go Australia (Travel Directions)
15th Floor Office Suite 1502
Sanlam Golden Acre
Adderley Street
(PO Box 3189)
Cape Town 8000
Phone 21 419 9382/3/4
Fax 21 419 5280

Go Australia (Travel Directions)
Suite 810 Musgrave Centre
Musgrave Road
(PO Box 51182)
Durban 4062
Phone 31 21 6061/2-5
Fax 31 21 7809

Sweden

Benns Rejser
Kastellgatan 17 (Box 7124)
S–40233
Gothenburg
Phone 317 740025
Fax 317 740228

United Kingdom

Leisurail
Merlin Business Park
Units 1-3, Coningsby Road
North Bretton
Peterborough
Cambridgeshire PE3 8BL
Phone 01733 335599 (information &
reservations)
01733 335556 (brochures)
Fax 01733 505451

United States

ATS Tours
2381 Rosecrans Avenue, Suite 325
El Segundo
CA 90245
Phone 310 643 0044
Toll free 800 423 2880
Fax 310 643 0032

Tranz Rail Sales Agents

Australia
Australia New Zealand
Phone 1 800 074 247 (toll free)
  07 5591 5555 (Brisbane direct)
Fax 07 5591 5636

Kirra Tours
Phone 1 800 888 242 (Toll free)
  08 8212 7833 (Adelaide Direct)
Fax 08 8231 2012

NZTP Travel
Phone 1 300 300 035 (Toll free)
  03 9288 0022 (Melbourne Direct)
Fax 03 8347 3288

Value Tours
Phone 1 800 222 001 (Toll free)
  02 262 5611 (Sydney Direct)
Fax 02 262 2780

Walshes World
Phone 1 800 227 122 (Toll free)
  02 232 7499 (Sydney Direct)
Fax 02 221 8297

Denmark
Benns Rejser
Phone 80 01 00 25 (Toll free)
Fax 097 41 28 27

Germany
Adventure Holidays
Phone 0911 97 99 555
Fax 0911 97 99 588

Netherlands
Wereld Contact Reisen
Phone 0343 530530
Fax 0343 520334

Singapore
GBC Pte Ltd
Phone 65 339 2233
Fax 65 337 1889

United States
ATS Tours (California)
Phone 800 423 2880 (Toll Free)
Fax 0310 643 0032

United Kingdom
All-Ways Pacific
Chalfont St. Giles
Phone 01494 875757
Fax 01494 874747

Austravel
London
Phone 0171 734 7755
Fax 0171 494 3528

Travelbag
Alton
Phone 01420 88724
Fax 01420 82133

Information Offices in New Zealand

Auckland InterCity Travel Centre
Central Railway Station
Beach Road, Central Auckland
Phone 09 387 8400

Christchurch Travel Centre
471 Moorhouse Avenue
Christchurch
Phone 03 377 0951

Dunedin InterCity Travel Centre
599 Princes Street
Dunedin
Phone 03 477 8860

Greymouth InterCity Travel Centre
Mackay Street
Greymouth
Phone 03 768 1435

Napier InterCity Travel Centre
Munro Street
Napier
Phone 06 834 2720

Nelson InterCity Travel Centre
27 Bridge Street]
Nelson
Phone 03 548 1539

Palmerston North Travel Centre
95 Princes Street,
Palmerston North
Phone 06 355 5633

Rotorua Visitor Information Centre
Fenton Street, Rotorua
Phone 07 349 0590

Wellington Travel Centre
Railway Station
Bunny Street, Wellington
Phone 04 498 2528

Whangerei InterCity Travel Centre
11 Rose Street
Whangerei
Phone 09 438 2653

Australian Tourist Commission Offices

Head Office

3rd & 4th Floor
80 William Street
Woolloomooloo, NSW 2011
or
GPO Box 2721
Sydney NSW 2001
Phone 02 9360 1111
Fax 02 9331 6469

Germany

Neue Mainzer Strasse 22
D6000 Frankfurt/Main 1

Japan

Twin 21 MID Tower, 30th Floor
2-1-61 Shiromi
Chuo-Ku
Osaka 540

28th Floor
New Otani Garden Court
4-1 Kiocho
Chiyoda-Ku
Tokyo 102

Hong Kong

Suite 1501, Level 15
Central Plaza
18 Harbour Road
Wanchai
Hong Kong

New Zealand

13th Floor
44-48 Emily Place
Auckland 1

Singapore

Suite 1703
17th Floor, United Square
101 Thomson Road
Singapore 1130

United Kingdom

Gemini House
10-18 Putney Hill
Putney
London SW15 6AA

United States

Suite 1200
2121 Avenue of the Stars
Los Angeles, CA 90067

25th Floor
100 Park Avenue
New York, NY 10017

New Zealand Tourist Board Offices

Head Office

Fletcher Challenge House
89 The Terrace
Wellington
or
PO Box 95
Wellington
Phone 04 472 8860
Fax 04 478 1736

Australia

Level 8, 35 Pitt St
Sydney, NSW 2000
Phone 02 9247 5222

Canada

Suite 1200, 888 Dunsmuir St
Vancouver
British Columbia V6C3K4

United Kingdom

80 Haymarket
London SW1Y 4TQ
Phone 0171 930 1662
Fax 0171 839 8929

United States

780 3rd Avenue, Suite 1904
New York, NY 10017-2024
Phone 212 832 8482

501 Santa Monica Blvd, Room 300
Santa Monica, CA 90401
Phone 310 395 7480

1111 North Dearborn St, Suite 2705
Chicago, IL 60610
Phone 312 440 1345

FURTHER READING

Travel Guides
There are numerous general travel guides available to all or parts of Australia and New Zealand. Many readers of this book will have their own favoured source for such information. For others, the "Lonely Planet" series includes general titles on *Australia* and *New Zealand* as well as individual titles on each of the Australian states and one entitled *Outback Australia*. All can be recommended.

General
Geoffrey Blainey   *The Tyranny of Distance*
Ian McNamara   *Australia All Over*
John O'Grady   *They're a Wierd Mob*

Scyld Berry's *Train to Julia Creek* and Nigel Kranth's *Matilda My Darling* are referred to in Chapter Six.

Present-day Railways
ARHS Sydney (eds.)   *Rail Scene Australia: 1995 Guide to Australian Tourist Railways and Museums*
Geoffrey B. Churchman   *The Midland Line, New Zealand's Trans-Alpine Railway*
Geoffrey B. Churchman & Tony Hurst   *South Island Main Trunk*
Anthony Dennis   *Ribbons of Steel: Riding the Indian Pacific*
Anthony Dennis & Michael Rayner   *Ticket to Ride: A Rail Journey Around Australia*
John Garner   *Guide to New Zealand Rail Heritage*
Roy Sinclair   *The TranzAlpine Express*
Derek Whitelock   *Gone on the Ghan (and other great railway journeys of Australia)*
Colin Taylor   *Great Rail Non-Journeys of Australia*
Colin Taylor   *Traincatcher*

Railway History
Phil Belbin & David Burke   *Changing Trains: A Century of Travel on the Sydney–Melbourne Railway*
Robin Bromby   *The Country Railway in Australia*
John Gunn   *Along Parallel Lines: A History of the Railways of New South Wales*
John Kerr   *Triumph of Narrow Gauge: A History of Queensland Railways*
Patsy Adam Smith   *When We Rode the Rails*

210

INDEX

The major cities and named trains are mentioned on many pages throughout this book. To reduce complexity only the most significant page references to these are given in this index.

Aberdeen 26
Addington xi, 183
Adelaide 38-9, 67, 86-7, 90, 198
Air and bus connections xi
Airport links x, xi
Albury 33, 66-7, 198
Albury-Wodonga 134
Aldgate 153
Alice Springs 22, 52, 68-9, 90, 104-5, 198
Almaden 90
Alpha 31, 90, 100, 120
Anakie 90
Ararat 149-50, 198
Armidale 26, 90, 92, 140-1, 198
Arthur's Pass 164, 187
Ashburton 164
Ashfield, WA 125
Atherton 90, 117
Auckland 168-71, 202
Austrail Flexipass 14
Austrailpass 13-4
Australian Tourist Commission offices 207
Australind 35, 70
Avoca, NZ 187
Ayers Rock 41, 50-6, 104-5, 198

Babinda 144, 198
Bacchus Marsh 90
Bairnsdale 147, 152
Balclutha 164
Ballan 90, 149
Ballarat 92, 149, 198
Ballarat Vintage Tramway 121
Ballyhooley Express 114, 143-4
Balranald 152
Barcaldine 31, 100, 146, 198
Barooga 148, 152, 198
Barraba 141
Barton 21
Bassendean Rail Transport Museum 125
Bathurst 21, 26, 111-2, 134-5, 198
Bay Express 161-2, 177-9
Bealey Bridge 164
Beechworth 152
Bega 27, 141

Belair 153, 198
Belgrave 90, 121
Bellarine Peninsula Railway 122
Bellata 146
Benalla 24, 152, 198
Bendigo 34, 92, 148, 198
Bendigo trams 122
Bennett Brook Railway 125-6
Beyer Garratt Locomotive 114
Big Pineapple Railway 114
Birdsville 98, 198
Blackall 146
Blackheath 139
Blackwater 31, 99
Blayney 21, 26, 27, 111-2, 198
Blenheim 163, 180
Bloomsbury 90
Bluff, NZ 185
Bodallin 35
Bogantungan 100
Boggabri 26
Bomaderry 136
Bombo 137
Bombola 27, 141
Bonnie Vale 154, 198
Border Loop 107
Bordertown 24
Boulder 126
Bourke 141
Bowen 40, 63, 198
Bowral 27
Boyanup Transport Museum 126
Brampton Island Railway 115
Branxton 110, 130-1
Brewarrina 141
Bribie Island 143
Bridgewater 90, 153
Bright 152
Brisbane 62, 82-5, 142-3, 198
Brisbane Tramway Museum 114
Brisbane XPT 25
Broadmeadow, NSW 25, 59
Broadmeadows, Vic 33
Broken Hill 27, 135-6, 198
Broken Hill Transport Museum 107
Buderim Ginger Factory, Yandina 118
Bunbury 58, 70, 198
Bundaberg 62-3, 132
Bundanoon 27
Bungendore 27, 90
Burkes Pass 166
Burnie 127
Burren Junction 26
Bus connections, NZ 188
Bus/rail connections, NSW 141-2
Bus/rail connections, Queensland 146-7

Bus/rail connections, Vic 152
Buxton 113
Byron Bay 25, 57, 60-1, 198

Caboolture 28, 31, 90
Cairns 28-31, 64, 90, 142-6, 198
Calen 29
Callemondah 132
Callemondah Yard 115
Campbelltown 24, 26-7, 137-8
Camperdown 34, 152
Canberra 27, 66, 133, 198
Canberra Rail Museum 108
Canberra Xplorer 27
Capital Connection 163
Cardwell 29, 64
Carmila 29
Casino 25, 61, 92, 94
Cass 187
Castlemaine 34, 148-9, 198
Castlemaine & Maldon Railway 122
Central Highlands Tourist Railway 122
Caulfield 32
Central West XPT 26
Cessnock 110
Charleville 31, 98, 199
Charters Towers 90, 102, 199
Cheepie 31
Chillagoe 90, 145
Chinchilla 31
Christchurch 182-3, 202
Cloncurry 31, 90, 102, 147, 199
Coastal Pacific 163-4
Cobar 141
Cobram 33, 148
Cockatoo Run 91-3
Coffs Harbour 25, 60, 199
Colac 34
Colonial Tramcar Restaurant 81
Condobolin 21, 27, 142
Cook, SA 69, 71, 199
Cook Strait ferries 179-80
Cooladdi 31
Coolangatta 25
Cooma 27, 90, 133, 199
Coomera 116
Coonabarabran 141
Coonalpyn 24
Coonamia 40, 68, 199
Coorong National Park 153, 199
Cooroy 29, 31, 143, 199
Cootamundra 24, 142, 199
Corinda 31
Corio 34
Coromandel 188
Corowa 152
Countrylink Discovery Pass 11